THE
PROGESS
OF

ART EDUCATION

IN
THE
ELEMENTARY
SCHOOL

THE
PROCESS
OF
Art Education
IN
THE
ELEMENTARY
SCHOOL

GEORGE CONRAD

PRENTICE-HALL, INC., ENGLEWOOD CLIFFS, N. J.

PRENTICE-HALL INTERNATIONAL, INC., *London*
PRENTICE-HALL OF AUSTRALIA, PTY., LTD., *Sydney*
PRENTICE-HALL OF CANADA, LTD., *Toronto*
PRENTICE-HALL OF INDIA (PRIVATE) LTD., *New Delhi*
PRENTICE-HALL OF JAPAN, INC., *Tokyo*
PRENTICE-HALL DE MEXICO, S.A., *Mexico City*

Library of Congress Catalog Card No.: 64-15648.

Printed in the United States of America
72294-C

for my son and daughter
MARTIN AND MARCIA

PREFACE

If any one thing guided me in writing this book, it was the belief that education should foster and give a useful direction to the uniqueness with which every child is gifted. Every child is potentially an artist because, as an individual, he has his own modes of responding to the people and things around him. The work every child will do is potentially valuable, both educationally and as a work of art, because its precise form is unpredictable.

Throughout this book runs a determination to define the characteristics of successful programs of art education, which serve as useful devices for encouraging the development of a socially useful uniqueness. Such a definition requires a persistent search for touchstones and guideposts that, because of the special character of art, must be unendingly tentative. If they were ever more than tentative, the essence of art would be destroyed. If I were asked to offer a theme for art education, I think the one that would strike me as most useful would be expressed as the attitude, "Let's try

it and see what will happen." Try what? Why, try anything! But try it! If we must find solutions in mindsets, in formulas, in stereotypes, in single all-embracing answers, we will certainly not be dealing with the special qualities of art. Art is an adventure precisely because it is unpredictable. Art is not a science, and the moment it attempts to use the methods of science, it must inevitably destroy itself.

The second guide to writing this book has been the belief that art education is at least as important as anything else in the elementary-school curriculum. For this reason, art must be given the same consideration as anything else that is very important to children's happiness, growth, and development.

A book about art education is seldom the product of just one person's experience. A great many people have worked to define art education, to clarify its purposes, and to formulate its programs. My experience in art education has been enriched by the contacts I have had over a period of many years with parents, teachers, and students. My debt to all of these people is profound, but its sources have been obscured by the multitudes of people involved. To all those who have contributed to any useful knowledge or understanding developed in this book go my sincerest thanks.

During the past few years, I have had opportunities to observe and participate in the art program conducted in the campus laboratory school of the Glassboro State College. The students and the teachers of that school have been most kind and generous with their help. All the teachers have contributed materials that have been of great value in the development of this book.

A number of teachers in schools throughout New Jersey have extended suggestions and examples of children's art work.

Special thanks are due Mr. Theodore Lynch, formerly assistant professor of art at the Glassboro State College and now consultant in art education in the Princeton Township Elementary Public Schools, for permission to use examples of work by his students in the Teaneck Public Elementary Schools.

Miss Olive Riley, director of art of the New York City Public Schools, gave permission to reproduce examples of children's art work done in the New York City Elementary Schools.

Mrs. Mildred Brenner, of the Toms River, New Jersey, Public Schools, has permitted use of some of the work of her students.

Mrs. Rea S. Kline, of the Runnemede, New Jersey, Public Schools, conducted some useful experimental work in her kindergarten classes.

Miss Bernice Magnie, supervisor of art of the East Orange, New Jersey, Public Schools, devoted much of her valuable time to conducting me through the schools of East Orange and permitting me to photograph work done by East Orange elementary-school students. Among the teachers in the East Orange schools, the following were most helpful: Mr. Frank Capasso, Miss Helen Crisson, Miss Susan Hartke, Mr. Richard Howard, Miss Patricia Lee, Mr. Myron Palmer and Mrs. Bernice Price.

One of the most important influences on my thinking has been the work of Marion Quin Dix, director of art education of the Elizabeth, New Jersey, Public Schools. The list of "evidences" in Appendix Two is compiled from materials developed by the art staff of the Elizabeth schools under the direction of Mrs. Dix.

The following persons offered me much excellent advice and editorial guidance during the writing of this book: Jerome J. Hausman, director of the School of Fine and Applied Arts of the Ohio State University; Ivan E. Johnson, professor and head of art education and constructive design, Florida State University at Tallahassee; and Edith M. Henry, associate professor of art at the Long Beach College in California.

I am indebted to Diana J. Powers, who untangled many of the language tangles that occur when a neophyte writes a book.

The index has been compiled by Dr. Eva Aronfreed of the Glassboro State College.

Whatever depth this book may have is due to the untiring devotion and encouragement of my wife, Sylvia Conrad.

GEORGE CONRAD

HOW TO USE THIS BOOK

This book will be most useful if the reader is aware that it is built around a central concept, which is *process*.

The thesis proposed in this text is that art is the spirit that can invigorate the whole of the process of learning, of flux, growth, and change. These are the things that seem to describe the children for whom the elementary-school curriculum is planned.

The concept of a process that can be developed through art activity requires that we probe, study, and become familiar with four basic problems. The answers to these problems are not really answers in the sense that answers to a question must be definitive and final. The reader will profit most if the discussion, developed as an "answer" to these problems, is considered part of the business of finding directions.

The four problems that provide the framework on which this text is built are:

1. Why is art important in elementary-school education?

2. What is art education?
3. How do we recognize the process of art education in the work of children?
4. How do we use art as a means to contribute to the education of elementary-school children?

Part One is a discussion organized around the first problem. This part will introduce the reader to the role of art in elementary-school education. Part One also introduces the reader to the backgrounds of art education, its philosophy and history. This material is developed from the belief that the methods of the artist suggest methods and purposes for achievement of the educational role of art in elementary school.

Part Two presents a discussion of the second problem: What is art education? Related to this is another problem: How does art education work? These two problems are treated together because the understanding of one leads to a need to understand the other. Art education is described as a structure that is designed in terms of the definable needs of elementary-school children in order to make the process of education workable. Part Two is treated as an outgrowth of Part One. The structure of art education is described as being made up of parts that give reality to the purposes and philosophy discussed in Part One.

Part Three applies the discussion about the structure, philosophy, and purposes of art education to the natural ways children engage in art activities. This discussion is intended to provide a basis for the building of an art-education curriculum.

The discussion beginning with Part Three and developed through Parts Four and Five defines the central theme that grows out of the concept of *process*. This theme is that *the needs of children and the natural modes of their art suggest a technique for the construction of an educationally valid art curriculum.*

Part Four is designed as a description of the kinds of skills that are most useful in art education. The skills fostered by art education are those that contribute to the intellectual and emotional growth of elementary-school children. For this reason, emphasis is placed on skills in invention, expression, and learning.

Parts Four and Five are intended to be responses to the third and fourth problems listed on page ix. The emphasis in Part Four is on problem number three and in Part Five on problem number four.

The Appendices are made up of material that can serve as a general guide to teachers. Appendix One describes the processes of evaluation, which are a part of the general discussion throughout the text. The purpose of this Appendix is to provide examples of useful evaluation techniques and record-keeping methods. Appendix Two may have special value as a means for helping teachers know the signs of an educationally valid art program for elementary school. The material in this Appendix can be used as a check list and, like the material in Appendix One, it involves the basic elements of the discussion developed throughout the text.

CONTENTS

xi

PART ONE

ART IN EDUCATION

GENERAL INTRODUCTION TO ART EDUCATION

Art can be an effective tool of the process of learning and growing. Art in child education is a dynamic force. Because it emphasizes the interrelatedness of thinking and feeling, art can increase the effectiveness of the whole process of elementary-school education.

Art education is unique in the school curriculum because it offers children opportunities to give organized physical form—a painting, sculpture, or other crafted construction—to their experiences, their concepts, their thoughts, and their feelings. When emotional and rational responses to experience are combined in a satisfying and unified way, using paints, clay, crayons, ink, pencils, chalks, or colored paper, the result can be an aesthetic experience.

The aesthetic experience comes into being because the combining of concepts with physical materials is a pleasurable activity. And the pleasure and completeness of the aesthetic experience can result in an effective means for achieving new and useful understandings. For this reason, the art activity can help children know more about their social and physical environment, so that they can fulfill their need for an increasingly satisfying and useful involvement in it.

Art in the elementary-school classroom provides a means for gaiety and pleasure to join with invention and knowledge. Art helps the child to know the pleasures that are traditionally considered the special privilege of the professional artist.

The Roman philosopher Plotinus considered the artist to be a divine intermediary between man and God; he maintained that the artist is the voice of divinity. This concept must have been derived, in part, from observing that the artist's sensitivities enable him to probe beneath the purely mechanical explanations of realities to achieve experiences and understandings that cannot be obtained by purely rational means. In achieving and expressing this profound understanding, the artist engages in processes of art activity that involve the pleasure of the aesthetic experience. The labor of the artist is a labor of love. When it does not involve pleasure, the labor of art loses much of its meaning, its scope of sensation, and its inspirational exhilaration. A completed art activity provides a kind of revelation available by no other means.

We have reason to believe that the joy in work—the mark of art activity—is an important cause of the beautifully formed expressions of human experience that have made our heritage qualitative. It is precisely this special kind of joy, derived from giving form to expression, that can become the educationally useful activity of elementary-school children.

We begin our discussion with the generalization that the methods of the artist can be used to create a valuable educational program in the elementary school. From his first school days, the child in elementary school can produce art forms, just as artists produce art. His involvement in art activities will lack the sophistication of the professional artist; it will lack advanced skills, trained sensibilities, profound knowledges, and the artist's extensive experience. But the core of the working, thinking, and feeling processes that are the living and working processes of the artist can be experienced and fruitfully used by young children.

EDUCATIONAL POTENTIALS OF ART ACTIVITY

Art has a unique capacity for interacting with human living. It will interact with, and become part of, the living and the thinking that is characteristic of children. When the art forms produced by children are childlike, when they represent the thoughts and feelings of children, we have some reason to believe that they also have educational value. One of the purposes of this book will be to demonstrate the ways in which child art expressions interact with and become an educational contribution to children's everyday living.

The most important resource in art education is the children with whom the teacher works. The special characteristics of childhood must be understood by the teacher in order to insure the effectiveness of the art education program. Once the teacher has gained some understanding of children, it may then become possible for him to know what useful educational relationships can exist between children and art. What are some of the general achievements that are possible through art education?

It is worth noting that in the opinion of some investigators, value in child art activity is largely dependent on the degree of inventiveness, imagination, and creativity that children bring to it. For example, Carolyn Tiebout [1] notes that children in the five- to ten-year-old group who did original work in drawing and painting demonstrated growth as follows:

1. They made more complete observations of their environment.
2. They exhibited greater perceptual ability in making discriminations.
3. They had better memory for details.
4. They showed greater inventiveness and originality in relating and arranging objects and other visual elements.

The techniques of the processes of art activity tend to develop the natural inclination of children to invent meaningful organizations of ideas and experiences and in this way to give constructive meaning to experience.

PROCESSES OF ART EDUCATION

In this text, art education is considered as part of the whole of the learning, the living, and the growing processes of children. The concept of process implies flux, a purposeful rhythm of work and change. In art education, "process" refers to the things children have done, the influence of past performance on present activity, and the

[1] Carolyn Tiebout, "The Psychological Functions Differentiating Artistically Superior Children From Artistically Inferior Children," *Psychological Monograph*, 45, No. 200 (1933), 108-133.

contributions of this activity to the children's physical, mental, and emotional growth.

Although a child engaged in art activity uses knowledge previously acquired, his act of making an art work is part of a process, a way of doing, that is ever new because it is the result of previous experience recombining with new experience to open new worlds of knowing and understanding. The process of art activity is a process of doing and becoming; and "becoming" implies change, the forming of that which does not yet exist.

Once an art object comes into existence, it becomes a means for helping the child see what he has accomplished. Experience, thought, and knowledge have been given a form. The completed art object can be evaluated. In this way the child will know something about how he can improve his work. He will also be helped to establish new directions for thinking and working. (Each art activity is thus a stage in a continuing process, a basis for knowing how to make other art works.)

The process of art activity is thought of as continuous and unending. But within this continuousness is a completeness of experience that is represented by each separate art work.

The activity of doing, of making an art work, helps the child give added depth and meaning to experience, a completeness which might not have existed without the creative activity.

The aesthetic experience grows out of this completeness of experience, but it is also dependent for its existence on the continuousness of experience. The very fact that each completed art activity and art form may result in new and richer art experiences helps the child feel satisfaction. This satisfaction is purposefully combined with recognition of a need to engage in new art activity. This recognition of completeness in flux, accomplishment, and need is the basis of the aesthetic experience.

In classroom practice, process evolves out of the children's needs. Art activity can be motivated and valid learning experiences can be provided if the teacher understands the important needs of children. Elementary-school children need, for example, to know more about their environment. Through science, they can be given opportunities to learn more about the materials that comprise the earth. Through art activity,

they can handle such materials, manipulate them, and become acquainted with their qualities. An example of a specific material is the yellow clay that might be found in the ground outside the school building.

The mere process of manipulating a material does not guarantee that the interest of the children in the process and their awareness of the importance of what they are doing will be maintained. Purposes for using the materials will have to be developed. The children have to be helped to know what they are trying to accomplish. The teacher should help them know more about the ideas, experiences, and cultural concepts that are part of their lives. This knowledge could become subject matter for forming objects from natural clay—particular animals with which the children are familiar, figures of specific persons, or models of machines, buildings, or even of communities. In each case, the relation between the materials and the experiences given form in the materials is purposeful. The process is not merely one of using clay to make a sculpture that looks like some object. The object will be a particular animal, for example, perhaps a pet; or an animal about which the children are gaining new understandings, such as a lion, a tiger, a snake, or an elephant.

Process grows out of the forms of child art that are natural for each phase in the growth of children. We do know that child art is distinguishable according to levels of physical, emotional, and intellectual growth. The art work of the kindergarten child is different in appearance from the art work of the seventh or the eighth grader. These characteristics of child art will influence the nature of need. For example, need in the kindergarten is not the same in quality as it is in the upper grades. The need to manipulate materials in order to become familiar with environment requires a different kind of emphasis in the kindergarten than in the upper grades.

Process in art education operates in a context consisting of children, their cultural characteristics, and the classroom teaching situation. It is of special importance to us that the nature of this context be given a definable form by means of specific teaching techniques. The way in which processes of art activity operate within the context of the classroom is our immediate concern.

An example of the relationships of need, the

character of the child's art activity, and the context of the classroom teaching situation may serve to clarify the relation of teaching to art activity and children. The need could be as fundamental as the need to find directions for growth, which is basic in the whole of the process of education. This need is the mainstream of the process of art activity.

In order to develop a process of finding directions for growth the teacher should provide children with opportunities to judge their efforts. This can be done in two major ways. First, the children can discuss their work individually with the teacher. Second, the teacher can engage the children in group discussions. By leading them in the critical assessment of their work, the teacher provides opportunities to learn about the job to be done and helps them accept responsibilities for the program that will lead to the completion of their work. These sessions will help the children understand what has been accomplished and what remains to be done.

In art education we are concerned with the achievement of quality in the art work produced by children; however, the degree to which the child achieves an artful picture, sculpture, or other craft object is not the only important factor. The things made by children during an art activity are valid if they are related to a phase of child learning, to behavior, and to the quality of the child's participation in the activity.

In art education, process and result are related. The way a thing is done is at least as important as the thing accomplished. The result of the art activity, the work of child art, becomes a part of the flux of learning and growing. The art object is a symbol, a marker, a sign of achievement or its lack.

ART EDUCATION AND THE CLASSROOM

A philosophy of art education has little meaning unless there is evidence that the techniques of teaching that can give it reality are available.

The requirements for an educationally effective art program are twofold. First, there must be an understanding by the teacher that the effects of art activity are evident in the behavior of the children. Second, there must be an environment and facilities which make effective art education activities possible.

The teacher must make a wide variety of suitable materials for art work available to the children. However, just giving children opportunities to work with materials is not enough. Children need to learn how to relate materials to thinking. They may learn to do this if the teacher makes it possible for them to explore their surroundings and then makes it possible for them to discover how explorations can be related to forms made with art materials.

The classroom should be organized in a way that will invite the children to become involved in art activities. The teacher should plan the room so that tools and materials will be available (easily accessible) to the children. The classroom will invite art activity if it reflects the work the children do. Work in progress as well as completed work needs to be seen continuously, and the displays should change as the children's understandings and knowledges change and grow.

SUMMARY

The art activity draws its major strength from the motivations to learning that grow out of the aesthetic experience and that are given vitality by the pleasure of the aesthetic experience.

Art education makes a major contribution to the process of education in the elementary school because it emphasizes the use of invention, imagination, the organization of real experience, and the construction of forms that give added meaning to children's experiences and learnings.

Art activity is an active learning process; it gains much of its strength from the children's direct involvement in processes of forming concepts into physical structures with their hands.

The process of art education has validity because it evolves out of the needs children recognize or are helped to recognize.

Although art education is most effective when it is planned in terms of the needs and experiences children know about and can understand, it is also necessary that children draw inspiration from the classroom itself. The organization of the classroom provides the environment that helps to motivate the children to activity. The classroom is thought of as a workshop that provides children with opportunities to develop concepts and understandings related to their own living.

SOME SOURCES OF CONTEMPORARY KNOWLEDGE

OF THE FUNCTION OF ART EDUCATION

Art education has a rich tradition and enough is known to make art a useful and necessary part of the education of all children. The first and basic job of the art teacher has been to construct educationally valid art curricula for the elementary school. This job is most effective when the teacher can work from a sound philosophy of art and art education. One of the basic assumptions the art teacher makes is that the art education program should give added depth and meaning to the education of all children in the elementary school.

Art education program planners need good and reliable knowledge about how children learn and grow and about what they need for useful, healthy, and happy living.

In recent years, art education planners have begun to discover a rich body of information about how people think, behave, and perform. When this information is correlated with the kinds of understandings the artist has intuitively known, a strong basis for art program planning in the elementary school becomes available. Work done by general educators and writings and research in psychology, philosophy, anthropology, and sociology provide a rich source of reference. Knowledge about people has helped to guide our thinking about how to design art education programs that will work for young people.

7

GENERAL PHILOSOPHICAL SOURCES

The philosophical sources of art are firmly rooted in some very ancient literature. In his book *Education Through Art*, Herbert Read makes reference to the great Greek philosopher Plato who, according to Read, believed that art should be the core of all education. This concept of the place of art in education has undergone changes through the centuries since Plato lived; but the general characteristics of the Platonic concept have been a useful guide to art education planners.

In more recent times, the American philosopher John Dewey has written about the functions of art in human experience. Both his book *Art as Experience* [1] and his essays advocating that children participate actively in the learning process [2] have provided us with a useful philosophy regarding the place of the art education program in the education of elementary-school children.

In his book *The Child and the Curriculum, and the School and Society*, Dewey placed emphasis on the need for an elementary-school curriculum that would use children's abundant energy in an increasingly constructive way. Dewey wrote that the child does not have to be "drawn out" (although the term is a better one than "pouring in," as if some kind of empty vessel needed to be filled with knowledge). The child is a human being with a great deal of vitality that needs to be directed and organized, not scattered, helter-skelter, so that we may avoid the usually unfortunate results of purely impulsive actions. One way to give effective direction and organization to youthful energy is through art activities. Dewey warns, however, that we cannot permit the child merely to indulge his interest in expression through the arts. If we permit the art activity to be purely permissive, the only kind of useful growth will be accidental. We can give direction through a program that makes the child responsible for evaluation and critical study of problems. This kind of process requires observation, memory, and imagination,

three things that lead to pictures, sculptures, or other art forms that will have a measure of poetic feeling.

In Part Two, our discussions about the structure of art education will reveal that as children mature they can make increasing use of their memory. We shall also find that observation gives depth and breadth to memory and that both memory and observation combine to increase the richness of experience. Knowledge of techniques and methods for working with art materials results in a process of thinking and performing that may become productive.

Thinking that draws upon memory becomes a form of cognition and habit. We could call this a process of conscious thinking and automatic reference. Habits result from familiarity with ideas, ways of doing things, and ways of expression. Such habits, based on previous experience, make rapid thinking and rapid recall possible. Such rapid recall may produce the flashes of insight known as inspiration. I shall call this combination of observation, critical evaluation, and previous experience "precognitive thinking." Precognitive thinking combines with active participation in learning, and it provides directions for performance. This performance may result in the production of poetic forms. These poetic forms, which will be referred to in this text as physically structured metaphors, become expressions of an entire process of learning and living.

When art teachers are able to prepare programs of art education for young children, they find that the abundant, natural energy of children is an educational resource. If a child does not have to sit perfectly still and quiet, he can direct his energies to the achievement of some educational goal. If he has to remain immobile, he naturally becomes restless and irritable, and his energies are drained away from the achievement of educational values. In art education planning, it is possible to provide workshop activities with established goals that are part of a large educational plan. The children are usually involved in this kind of planning and are thus able to give a direction to the expenditure of their own energies.

The art activity makes ideas and experiences useful and meaningful to children. They may not always be completely sure of their purposes, but

[1] John Dewey, *Art as Experience* (New York: G. P. Putnam's Sons, Capricorn Books, 1958).

[2] John Dewey, *The Child and the Curriculum, and the School and Society* (Chicago: The University of Chicago Press, Phoenix Books, 1960).

they do know that they can search for a purpose through the art activity. They do more than merely listen, for example, to descriptions of life in some far-away country: they participate in the study of such life and finally make a picture, sculpture, chart, or construction that gives reality to their investigations.

Some of the important and revealing statements about the function and the resulting structure of art curricula were made by the group of architects, painters, sculptors, and writers who formed the faculty of the Bauhaus, an art school organized by the architect Walter Gropius. The Bauhaus was established in Germany during the early part of this century; its curriculum was built upon the belief that sensory skill can be educated and upon the realization that the contemporary artist needs to develop understandings of varied and diverse relationships among materials, tools, purposes, and ideas.[3]

The Bauhaus performed the important function of questioning the traditional dogmas regarding the education of the artist. No longer was art to be concerned with the making of mere replicas of experience. The interaction of the human personality, its experience, and its sensory equipment were to be a significant, tangible, and useful part of the process.

The Bauhaus produced fruitful results because radical changes in human living brought about by the Industrial Revolution made necessary an entirely new and revolutionary process of art education. The importance of the Bauhaus' contribution to our understanding of art education rests on its clarification of the relationships of tools, concepts, technological processes, materials, and the quality of human perception and experience.

The Bauhaus' concern with the education of the perceptive senses and the use of tools and materials as a means for giving form to one's perceptions indicated new directions for the formulation of purposes in art education. The Bauhaus was able to indicate a procedure for making use of modern technology to improve the expressive power of people. In this way it also provided a means for people to achieve emotional security in spite of a science and technology that could blunt the human sensory apparatus and destroy the urge for expressive power.

In more recent years, Lewis Mumford has described the relationship between art forms and the technologies that help give them a tangible structure. In an essay entitled, "The Tool and the Object," [4] Mumford describes the interaction between cultures and their technologies. The central theme of the essay is based upon the belief that techniques and technologies do not precede human expressive power and spiritual achievement. The importance of this understanding to art education is clear. We must be concerned with tools and techniques, but we must realize that they are only a means for implementing, aiding, and providing tangible means for human growth through spiritual expression.

Mumford's contribution to our developing knowledge about art education is valuable. It helps clarify the Bauhaus' concern with the interaction of human personality and technological achievement. Our technological prowess is valid only insofar as it helps us build "great symbolic structures which reveal and enhance every dimension of human experience—extending man's memory, deepening his sense impressions, rousing his hopes, making more sensitive his feelings, widening the range of sympathy and understanding and loving reciprocity with his fellow creatures." [5]

The combination of the technical knowledge and programs for art curricula proposed by the Bauhaus and the expression of a modern humanism by writers such as Mumford has provided direction for the planning of contemporary school art education programs.

It must be remembered that because the Bauhaus was an art school for the training of professional craftsmen and artists, its curriculum is

---

[3] Lazlo Moholy-Nagy, Vision in Motion (Chicago: Paul Theobald and Company, Publishers, 1947). This book describes the curriculum of the new Bauhaus as it was developed in Chicago. The original Bauhaus was established in Dessau, Germany; however, the Nazi government made its continuation in Germany impossible. The curriculum of the new Bauhaus as described in Vision in Motion was developed for an independent art school named the Institute of Design. This school is now a part of the Illinois Institute of Technology.

[4] Lewis Mumford, "The Tool and the Object," in Art and Technics (New York: Columbia University Press, 1960), pp. 33-58.

[5] Ibid., pp. 33-34.

not directly applicable to a program of public education designed to meet the needs of all kinds of elementary-school children. But the heart of the program—its concern with a method of combining human experience with processes, tools, and materials in order to improve the quality of human living—provides much useful information regarding art in education.

Much of the work that has added to our contemporary knowledge of art education comes from many other areas of study and was not specifically intended as a contribution to the literature of art education. Writers in the fields of art history and cultural anthropology, such as Margaret Mead,[6] Herbert Read,[7] and Susanne Langer[8] have provided us with information regarding the nature and purpose of art. We have also gained insights from writings of creative workers who have described their methods of working and thinking in the fields of science, mathematics, architecture, and literature.[9] The work done by modern painters, sculptors, and other craftsmen has greatly improved our understanding of the purposes of art activity. And the general fields of art, philosophy, and psychology have provided us with much useful information.

SOURCES IN PSYCHOLOGY

Modern psychology contributes a vast body of information that is useful in understanding the functions of art education. The relations between perception and the organization of human thinking in terms of visual-plastic forms, that is, ideas given structure and form through the utilization of pliable materials, have been described by such workers in the arts as Gyorgy Kepes in his book *The Language of Vision.*[10] The materials for Kepes' study were largely drawn from the work of the Gestalt psychologists.

Gestalt psychology has been particularly helpful. The Gestaltist is concerned with patterns of growth and structuring of forms, with perception and its relation to conception and the forming processes. Perhaps most significant is the Gestaltist's realization that the physiological and the neurological human is related to the processes of organizing and forming. This psychology provides reliable information and useful guides to writers on art and human behavior.

On the basis of Gestalt psychology and his own sensitivity to the quality of the processes of art activity, Kepes found that arrangements of visual forms can provide a means of effective, efficient communication; but even more important was Kepes' realization that the very act of perceiving and assimilating visual experience involves the spectator in a process of "shaping sensory impressions into unified, organic wholes."[11] From this point of view, the observer participates in a process of art activity as a natural part of living; and by providing a means to make use of this knowledge, the process of art activity promises educationally valuable results.

In his book *Art and Visual Perception,*[12] Rudolf Arnheim also relied heavily on the work of the Gestalt psychologists. Arnheim's work is specially useful to our understanding of art as an educational tool because he places emphasis on the relationships among visual perception, the visual image, the processes of art activity, and the involvement of the human being in giving plastic form to experience. In this connection, Arnheim has developed a study of the evolution of visual perception, knowledge, and thought in the art work of children.

Our understanding of the role of imagination and conscious and subconscious perception has been clarified by Jean-Paul Sartre's *The Psychology of Imagination.*[13]

In works such as Ralph W. Gerard's analysis of imagination,[14] we have a description that may help us provide for an educative function of

[6] Margaret Mead and Martha Wolfenstein, eds., *Childhood in Contemporary Cultures* (Chicago: University of Chicago Press, 1955).

[7] Herbert Read, *Education Through Art* (New York: Pantheon Books, Inc., 1958).

[8] Susanne Langer, *Problems of Art* (New York: Charles Scribner's Sons, 1958).

[9] An excellent source is Brester Ghiselin, ed., *The Creative Process* (Berkeley and Los Angeles: University of California Press, 1955).

[10] Gyorgy Kepes, *The Language of Vision* (Chicago: Paul Theobald and Company, Publishers, 1948).

[11] *Ibid.,* p. 15.

[12] Rudolf Arnheim, *Art and Visual Perception* (Berkeley and Los Angeles: University of California Press, 1957).

[13] Jean-Paul Sartre, *The Psychology of Imagination* (New York: The Citadel Press, 1961).

[14] Ralph Gerard, "The Biological Basis of Imagination," *Scientific Monthly*, 62 (1946), 477-99.

imagination in the art processes. Gerard was able to demonstrate that the mere process of bringing images to the level of awareness does not insure the existence of imagination. Imagination is a force in constructive work when it is accompanied by the elements of creativity. Without creativity, what we took to be imagination is only hallucination—energetic but purposeless. In the processes of art activity, we have to be aware of these distinctions. The confusion resulting from a lack of such distinctions would seriously hamper construction of useful art education programs.

Gerard claims that imagination may be a product of impulse, of the irrational, or of subconscious elements and intuition; however, it can achieve the status of qualitative imagination only when these factors are curbed and directed by reason.

In an essay that provides additional depth to Gerard's writing, Gardner Murphy writes that learning, or the freeing of human intelligence, is possible when we can achieve a proper balance between impulse and reason.[15]

Lawrence Kubie has done descriptive writing regarding a psychoanalytical approach to creativity, learning, and the freeing of human intelligence to achieve its highest possible potential.[16] Kubie presents an interesting opinion regarding the role of expression through art forms. In many respects, he offers guides that, if properly applied, may be useful in discovering a means for achieving a proper balance between the rational and irrational aspects of human beings. The achievement of this balance constitutes a major challenge for education.

The general accord reached by writers such as Kubie and Murphy appears to substantiate the old belief of art educators referred to by Gardner Murphy: "there is . . . within us a world of *inner* stimulation and challenge, an *inner* world of physiological response, of memories, of images, and of fantasies about which we have always known, but about which we know vastly more today as a result of the labors of physiology and psychoanalysis."[17]

Art educators and artists have long believed in the value of art to society and to the individual; today science is substantiating this belief. Because the processes of art activity make use of the very factors that modern science is discovering to be basic to the processes of education, it is important that we, in the field of art education, understand and define the involvement of all people in the art processes. The educationally orientated definitions of intuition that we now have available indicate directions for the development of art education programs. Jerome Bruner, for example, provides a helpful discussion of the role of intuition in the learning process.[18]

Because art is so concerned with visual perception of experience, it can find valuable guides in psychology. Early work, such as that done by the Gestalt psychologist Kohler, led to the description of art processes as we find them in the writing of Arnheim and Kepes. With our present abundance of reliable research, it may be possible for us to refine and strengthen our knowledge of the related processes of art activities and visual perception.[19] Studies in the psychology of perception are important because they can indicate directions, techniques, and purposes for the development of curricula for art education.

SOCIAL AND CULTURAL SOURCES

Our concern with the psychology of learning through art must not blind us to the importance of sociological and cultural sources. These two factors, inextricably related, form the soil in which psychological and physiological processes find their roots and are able to grow.

The history of art illustrates that the nature of an art process and the form given to an art work have been influenced in a very fundamental way by economic, cultural, and socio-political forces. It is possible to cite any number of examples in which abstract elements such as line and design are related to socio-political, economic, and cultural forces. A good example is the case of the ancient Greek Sophists who found in their sculp-

---

[15] Gardner Murphy, *Freeing Intelligence Through Teaching* (New York: Harper & Row, Publishers, 1961).
[16] Lawrence S. Kubie, *Neurotic Distortion of the Creative Process* (Lawrence: University of Kansas Press, 1961).
[17] Murphy, *op. cit.*, pp. 37-38.

[18] Jerome S. Bruner, *The Process of Education* (Cambridge: Harvard University Press, 1961), Chap. 4.
[19] William N. Dember, *The Pschology of Perception* (New York: Holt, Rinehart & Winston, Inc., 1960). J. J. Gibson, *The Perception of the Visual World* (Boston: Houghton Mifflin Company, 1950).

ture the first expression of an approximate demo-cratic ideal. This ideal is most evident in the sculptures of Praxiteles and Lysippus; it replaces the earlier aristocratic idealization of the human body found in the work of earlier Greek sculptors, such as Polyclitus. The sculpture that approximates the Sophist ideal is dominated by a dynamic quality, an emphasis on the energy of line and mass, and the complete elimination of principal viewpoints. This is an innovation that reached a high level of development in medieval Europe when a new form of cooperative community-building resulted in Gothic cathedral architecture. Such art forms as these eliminate principal viewpoints; the spectator is compelled to walk around or through the sculpture or building in order to obtain an image of the whole. No single view is complete in itself. The spectator is thus made aware of the relativity of each part just as every truth, every norm, and every standard is relative and alters as the point of view is altered. The opposite of this flexible design is found in despotic regimes, such as certain of the Egyptian Kingdoms, where the mass of a form is monolithic and static. By contrast, in Athens in the Age of Pericles, both creation and thought were combined to produce art forms that established an understanding of democratic expression. The art of a popular democracy, then, is expressive of the spirit of economic liberalism, of the belief that man himself is the measure of all things.

We have some reason to believe that economic and cultural factors have much to do with the way in which children perform in art activities. Certainly, there can be little question regarding the significance of their cultural backgrounds.[20]

The character of the art forms found in the work of children is obviously controlled by the sociological environment in which the child lives and the length of time he has been exposed to his culture. The younger child is less influenced by these forces. We have reason to believe that there is a correlation between the evidence of sociologi-cal characteristics in art work and the development of social forms such as speech, patterns of behavior, and adaptation to cultural mores.[21]

SOURCES IN WRITINGS ON ART EDUCATION

An important contribution in the specific field of art education is the descriptive research and writing of Viktor Lowenfeld.[22] This work adds a new depth to our understanding of the meaning of children's drawings.

The general relation of art to the totality of the educative process has been described by Herbert Read in an analysis in which he proposes that we make art the center of all education.[23]

Since the end of World War II, progress has been made in our understanding of the nature of the creative process. Although for many years art teachers have considered creativity to be an important aspect of the contribution art makes to education, they have been vague about what constitutes creativity, because little information or organized study of the process was available. We now have such studies, and their results reveal that creativity is an essential element in all human accomplishment. Most important is the knowledge that the processes employed in the art activity are precisely those that are basic and absolute requisites for the act of creativity.

The relationship between creativity in art and creativity in science was described in two independent studies which were conducted in two different locales under separate grants; the studies had different approaches, research procedures, and general purposes. These are the work which was directed by J. P. Guilford [24] and the study made

---

[20] An excellent source for discussion of the socio-economic and political influences that help shape the art forms will be found in Arnold Hauser, *The Social History of Art* (New York: Vintage Books, 1957), Volumes I, II, III, IV.

[21] Other works that demonstrate the effects of sociological and cultural forces on the art activity are: Franz Boas, *Primitive Art* (New York: Dover Publications, Inc., 1955); Russell Lynes, *The Tastemakers* (New York: Harper & Row, Publishers, 1954); Margaret Mead and Martha Wolfenstein, eds., *Childhood in Contemporary Cultures* (Chicago: University of Chicago Press, 1955).

[22] Viktor Lowenfeld, *Creative and Mental Growth*, 3rd ed. (New York: The Macmillan Company, 1957).

[23] Herbert Read, *Education Through Art* (New York: Pantheon Books, Inc., 1958).

[24] J. P. Guilford, "Creative Abilities in the Arts," *Psychological Review*, LXIV (1957), 110-18 and "Psychology of Creativity," *Teachers College Record*, February, 1962, pp. 380-92.

jointly by Viktor Lowenfeld and Kenneth Beittel.[25]

The Owatonna Art Project was the pioneer study of how art can function in the education of people and how it can be related in a useful manner to the whole of the school program and community life. This project, begun in 1933, was conducted by the University of Minnesota. Under the leadership of Edwin Ziegfeld, a plan to make art an important part of the school program was put into operation in a town named Owatonna. It was proposed that art activity be based on the natural aesthetic interests of the people who would participate in the program. The core value of the plan was found in its demonstration that the function of the teacher need not be restricted to teaching art during a designated art period. The major achievement of the plan was the development of a program that gave an aesthetic emphasis to the general educational pattern of the whole school. In practice, all subject areas were affected by the art program.[26]

Now, because of improving facilities for professional work and information made available by the organized effort of pioneers in the field, we can build upon established knowledge to gain increased understanding of the processes and purposes of art education. The implications of our primary sources for contemporary thinking in art education are evident. The body of available material provides us with the resources necessary for the establishment of specific objectives and directions for the achievement of educational value through the means of art education.

In the chapters of this text which follow, we shall investigate the implications of our contemporary knowledge of human personality and of sociological and philosophical literature. By building upon the results of these investigations plus the experience of earlier art educationists, we will be able to define the most fruitful directions for education through art.

[25] Viktor Lowenfeld and Kenneth Beittel, "Interdisciplinary Criteria of Creativity in the Arts and Sciences," *Research in Art Education*, 9th Yearbook, National Art Education Association, 1959.

[26] Owatonna Art Project, *Projects in Art Education* (Minneapolis: University of Minnesota, 1944).

Three

GOALS OF ART EDUCATION

The goals we establish for art education are intended to improve the ways in which people live, think, feel, and do things. The methods of the artists, like the methods of the scientists, are an important source of reference for the planners of art education programs.

THINKING PROCESSES IN ART ACTIVITIES

Evidence available to us from work, writings, and other documentation of the working habits of artists and scientists emphasizes the importance of both unconscious and conscious modes of thinking. Artists and scientists depend on such combinations of thinking to develop directions for their work. Such thinking is related to the role of impulse. We have said that impulse is not very useful unless it is directed. Dewey wrote that the abundant energy of children makes it possible for us to help them give a purpose and direction to their impulses. In much the same manner, the scientist and the artist find valuable sources of meaning and inspiration in impulses that originate in subconscious or unconscious thinking. When the artist or scientist can combine these modes of thinking, he may be able to create meaningful concepts or to invent forms that will contribute to the richness of human heritage.

LEARNING THROUGH ART ACTIVITIES

Art education can provide children with useful learning processes. The processes of art activity can give children an opportunity to apply reason to their impulses. In this way, the children can learn to produce expressive forms by learning to invent, to use their imaginations, and to draw from their experience.

The processes of learning through art begin with modes of thinking, knowing, and doing that are common to all creative human endeavors. This merely means that the roots of art activity are deeply imbedded in all human experience.

The common root of art and all other productive human experience is defined by Gardner Murphy as impulse that permits thinking to take root and grow. The impulse—the emotional motivation to thinking, learning, and knowing—can condition and give form and direction to learning, but it can also be given purpose by reason. The relation between reason and impulse is interactive. Without this interaction the processes of art activity would be handicapped. The existence of a conscious rationality is made possible because of a desire on the part of the individual for an association with reality.[1] The specific contribution of the art processes to the process of learning is the unique character of the process of forming symbols from images of perception. The projection of the perceived image on the screen of the mind and the formulation of visual symbols according to a meaningfully organized pattern or structured form involves a process of learning of a high order.

REASON AND INTUITION

A goal of art education, and one that deserves a strong claim on our attention, is the utilization of deductive or inductive reason and intuition. The latter may be defined as unconscious thought processes.

In an enlightening discussion regarding the work of the physicist, Albert Einstein notes that one must ". . . arrive at those elementary laws from which the cosmos must be built up by pure deduction. There is no logical path to these laws:

only intuition resting on sympathetic understanding of experience can reach them."[2]

Intuition alone would be a barren prospect for any fruitful effort. It is significant that the scientist, as well as the artist, is fully aware that intuition and reason must be wedded to a motivating emotion.[3] Apparently, it is this emotional factor that provides the force to make any kind of process possible. It is exactly the force of emotion that Einstein describes as the source of energy that makes possible the work of the true scientist. Discussing the work of the physicist Max Planck, Einstein notes that many persons attributed Planck's achievement to an extraordinary willpower and discipline. In Einstein's opinion, this was not the case. Einstein wrote, "The state of mind which enables a man to do work of this kind is akin to that of the religious worshipper or the lover; the daily effort comes from no deliberate intention or program, but straight from the heart."[4]

Children seem more inclined to depend on intuitions and responses generated by irrational emotions than to subject their thinking to a stringent rationalism. A purpose of art education is to achieve a balance between the various modes of cognition, precognition, and experience. The art activity and the forms of art are well suited for this purpose. The forms of art and the processes of forming art objects can become a means for balancing and unifying the modes of thinking and doing needed for healthy living.

INDIVIDUALITY AND UNIQUENESS

The achievement of a rich and useful uniqueness in personality and its expression in art activity and art forms is a goal of art education. Since the uniqueness of the child is also the concern of all education, art education shares the purpose of education in general.

---

[1] Gardner Murphy, *Freeing Intelligence Through Teaching*, p. 22.

[2] *Essays in Science* (New York: Philosophical Library, Inc., 1934), p. 4.

[3] In the following discussion of the contributions made by art education to the learning processes, specific reference will be made to two books in which the authors have described the relationships between intuition and reason: Murphy, *Freeing Intelligence Through Teaching* and Jerome S. Bruner, *On Knowing, Essays for the Left Hand* (Cambridge: Harvard University Press, 1962).

[4] *Essays in Science*, p. 5.

Art education provides a means for fostering and developing what is unique in each child; it places a premium on the differences that are natural to people. The individual's special ways "of seeing, of thinking, of inventing, of expressing mind or invention" will be of value to the present and future condition of human society. Individuality, however, is not a complete and unqualified idea. The individual, in spite of his uniqueness, can be useful only in relation to the social group.

Herbert Read recognized this problem when he began to define the educational functions of art.[6] In order to demonstrate that art is necessary for the education of all children, Read found that he had to begin with the cultivation of individuality. "The purpose of education [writes Read] can only be to develop, at the same time as the uniqueness, the social consciousness of the individual."[7] Uniqueness is indispensable for the progress of community life; it provides richness and variety to patterns of social relationships.

EDUCATION OF THE SENSES

Children need to know how to respond to experience and how to make use of their responses. Art activity provides a means for forming concepts from experience. But to form these concepts, children need to develop their senses of seeing, hearing, smelling, and touching.

The art education program must provide a program for the education of the perceptive senses.

CULTURAL GOALS FOR ART EDUCATION

Children bring a varied cultural background to the art activity. The art education program should begin with those cultural characteristics that are most important to the children.

In an essay entitled the "Interrelation of the Arts," Thomas Munro describes what he considers to be the "two comprehensive goals of liberal education."[8] The first of these goals is the accomplishment of ". . . balanced growth and healthy maturing of individual personality, including the ability to make successful interpersonal adjustments."[9] This is a goal that is directed toward psychological growth, which is deeply rooted in the sociological and the cultural.[10] We have evidence that people are shaped as much by their cultural environment and traditions as they are by their physical, mental, and emotional make-up. For this reason, it is necessary to note how art education draws from and implements the child's understanding of his relation to and his interaction with his cultural atmosphere.[11] Munro refers to the second of the goals of liberal education, which are concerned with the cultural and the social, as ". . . the selective transmission of world culture. It conceives of the educational process as feeding a wide range of knowledge, experience, skills, attitudes, and standards of value to each student in the best possible order."[12] These two broad goals of education are intimately related. As we have indicated, the sociological and cultural environment provide the soil in which the human grows.

To these broad goals of education, we must add a third, actually a combination of the two proposed by Munro: to help young people adjust to the cultural environment, to add to it, to aid in its continuous reconstruction or evaluation, and to be a contributing part of the culture.

Munro suggests that education in the arts is the proper means whereby the combined goal of cultural and psychological growth can be accomplished.

Experience in teaching art has demonstrated that involvement in the processes of art activity serves as an effective means for developing understanding and appreciation of cultural forces and traditions. For this reason, the program of art education must be organized to direct understanding in this direction. In the elementary school, the most effective appreciation and the most useful involvement in cultural understandings can grow out of the art activity.

[5] *Education Through Art,* p. 5.
[6] In *Education Through Art.*
[7] *Ibid,* p. 5.
[8] In *The Creative Arts in American Education* (Cambridge: Harvard University Press, 1960), pp. 10-11.

[9] *Ibid,* p. 10.
[10] See Chapter Two of this text.
[11] See especially Leslie A. White, *The Science of Culture* (New York: Grove Press, 1949), Part 2.
[12] "The Interrelation of the Arts," *op. cit.,* p. 10.

Four

ART EDUCATION IN THE

ELEMENTARY-SCHOOL CURRICULUM

In a subject-centered curriculum, the emphasis is on the disciplines that make up the experiences of human living. In many curricula the emphasis is placed on selected disciplines rather than on the large areas of human activity. In such curricula, there may be a danger that the relationships among disciplines will be lost: children may separate one subject area or discipline from another. This results in fragmentation. Children need to know that each thing we do in our living is the result of a coordinated use of many different kinds of learning. We make choices on the basis of our knowledges, intuitions, and experiences with many different subjects or disciplines. The architect, for example, must know engineering principles in order to design a building. Such principles involve mathematics, concepts of function, sensitivity to design, and knowledge of the kinds of things other architects have designed. The elementary-school child may find that a poem provides him with references to experience, with insight into the expressional power of language, and with a model of a technical structure of language for expressional purposes. At the same time, a poem may be the expression of a social order, a culture, or a philosophy of life. Each child needs to consider all this within the frame of reference of his own way of thinking and behaving and that is partly the result of his cultural background, his physical and emotional make-up, his interests, and his immediate needs.

ART IN THE ELEMENTARY-SCHOOL CURRICULUM

The concept of art as a part of the whole elementary-school curriculum is based on a concept of the curriculum as a structure built upon the most basic needs of growing children: food, clothing, shelter, recreation, health, human relations, and consumer education. The need for self-development is fundamental. As teachers, we should be aware of the relation between the needs of children, the elementary-school curriculum, and art education.

In a learner centered or child centered curriculum, we think of the child as a composite of three large areas of experience with which he interacts continuously. He affects and is affected by these broad areas of experience that make up his world:

1. Human expression and communication.
2. The natural environment.
3. The social environment.

According to Chart 1, the core of these experiences is the child, whose needs radiate outward in a chain reaction of a series of interactions that form the dynamic framework of a curriculum. In such a curriculum, art may find its proper functions in the living of children. Thus, the needs of the individual child may be conceived as beginning with modes for finding healthful and useful avenues to make possible the most healthful and constructive kinds of growing. These needs for growth, or self-development, provide a basis for educational planning and for the construction of a curriculum.

If the curriculum is thought of as three intersecting circles, as described in the Lester Dix Diagram (Chart 1), the core of the three areas of experience comprises the factors of the child's self-development, which is the purpose of this curricular program. Note that none of the areas of experience, or the disciplines within the areas, can be isolated. Thus, the arts, which form the area of human expression and communication, interact with, and become parts of, the natural and social sciences. If the child requires health, recreation, speech, or family education, he must find his useful educational experiences in areas that are blends of the arts and the social and natural sciences.

CHART 1

A PLAN FOR THE EMERGING CURRICULUM

Adapted from Lester Dix, *A Charter for Progressive Education* (New York: Teachers College, Columbia University, 1940).

The interaction of the child with his environment becomes the source of learning experiences. Influenced by his experiences, he, in turn, acts upon and makes changes in experience according to his memory of other experiences which provide a means for comparison. The ability to compare and relate is an important part of the process of education. In art education, the evidence of this activity is the structuring of art forms.

Through art activity, the child can make changes in his environment and he may, in turn, be affected by the changes he makes. For example, the need for communication and expression through speech may result in creative writing or the production of a dramatic presentation. This may result in the making of puppets or marionettes and a setting such as a stage, scenery, costumes, or props. The important thing is that these things happen because the child's vitality is being given a direction and a purpose. He must act upon his needs. Prepared forms, marionettes, stages, and other related paraphernalia would not permit active structure of understandings into forms that are the product of thinking, skills, and understandings. The interaction of the arts with speech, writing, or some other form of communication provides a real form, or organized structure, that will help the child define experiences, ideas, and concepts; it will help him clarify understandings, increase the scope of experience, and give experience richness, depth, and breadth. The skills required to give form to experience will certainly depend upon the child's possession of knowledges and disciplines.

This concept of the relation of art to the whole of the elementary curriculum is based on the assumption that a curriculum such as that described in the Lester Dix Diagram will be the basic model used in the elementary school. In practice, curricula in different schools vary. Thus, the problem of the teacher becomes that of finding a means for making art an experience that interacts with the whole pattern of the child's growing and achieving.

ARTS RELATED TO EACH OTHER

The relationship of the arts to each other is a natural one. The teacher will find that some kinds of experiences lend themselves more easily to one art form than to another; however, there will be much overlapping. Sound, for example, may be expressed in pictures, in poetry, or in music. But one form may be more forceful, more expressive than the others, and learning how to discover that form requires opportunities for experimentation.

Chapter Seventeen of this text presents a discussion of the ways in which the senses interact during the processes of art activity. Each art form places a different kind of emphasis on different groups of the senses. Each kind of experience needs to be known in a different way. We know the beauty of color through sight, the beauty of sounds through hearing. In the same way, each of the disciplines will require different kinds of sensory experience for their understanding. Children might know something about the battle campaigns of George Washington by reading or hearing about them, but they will know more about them if many of their senses are called into action. Understandings will be far more vivid if children are able to form them into pictures, poems, music, or dramatic presentations.

Each of the arts requires relationships with sensory experience beyond its own characteristics. Music, for example, places major emphasis on the sense of hearing; but the sensory activity needs to be supplemented by other kinds of sensory experience: rhythm, kinaesthesia, suggestions of color, and responses to visual experience that are translated into the musical medium. The typical example of this is operatic or "program" music. These characteristics may lead to associations of music with the dance and with dramatics. Through such means, the rhythm, color, and pattern of music can be given a visual form.

The ways in which interactions can be established between music and art depend upon the requirements of a particular situation and most often grow out of a situation. For example, dramatic presentations may serve as a means for giving added meaning and clarity to otherwise abstract ideas or they may give a more objective reality to stories or areas of study in science, history, civics, or poetry. This list should be extended to include any area that, in the teacher's opinion, may benefit from dramatization. In order to make the dramatization as vivid as possible, pictures, costumes, background scenery, charts, graphs, and maps will be useful. Music may be used to increase the emotional impact of the dramatization.

Music and art are akin in a variety of other ways. One of the best-known is their common interest in pattern, color, and rhythm. This relationship has been exploited in the practice of painting to music. Children listen to a musical composition and then try to give visual form with color, line, pattern, and texture to the color, sounds, and rhythm of the music.

Association between art and music at the primary-grade levels has been successfully used in such activities as the rhythm band, a well-known means for making music with instruments made by the children—drums, clappers, or simply objects filled with a material that will rattle when shaken, all decorated in a manner that expresses their tone and musical qualities.

ART AND THE SCIENCES

The art activity becomes a useful means for giving a reality to the abstractions of mathematics. Constructions made with various kinds of materials can utilize mathematical concepts. For example, children can use wire, toothpicks, or ceramic clay to construct models of buildings, bridges, or airplanes. Such constructions can be developed from geometric forms, from numbers of units, or according to engineering principles that require the application of mathematical principles.

In the primary grades, art activities can be used to give form to ideas relating mathematics to commerce or industry. Children can build replicas of markets with merchandise and computers. In this way, the simpler forms of arithmetic can be dramatized. In the upper grades, children have opportunities to apply mathematics to the construction of forms that give meaning to geometric structures. In the social sciences, children have opportunities to construct dioramas that are replicas of social organizations, of places in which people live and work. Diagrams and pictures help clarify verbal explanations of social situations or historical events.

AESTHETIC IMPLICATIONS

Illustration of the relationship of the visual arts to mathematics, music, and dance is especially useful if interactions of the subjects clarify and deepen their meaning, providing an aesthetic experience. The aesthetic experience may evolve from the logic that can become an important part of sensory interaction and sensory experience. In order for sensory interaction and a resulting aesthetic experience to take place, the children will have to become involved in processes of imaginative thinking, creative action, and analyses of cultural qualities and situations. Sensory interaction may take place when the forms of the ballet seem to relate themselves to the circles and ellipses in the geometry book; and if those moving circles result in a swirling painting or wire construction, then we have some evidence of an aesthetic experience.

OTHER RELATIONSHIPS AND INTERACTIONS

The interaction of several subject areas is not restricted to the group of activities we have listed. All areas of human living can be organized in this way. The accomplishment of this organization is a creative problem for the teacher or curriculum planner. The method consists of establishing relationships among the modes of sensory behavior that are dominant in each of the activities.

Modes of sensory behavior, however, are not the only considerations which determine the method of achieving educationally effective relationships among the area of art activities and subject fields. It must be noted that each subject field places a specific emphasis on modes of thinking. For example, in beginning mathematics the mode of thinking is rational. In music the mode is largely based on the pleasure children can derive from sound and rhythm. This does not mean that any one mode is used to the exclusion of all others. In spelling, for example, we may emphasize memory, but logic, a feeling for sounds, the relations of syllables, and the visual appearance of a word may play an important part in the development of spelling skill. It might follow that in a subject field such as spelling, the obvious modes are visual, audio, rhythmical, rational, and emotional. Words are capable of suggesting images. Nouns do this in an obvious way, but verbs and adjectives can do it on more abstract or imaginative levels. Noun images can quickly be related to verb, adverb, and adjective qualifications and colorations.

ART ACTIVITIES FOR THEIR OWN SAKE

Art activities are not always most effective simply because they interact with other subjects or areas. Many art experiences are educationally useful because the children experiment with materials to find ways of creating shapes, patterns, structures, and forms that are aesthetically satisfying. Children at all grade levels need opportunity to play with art materials, to explore and invent just for the excitement and the pleasure of such an experience. Working with materials, they also learn new things about the art processes.

PROVIDING TIME FOR SCHOOL ART ACTIVITIES

When do art activities for a class take place? How much time should be allowed for art activities? Teachers will sometimes say that no art activity took place during a particular period—a week, a month, or even a semester—because the "practical" subjects were too demanding; there was just no time for art. But "time for art" will be allotted when both children and teacher recognize that art is needed to give objective form to ideas, to make learning more effective, or to provide aesthetic experience.

It is easier to recognize the need for the learning process than the need for art as an aesthetic experience. The aesthetic values of involvement in art activity may be recognized as the result of participation in art activities that interact with all of the learning that takes place in the school day. For this reason it is useful to know how art interacts with learning.

We begin with the understanding that learning is most effective when it is based on a recognition of need. The art activity must be known as a learning process that is part of a total pattern —of thinking, knowing, experiencing, and doing —that ultimately leads to the fulfillment of needs. Since this is a process made up of interrelations and interactions among many modes of doing, knowing, and experiencing, there is little reason to divide the school day into periods of time with each period devoted to the study of a limited area of knowledge. The following example may help to clarify the way in which different areas of learning and knowing interact to create a time continuum.

There will surely be recognition of the child's need to understand the role of food, clothing, and shelter in his life. The curriculum may provide studies of manufacturing practices, agriculture, geography, distribution techniques, or merchandising practices in modern business. Studies of clothing may be related to studies of the use of certain kinds of cloth and design characteristics, which make clothing function satisfactorily, for example, to supply warmth in winter or cold climates and coolness in summer or warm climates. Other studies of clothing may be concerned with sources of supply for textiles, the kinds of materials that may be used, and the manufacture and design of textiles. The children can make hand looms with which they can weave textiles, using techniques they have studied that were used by other peoples in other times and places, or they may use processes they invent themselves. They can design fabrics and clothing in an effort to discover how textiles and clothing can be adapted to certain conditions. By designing and making their own fabrics, the children will relate to their work and will become aware of the tactile and visual characteristics of materials. In scientific studies, the children can compare the materials and processes related to animal textile fibers and synthetic man-made textiles.

Art activities, which will be a natural and necessary part of the study of clothing, will involve designing and making clothing in terms of the technical characteristics of the materials and the merchandising, cultural, and climatic requirements.

If approached in this manner, the study of clothing involves the interaction of many different disciplines, all of which may benefit by interaction with art activities. Through science, children discover how fabrics are made. By working with looms of various kinds, they discover something about the relation between technical manufacturing processes and techniques of clothing design. Comparative studies point out the differences between hand-operated looms and the highly developed machine weaving processes in modern factories.

Food and housing studies also involve interactions among many disciplines. The study of food requires an understanding of the relationships of agriculture, industry, and various social and economic factors. Housing studies involve learnings related to the design of homes and communities, and these designs reveal additional information, such as the functions of community agencies and the relation of school, church, and industry to the local scene. Understanding the community and its needs can become an important part of this type of study. Purposeful art activities involve construction of landscape models and making descriptive charts, maps, and diagrams.

If the art activity is thought of as interacting with everything a child needs to know and understand, time for art does not have to be "found" in a busy school day. All of the purposes of elementary-school education are met through the interaction of art activity with the most basic learning processes.

WHO TEACHES ART?

In an elementary-school program, where art becomes an area of the curriculum, every teacher teaches art. It is the general teacher who can relate art activities to the subject fields. Art becomes the means for expression and communication needed by every teacher for every discipline in the class working program. In the primary grades, the relationships between art and the other disciplines are more closely knit than they are in the intermediate and upper grades. The older children, partly because of their growing critical awareness and partly because they are acquiring greater amounts of information and are able to construct relationships between greater amounts of detail, require increasingly specialized knowledges. Increased specialization results in more precise distinctions among the disciplines. When this happens there is more need for the children to know the context within which each discipline exists and the relationship of this context to day-by-day living. If such concepts are destroyed, education itself becomes fragmented.

For this reason, it is important that the teacher be able to relate the disciplines to areas of the curriculum. The relationships of the arts to the natural and the social environment must not be obscured. Because the total relationship of the areas of the curriculum to the child's processes of growth is a continuing responsibility of the teacher, the general elementary teacher must always be aware of the relationship between art and other areas and disciplines. The teacher's basic frame of reference is provided by the relation of the child's growth to the activities that grow out of the curricular program.

It is necessary for the general teacher to assume responsibility for the art education of elementary-school children regardless of grade level. At the same time, the teacher must be aware that older children need more detailed information and technical knowledge than do younger ones, but it is hardly reasonable to expect the general teacher to have all the technical knowledge that older children need. For this reason, the special art teacher is a necessary member of the elementary-school faculty. A special art room is also desirable for art activities that are not directly correlated with a discipline. This does not mean that the art teacher will not be concerned with correlations; some correlations, at all grade levels, may require art teacher guidance. Similarly, many art activities that are not correlated can be carried on by the general teacher in the general classroom.

If the elementary-school curriculum is developed from a concept such as that illustrated in Chart 1, an art program is an indispensable part of the whole curriculum. For this reason, the general classroom teacher in the elementary school must be prepared to direct a program based on the three major areas of child experience. A purpose of this text is to provide knowledges that will help prepare the teacher to assume such responsibilities.

PART TWO

THE STRUCTURE OF ART EDUCATION

Five

SOURCES OF STRUCTURE IN ART EDUCATION

The structure of art education is formed from the natural thinking and working characteristics of children. These characteristics are organized within the context of a teaching procedure, a culture, and the purposes of the art program. To describe the parts of the art education structure, we must describe the things the teacher and children do during the course of an educationally valid art activity.

WORKING WITH ART MATERIALS

Children often find pleasure in manipulating art materials and tools, a form of play for its own sake. The teacher should determine when this kind of playing can become a means for motivating an educationally useful art activity. Once this decision is made, it is necessary for the teacher to devise techniques for helping the children become aware of how materials can be formed into objects that will have a meaning and purpose for them.

The first step toward the development of an educationally useful art activity is made when the teacher can begin to help the children relate their thinking, experiences, and purposes to art materials and the processes of working with art materials. The achievement of this purpose will take place when the children are able to make art forms which they feel are successful expressions of their experiences and their concepts of experience.

The quality of motivation to art activity may influence the effectiveness with which relationships are achieved between the children's thinking, experiences, goals, and art materials.

MOTIVATION

In this text, we will discuss role-playing, group discussions, field trips, and evaluation processes as some of the ways with which to direct the energies of children. Motivation provided by the teacher may be most effective when it is based on the attitudes, impulses, interests, experience, and natural inclinations of the children.

In the process of art education, we try to use the inclination to play with materials as a means to help children make ideas and experiences into meaningful and communicable art forms. A child may like the way paint can be made to form exciting patterns of color on white paper. From this pleasure he can learn how color can be used to make a statement about the appearances of spring or summer flowers, the color of a sky at sunset, the relation of colors to each other in a winter landscape, or the colors one might see at a football game.

Motivation provided by the teacher includes helping the child form a clear understanding of the problem at hand. We can refer to this understanding as clarity of perception.

MOTIVATION AND PERCEPTION

The word "perception" is used because in art activity we try to help children observe and be aware of experiences. Perception must be related to art materials and purposes and to ideas about an experience. The teacher may ask the children to paint pictures of their pets. They should then talk about, and experiment with, paint and the various ways paint can be used to form images of their pets. If the children are allowed to go ahead and paint, the results of such a permissive art activity might be some pleasing pictures of pet animals; but if we are concerned with having the children develop their sensitivity to how ani-mals look, to how they can express ideas about animals, and to how paint can provide a useful means for making specific kinds of visual statements about animals, it will be necessary for the teacher to plan for the achievement of such purposes.

The development of children's skill in perceiving and relating perception to expressions of ideas and experiences is a typical general purpose of art activity. In most primary groups, the teacher should try to help the children develop sensitivities to the unique characteristics of particular objects and experiences. The habit of making very broad generalizations is a typical sign of immaturity. The drawings made by the youngest children may be pictures of people. But it is significant that such pictures are usually not about a particular personality; they are most often just pictures of anyone. In conducting art activities, the teacher should help the children perceive and think in a specific rather than a generalized way. This kind of a detailed understanding is most likely to exist if the teacher can help the children describe their perceptions and experiences with gestures, words, sounds, and stories before they attempt to paint them.

The teacher, through the use of motivation techniques, helps the children relate perception to the processes of manipulating art materials. The shapes the children give to painted forms are devised in terms of specific understandings; in this way, the art activity is used to sharpen perception.

THINKING AND FEELING

During the processes of motivation, the teacher should provide the children with opportunities to express their feelings about the things they are going to paint. The feeling or emotional attitude of the children should become a part of the process of their art activity and of any of their other means of expression. Helping them relate their feelings about an object or experience to the art forms they are creating is probably easier with the less inhibited primary grade children than with the older groups. The very young do not easily separate their feelings from what they know about things that are important to them. The teacher should try to establish a qualitative relation between feelings and objective knowledge.

This relation between feeling and thinking should become a mature habit of thinking among the older children. Feelings often result in adding strength to what we have to say about something, whether the expression be verbal or pictorial.

The teacher can encourage children to relate their thinking to their feelings by showing proper respect for the feelings the children express. The children should be encouraged to express their feelings, as well as their factual knowledge. When a child paints a picture of a dog monstrous in size, he needs this opportunity to describe his feeling of bigness. The picture of a policeman in Figure 24-1, with exaggerated emphasis on the policeman's raised hand and white cape, shows an emotional emphasis; the child knows that with this important gesture, the policeman stops traffic so that children can safely cross the busy street.

The teacher must be aware that all childhood or adult thinking is not deliberative. Many of the things we do are not premeditated, but result from what we know as intuition, inspiration, impulse, or "a feeling" of rightness. Thinking that is not always deliberative will be referred to in this text as precognitive thinking.

There are other kinds of thinking that the teacher should encourage the children to use in their art activity. One of the most important is imaginative thinking, sometimes called creative thinking. There are slight differences, however, in the meanings we give to imaginative and creative thinking, differences that will be noted in our discussions about imagination and creative action. But because the two are so closely related, we are perfectly justified in coupling them and using the term "creative-imagination."

So far, we have said that the structure of art education is comprised of motivations to art activity, the manipulation of art materials, impulse, inspiration, intuition, precognitive thinking, imaginative thinking, and creative action. Now we shall see how these parts can be related to each other so that they become a useful means of education. First, the teacher must develop techniques to motivate and enlarge upon classroom art activity—techniques designed to call into action the other parts of the structure. These parts will, in turn, initiate the process of forming visual-plastic concepts or metaphors from the symbols children make to represent their experiences.

BEGINNING THE ART ACTIVITY

Art activity begins when the youngest children start to become involved with art materials, even before purposes are formulated. All art activities are not begun in this way, but the introduction to materials and tools may occupy a period, perhaps of one hour, in which children simply play with materials. Motivation to purposeful art activity can grow out of this initial interest.

The youngest children may use paint for the pure pleasure of smearing it on paper (and on themselves, and on everything else that is close to them). But the interest the child has in the materials may make it possible for him to be led to establish relations between the forms he can make and the things he sees, smells, hears, and talks about. Ask a child who is daubing paint on paper for the first time, "What are you making?" He may not know, but there is nothing to prevent the teacher from talking about how a circle could become a face if it had two blue spots for eyes. The teacher can then ask the child, "Whose face could it be?" If the child becomes shy, the teacher can ask some of the other children in the group what they are making. There is a good chance that ideas will begin to grow, and the children will begin to relate their painting to ideas.

Inventiveness and imagination are stimulated by showing the children how chalk can make brilliant masses of color when applied to paper, how paint can be effective when applied to large or small sheets of paper with large or small brushes, sponges, or any other kind of applicator. This phase of the classroom activity is concerned with exploration of the materials. It is the process of finding relationships between ideas and the things that can be done with materials. When children begin to make pictures, they sometimes recognize forms that result from ordinary manipulations. The youngest children in the kindergarten make circular scribbles that suggest things which, to their generalized ways of thinking, are circular: the sun, a face, or the center of a flower. The important thing is that associations are made between manipulated art materials and things the children have seen and know. An elongated oval, made with the sweeping motion of an arm, may suggest a dachshund to the child, who then adds a circle at one end for the head, two dots for eyes, four short lines on the bottom for legs, and a short line at the end opposite the head for a tail.

ASSOCIATION FORMING

Association and invention become close allies in the art activity. Association becomes the mother of invention; or invention may lead to the formation of successful associations. Association grows out of the processes of exploration.

When does exploration end and association begin? There is no pat answer to this question. A great deal depends upon when children are ready to make associations. Some will establish associations almost immediately; others will not make them at all until they begin to see what some of the other children have begun to do. This is an important aspect of any group activity. Children learn from each other. When they begin to establish relations between colors, shapes, textures, or patterns and some idea or experience, they are beginning to make art forms that are meaningful to them. It is at the beginning of the process of making associations that the teacher needs to help the children talk about their work, to tell the others in the group what they are doing.

There can be little value in permitting exploration activities to perpetuate themselves and become a form of play for its own sake. Opportunities to show the children how associations can be made will be found in selected pieces of work, to illustrate how ideas can be found in the manipulative results. The teacher can hold up the work of a child and ask the class to tell her what it is about. Or she may ask the child to talk about what he is trying to make. Another alternative is a discussion opened with pointed questions such as, "This shape reminds me of an animal. What does it look like to you?" This practice is a method of creating opportunities to lead the children into making associations.

Relating materials, manipulative processes, and experiences to one another can become a group activity. The method will not be appropriate to every group; but if it can be used successfully, a slow group may be helped to understand these relationships. The teacher must use her good judgment. The technique begins when the teacher asks the children to suggest how a picture can be made to show the appearance of a particular object or the feeling or mood of a specific experience. The child who talks about houses may need to know how to show the size of a particular house. Another child may want to know how to express the blueness of a sky. Still another child may need a technique for showing how tall his father is. Such ideas may be expressed with a gesture of the arm to draw a line on a blackboard or sheet of paper pinned to a wall. The teacher can ask the children how she should make a line or a mass of color with crayon or paint on paper. An alternative method might be to have a child do this according to the instructions of his classmates. In this way the group will guide an individual who, in turn, will demonstrate methods. Or the children could take turns selecting colors and painting them on a large sheet of paper to show, for example, how red a fire engine is. They could paint lines with descriptive gestures of their arms to show each other how fast a fire engine can go. They could find colors which, when painted alongside each other, become symbols for the kinds of sounds a fire engine makes.

CONCEPTS

The expression of experiences through art materials can evolve into concepts, which may have metaphoric or poetic values. Concepts expressed as art objects result from thinking and feeling about experiences and ideas and giving this thinking and feeling a tangible form. Such concepts become something more than bald statements of facts. They are a blend of many kinds of feeling, thinking, imagination, associations, and creative arrangements of shapes, colors, textures, lines, and patterns. They are formed ideas and expressions that can evolve from the new experiences of art activity and are related to the organization of art materials, symbols, and processes.

Concepts may result from some of the insights the children develop during the period of motivation to art activity. These insights are the products of a planned and purposeful interaction of ideas and thoughts. The techniques for aiding the development of concepts are similar to the methods the teacher uses to start art activity. The teacher helps the children talk about their experiences, to describe their feelings and thinking in many different ways.

If the children develop meaningful concepts and become involved in a well-organized process of art activity—one which makes maximum use of the parts of the structure of art education—the resulting art work may have a good measure of aesthetic value.

CONCEPTS, EXPERIENCE, AND CHILD ART

The crayon drawing of a fire engine, Figure 5-1, is an example of a concept that grew out of the experience of making a picture about a fire engine. In this picture-making experience, the child discovered a way to say exciting things about fire engines, although the drawing itself may not be an exact image of the concept the child developed. Young children are not always able to put as much of their concepts into their drawings as they want to. This may be one

of the reasons why children like to talk about their art work. Talking gives them an opportunity to add detail to the expression of the concepts they have formed. The growth of the concept does not end with the completion of the picture. Apparently, new thoughts, feelings, ideas, and experiences continue to make the concept evolve and grow.

The drawing of the fire engine is an example of how thinking and feeling are given form, direction, and purpose in an art activity. Impulse is not permitted to scatter. The impulse merely to make noises like a fire engine or to draw wild red colors racing across a sheet of paper becomes a form that represents what the child would like to say. In this picture, we have an example of a vivid experience that has been directed through perception, feeling, and recollection of other and similar experiences, to form an organized product of imagination and creative action.

The crayon drawing of a fire engine is an example of how concept intermingles with art materials to form a visual expression of a child's

5-1. FIRE ENGINE
Crayon. *Author's collection.*

experience: the sound, speed, and fury of a fire engine rushing to a fire. This is the kind of thing that excites the imagination of a child. The art process came into being partly because of the excitement of the fire and the idea of the fire engine, but the art materials played an important role in helping to form the concept. The crayons were bright in color and the clean paper was inviting. These things provided an important part of the motivation to the activity.

The fire engine is drawn as a long red hook-and-ladder truck. On the rear end of the truck is a fireman, who is hanging onto the truck because it is going so fast. If he did not hang on with all his strength, he could easily fall off.

There are very definite feelings woven into this concept of the fire engine. Its great speed is shown by comparison with the bird above, who flies very fast but has a hard time keeping up with the fire engine. Long red lines trailing from the rear of the truck are familiar symbols of rapid movement. But some of the things in the picture are only vaguely associated with fire engines, and what they represent was not clear even to their creator. At the front of the truck, for example, there is a large bell-like shape. This could be the cab in which the driver sits. The child was asked to tell the teacher about this. He answered that it could be a bell; then he changed his mind and said that it was the place for the fire engine driver. At another time, the child said this was the great bell that makes loud warning noises as the truck races down the street. The bell was drawn very large because it makes such a loud noise.

The fire engine drawing is, in part, the product of imaginative thinking, exemplified by the relation between the bird and the speeding vehicle. The processes of creative action, precognitive thinking, feeling, and perception combine to form a concept. This concept is made from the speed of a bird, the image of desperation in the fireman hanging onto the rear of the truck, the large bell which stands for the noise of the fire engine as it warns everyone of a dangerous mission, and the brilliant red color which has been made with attractive red crayon applied to a white surface. The child has learned that a color's full value is most easily seen against a white background.

The forming of concepts, their special character, and the ways in which they influence the ever changing and ever unique processes of conception

must be determined by the symbols which are the child's created signs, by the elements which are able to form a language. This is the language with which the child can communicate. The fire engine, the bird, the ladder, and the bell are some of the elements of this language.

INTERACTION OF CONCEPTS AND SYMBOLS

The child's crayon drawing of a fire engine illustrates the way in which the concept of a fire engine is expressed through the use of symbols. The early appearance of symbols in children's art work may represent the achievement of purposeful relations between the process of manipulating art materials and the forming of communicable expressions.

Our observation of children's art work indicates that the symbol comes into existence after the child has become aware that the colors, shapes, textures, and patterns he makes can come to mean something familiar. We cannot always assume, however, that manipulation of art materials comes before children invent or discover symbols in their art work. We assume that the scribble drawing comes before the symbol. It may very well happen that a child will begin to work with a definite idea of what he is going to make. We have some reason to believe that the older children in kindergarten, and of course children in the upper grades have had enough experience with art work to know how to achieve a representation of an idea, an experience, or an object they have seen. But it is also true that we can expect children's thinking about what they are making during an art activity to change as they work. We have already indicated that the natural manipulative processes cause forms to emerge; some are caused by accident and some by the natural inclination of an art material to suggest symbols and ideas previously unthought of. It might happen that a child, while working, will simply decide that he has a better idea. Or it might happen that the child will become intrigued with the materials with which he is working and will make his ideas fit the natural forms that evolve from the manipulative processes. Ideas may also come into being because each child sees ideas in the work of the other children around him that he would not have thought about if he were working in isolation.

Symbols come into being in many ways. There is no reason to believe that there is only one acceptable way for a child to form a symbol. The important thing is for a child to learn to form symbols that are sufficient to embody a worthwhile concept.

The symbols children use in their art work are the signs they feel stand for things they see, hear, know, taste, feel, think and talk about. The symbol is a familiar sign that for the child stands for a host of sensations, associations, and understandings. For a small boy, a feather stuck in a hat can be a symbol for all the imaginative associations he makes with American Indians. For a little girl, a stick can be a symbol for a wand, which could be waved by a fairy to create fantasies impossible in the real world. In much the same way, a small child in the kindergarten makes a circle with the full movement of his arm, and the circle becomes a face. The gesture is translated into a round mass with dots for eyes, a small circle or oval for a nose, and an up-and-down curving line to symbolize a smile or sign of sadness. The symbols of child art—the circles, triangles, or rectangles with which the child makes a dress or a roof for a house—are often the simple product of an arm movement, a gesture that is an uncomplicated description of the world in which the child lives.

The art activity helps children understand their experiences; it helps them give purpose, order, and direction to their thinking about the things they have done and the things they have seen. The art activity helps children relate their mental images to the formed and structured symbols that they make as signs of their experience. A child draws a picture of a house as a rectangle with a triangle on top and smaller rectangles or squares for windows and doors. This becomes not so much a picture *of* a house as a statement in symbols *about* a house.

The images made by children in their art activity are the products of a motor movement, a kinesthetic rhythm of arm and hand. The motor movement is a gesture that describes an experience. In this way, art provides children with a language uncomplicated by the abstractions of words. It may be difficult for children to use words to convey their thoughts and feelings about the things they see and know. But a body rhythm, a muscular description—in short, kinaesthesia—

may provide a means for children to say more than they could with words. The art activity can become a means for providing children with opportunities to communicate. The language of the art activity will become the language of image-symbols.

In the classroom, we can watch the children form symbols into expressive structures. These structures are metaphors, signs meant to convey meanings, figures of visual communication. The sun is a circle with radiating lines. The earth is a base line, a ground symbol made by drawing a line at the bottom of a sheet of paper. The space of nature is the space between the ground line and a line at the top of the paper which is the sky. These images are the signs of experience. Flowers and animals are also made from such generalizations. Trees, houses, friends, family, and self are all originated in the typical forms of the gesture.

In the process of art activity, the symbol represents an image of experience. Symbols are collected by children during acts of perception. In art, the visual symbol may be closely related to the image of an original perception. But the symbol is not a replica of the image of perception; the symbol stands for an experience. The child puts his symbols together, according to the limits of his skill, to form a metaphor that expresses his thinking, feeling, and purposes as they are related to his learning about experience.

Symbols are important to the processes of thinking because they are a direct and simple means for representing the child's world. Because art education makes use of visual symbols closely related to images of perception, it is possible to consider the processes of art education as a short cut to the development of useful thinking processes.

The processes of art activity are direct avenues to effective development and growth of the human personality because they provide immediate and useful selections from the raw materials of perceptual experience.

MEANING IN EXPERIENCE:
MAKING THE IMAGE-SYMBOL STRUCTURE

The process of forming image-symbols in art works is dependent on the existence of qualitative concepts. We cannot determine whether a

5-2. CIRCUS
Mural. *Teaneck, New Jersey, Public Schools.*

concept is qualitative merely by applying an established standard. There is no way in which we can predict exactly what will happen when concepts are formed. The best we can do is to form a general understanding of the kinds of things we might expect the concept and the concept formation to be like.

Qualitative concepts are generally relative things. We can determine that a concept is qualitative if it demonstrates greater ability to understand experience, more detailed knowledge, increased abilities to establish relationships with other experiences, and an approach to understanding in terms of a variety of types of perception. When children form qualitative, concepts, they often show increased sensitivity to color and its relationship to the general character of experience and an improved ability to perceive unique expressional characteristics in movement of figures, lines, shapes, and the relationships between objects. Also included here might be evidence of sensitivity to varieties of texture, methods for creating a sense of movement related to expression, and techniques for demonstrating the effects of sound.

Figure 5-2 illustrates the way these general touchstones can be applied. This is a painting made by a small group of first grade children, whose purpose was to paint a circus. If this painting is compared to the one by a kindergarten child, Figure 7-5, it will be noted that Figure 5-2 is richer in detail. The subject "circus" for the kindergarten child suggested clowns. For the first graders, the subject "circus" suggested a multitude of actions. The first grade children have actually painted performers in action, and they have shown relationships between performers and clowns.

Figure 7-5 shows a change from purely muscular sensations and personal pleasure in movement to a beginning concern with the objective world around us. In Figure 5-2, the children have sensed the rhythms of movement and have demonstrated a feeling for the distortions of size and the rhythm of the acrobats. They have also found symbols for exaggerated motion and size. In this case the children were able to develop concepts of things they had experienced either vicariously or directly, they were able to combine both personal and objective sensations, and they were able to create symbols for the sensations and visions they associate with the subject. The total image is detailed and many faceted. In the kindergarten painting the variety of symbol, the detail, and the balance between objective and subjective perception is in no way equal to that found in Figure 5-2.

The concepts given a form in Figures 5-2 and 7-5 are qualitative in terms of the kind of personal development they indicate for the children who made them. In the work of the first graders, there is evidence of a high level of perceptiveness, emotional expressiveness, objective detailing of the experience, and the relatedness of the parts of the experience of a circus. The painting by the group of first grade children shows evidence of quality because of the manner in which the forming of the symbols into a whole and unified image-symbol is carried out. The kindergarten child's painting shows equal evidence of quality; but the accomplishment of the kindergarten child would not be considered an accomplishment for the first graders, from whom we expect more detailed and organized expression. In the case of Figure 5-2 we should note that the nature of the material, in this case paint, plays a large part in the kind of forming that has taken place. Paint is applied in broad masses. The children used lines of paint, which became planes and masses. The direction of the planes and the direction, shape, and size of the brush strokes determine the particular rhythmical movement that illustrates the rhythm of a circus.

This illustration of a circus demonstrates that *forming* is a process of creating visual structures from concepts. These structures are new images; they are not imitations of things that may be seen at a circus. These forms express characteristics of a circus action. Deformation of figures and emphasis placed on movements become part of the process of devising symbols from images of perception in order to express feelings and

ideas. The result is an image-symbol structure. The appearance of this image-symbol structure is as much determined by concepts, both seen and felt, as it is by the kind of material used to form it. The paint and its brushing qualities give the whole expression a quality that would have been different if chalk, colored paper, or wax crayons had been used instead.

It follows that the images made and related to each other, to ideas, concepts, and materials are the ingredients of the forming process; the way in which these ingredients are handled gives the final form, the work of child art, its unique qualities.

INTERACTION OF SYMBOLS, FORMS, CONCEPTS, AND MATERIALS

The painting about a circus defines several important ideas or understandings about the process of making a picture as a child art activity.

The interaction between symbols, forms, concepts, and materials is an important part of the process of learning through art. We have some reason to believe that concepts become a part of the images children make during the process of creating an art form. In this particular painting, the concepts were fairly well formed before the picture was made. However, the children's concepts of the circus underwent several changes as the process of arranging shapes, colors, textures, lines, and patterns caused the children to see their concepts in a different light. The development of an evaluation process (thinking about what they had done and what they should do) caused the children to make changes in their concepts.

The relation between concepts and the forming processes are not always the same as they were in the painting of the circus. Concepts do not always dictate what a form will be like. We have seen that concepts are the product of the interaction of art activity with other concepts. Although the concept or concepts may originally motivate the children to participate in the art activity, after concepts begin to translate the data of perception into materials, the materials act to influence and change the concepts in terms of their own unique qualities.

The interaction of concepts with materials and the changes that take place in each lead to the possibility that symbols formed during the manipulative processes are not necessarily childish stereotypes. The richer the interaction of concepts, materials, and manipulative processes, the more likely it is that symbols may be unique, inventive, and imaginative. Interaction of concepts, materials, and manipulation is of a nature that makes the order of action indefinable. It is possible that there is no rigid order of action: interaction may be simultaneous. It may also happen that concept, manipulation, and the original motivation, thought, and feeling are interwoven in a fluxlike stream that shows little definable change from one part of the process of art activity to another.

THINKING WITH IMAGE-SYMBOLS

The process of using symbols to form concepts into meaningful and poetic structures is also a rapid and effective means for thinking about experiences. When we think about our experiences and about the ideas that grow from experiences, we begin to understand them better. The ancient people who began the long chain of human history by making paintings about their lives and thoughts on cave walls took this for granted. In the same way, all of us find it helps to think more clearly when we can give our ideas a picture form. This is one of the ways children, too, can gain increased understanding about their experiences. When children can arrange ideas and experiences in forms made from art materials, or other materials that can be shaped, they may be better able to organize their thinking and to understand relationships between ideas.

TECHNIQUES FOR FORMING VISUAL METAPHORS FROM IMAGE-SYMBOLS

The process of forming concepts into images from the raw materials of experience is a creative act. The shapes of the images children make are often determined by the process of working with art materials. Although a child may begin to paint a picture of a fire engine, as in Figure 5-1, the act of making the drawing may cause unexpected things to happen. The crayon permits the child to make lines that could not be made with paint. The side of the crayon makes its possible

for the sky to take on a texture that creates an atmosphere not originally associated with the experience. While the child was working with the crayon, he noticed that when the side of the crayon was lightly drawn across the yellow sun, in the upper right hand corner of his picture, the sun seemed to shine through a haze. This was an appropriate metaphor as far as the child was concerned. The process of manipulating the art materials caused him to find a way to express the atmosphere one encounters at a fire. This is the kind of discovery that leads to both the clarification of experience and the forming of a poetic symbol. However, such discoveries are made only if the child and the teacher are alert enough to see the possibilities available for forming materials into symbols and symbols into metaphors. If the child begins to make some art form with predetermined ideas about what should happen, he immediately limits his possibilities for imaginative creation of a poetic visual metaphor. The art activity profits most when it can begin with a "let's see what will happen" attitude.

The open-ended approach to thinking about experience is most useful if the child is not hampered by conventions consisting of rules about how a form should be made. If the child who made the drawing of the fire engine had been limited by rules of drawing and rules about how to work with crayon, he would not have made some of the discoveries which transformed the drawing into a visual metaphor, a poetic analogy.

THE METAPHOR, THE IMAGE-SYMBOL, AND THE EXPRESSION OF FEELINGS

Some areas of the school curriculum have to be concerned with definitive or descriptive means. Descriptive subjects are those that describe rather than express. To describe the facts of geography or the inflexible outcome of the addition of two and two, leaves little room to invent poetic analogies, effectively expressive metaphors, and unexpected conformations of paint or clay that convey concepts of a child's reactions to the life around him. Some of the subjects or areas with which children become involved have to be descriptive. However, descriptiveness of this kind in art would defeat the purpose of the art activity.

In the literature of art education, we refer to

descriptive art forms as pictures that are literal representations of things as we think we see them. The desire of children for such descriptiveness does not seem to appear until the end of second grade. It may be that a cultural attitude leads children to associate skill with the ability to make literal descriptive pictures. Children begin to prize this skill as soon as they adopt this cultural attitude. They adopt such an attitude as soon as they become aware that authoritative adults consider such skill to be a good thing. It is unfortunate that when children consider skill in descriptive drawing to be admirable and desirable they are often not ready to acquire this kind of skill. As a result, the children are prone to frustrations because they believe they can not make acceptable drawings.

If a teacher were able to instruct first or second graders in the use of skills that would enable them to make descriptive drawings, the children would lose important learning opportunities. The demands of such descriptive drawing would prohibit thought, energy, and time for discovery. Discovery results from art activities that direct the children's energies to the important processes of imaginative exploration, creative action, and manipulation of art materials in order to form effectively expressive poetic metaphors.

The structure of an effective art education activity is dominated by modes for helping children discover metaphoric forms that embody the experiences which are part of their own living. The teacher who is aware of the importance of this understanding will have little difficulty in helping children find suitable directions for the development of art activity. For example, some of the things children know best and feel most strongly about are their own parents or even themselves. The drawings shown in Figures 5-3, 5-4, and 5-5 illustrate the various ways in which this approach can be developed.

Figures 5-3, 5-4, and 5-5 are evidence of the contrast between symbol formations that involve the entire process of perception, symbol making, and forming in response to feelings. These drawings also suggest what may happen when a teacher bypasses the procedure suggested by the structure of art education. Figure 5-5, for example, represents the work of a child who had previously formed ideas about how a self-portrait should look; the child followed a procedure that he be-

5-3. PARENTS
Crayon. *Author's collection.*

lieved would help him achieve his purpose. More about this later. First we need to consider the useful values found in the teaching techniques that made it possible for these drawings to be created.

Figure 5-3 is a picture by a first grade child of his mother and father. This child's father is a very big man. The father's bigness is drawn from the eye level of a very small boy. The mother is also very big, but she is not as big as the father. It is interesting to note the devices the child has used to communicate feeling. The mother wears a dress with many buttons extending from the top to the bottom. This device, which is an invented image-symbol, serves to establish a sense of height in the figure. The father has a rough beard. This is another invented image-symbol that, like the buttons on the mother's dress, becomes a metaphor. Apparently, small boys are aware that that which scratches them when a

the correlating of feelings and thinking that are so evident in the illustrations of a child's parents and of one little boy's conception of his father.

Figure 5-5 is an attempt to describe; however, it succeeds very little in describing anything. It is not a structured metaphor made from image-symbols. As a bare description, it possesses little if any educational validity because some of the most important processes of art activity have been bypassed. The elements of thinking and feeling are not related to the image in the same way as in Figures 5-3 and 5-4. Equally as important as relating concepts and feelings through image-symbols of the perceived object would be an effort to form the symbols of concepts into a meaningful structure. Figure 5-4 is an example of such a structure. The structure is direct and simple; the long lines are the lines of a tall and firm man. It is a statement full of economy. With two lines on each side of the figure, the child has made a sign for hands and guns. A single line on the bottom of the boot on each foot is an economical metaphor for a boot heel. On the top of each boot is a simple curved line that stands for the metaphor of a cowboy boot top. By contrast, the imagery of Figure 5-5 is the

5-4. PARENT
Crayon. *Author's collection.*

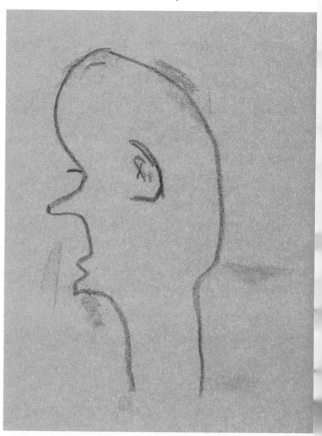

loving father plants a kiss on a tender face is the harsh, coarse beard with which fathers must contend. The child is also aware that father and mother are companionable or loving. In his drawing, the child has made his parents hold each other's hands.

Figure 5-4 is a first grade boy's proud and very definitely stated image-symbol of his father. His father is a very big man, and he is brave and bold just like a cowboy with two guns and cowboy boots.

Figure 5-5 is an entirely different kind of picture. This is not the result of thinking about a face or a human head. This drawing was made by a little boy who was asked by his teacher to draw a self-portrait. The child did exactly as he was asked; he placed his head on the drawing paper and traced around it. The result is obviously lacking in the expressiveness, the symboling, and accidental result of tracing the head; there is no evidence that these lines and shapes are symbols for vision and feeling.

DESCRIPTIVENESS AND TECHNIQUES USED TO FORM EXPRESSIONS

Descriptiveness and nondescriptiveness have been studied by art educators. Two studies of particular interest are the discussions by Viktor Lowenfeld [1] of the "visual" and "haptic" and Herbert Read's study of the function types.[2]

Visual refers to people who are concerned with the appearance of things. Visual-minded children are spectators who perceive mainly with their eyes. The visual-minded person describes experience as a reporter might report an event for a newspaper. The second type, the haptic, is the direct opposite of the visual. The haptic child is concerned more with the way he feels about experience. The expressions of the haptic child are the result of an emotional involvement. Extreme types of the visual or the haptic are rare. Most children are combinations of the two, with an inclination toward either the haptic or the visual.

Lowenfeld warns that we must not force the visual types to be haptic or the haptic types to be visual. Children should be permitted to follow their own inclinations. If, for example, we force the haptic child to be visual or the visual child to respond more frequently and with increased depth of feeling to body sensations and subjective feelings, we may cause the child to become inhibited and disturbed.

The most important thing for us to understand about visual types is that they are not purely descriptive. Visual children can form metaphors from the raw material of experience. Pure descriptiveness or the attempt to construct unimaginative replicas of experience may be a small part of the inclination of visual types; however, they can progress beyond mere description of their experiences. The visual-minded child first defines the experience of seeing; he sketches the broad outlines. During a second stage of observation, the visual-minded child analyzes the parts of his total impression of an experience. During a third stage, the child reconstructs the parts into a new form. Lowenfeld notes that mere observation of detail is not always important. For the visual-minded child, it is necessary to be aware of and to see the changes that take place in the details of an experience. These details will be related to and will be the results of influences existing in the surrounding environment.[3]

The haptic child does not transform his subjective experiences into visual forms. Haptic types will be satisfied with organizations of tactile sensations. The appearance of forms in the art work of haptic children will be determined by sensations rather than by objective fact. For this reason, the art work of the haptic child will contain an emphasis on the textures of surfaces and on the exaggeration of body parts. This exaggeration will become a device to draw attention to the aspects of the experience that are most important to the child. The haptic child places emphasis on what "feels" right.

The significance of this discussion by Lowenfeld is the indication it provides of an important element in our structure of art education. No two children need to express the same experience in the same way. Children will respond to experience according to their own modes of perception, understanding, and interpretation.

The effectiveness of the process of art activity will be partly dependent on the teacher's ability to know whether or not a child is predominantly visual or haptic. The teacher must make a distinction between the visual, the nonvisual, and the purely descriptive. Figure 5-5 is an example of the descriptive type. A child who succeeds in making forms that describe objective facts as we see them is descriptive. Descriptive forms may lack imaginative thinking, inventiveness, enriching associations, analogies, and poetic metaphors.

Herbert Read describes the descriptive type as belonging to a category that enumerates the data of visual experience. This type is named the enumerative. Concepts of structure, relationships, and meanings that are part of the experience of perception are of no consequence to this type.

It is possible for the enumerative type to be involved in an educationally useful process if he

---

[1] *Creative and Mental Growth.*
[2] *Education Through Art.*

[3] *Creative and Mental Growth*, p. 265.

can project himself into the experience of seeing, if he is able to derive emotional sensations from experience. These sensations add the element of feeling to the objective enumeration of detail. In this way, it becomes possible for the child to develop an understanding of relationships. Such an understanding aids in the eventual achievement of a useful art process. This kind of self-projection, which involves the use of imagination, leads to the combining of invented elements with objective perception and provides for the child's recognition of the problems involved in relating materials to expression.

This discussion of the visual, the haptic, and the enumerative type is concerned with the reality of classroom experience in art. It will be found that children are inclined toward one of these categories. Each category presents the teacher with a particular kind of teaching problem. The subjective child needs to be helped to associate objective experience with his sensations. The visual child should be helped to relate subjective feeling to his reporting inclinations. However, neither of these two types presents a serious problem. In each case, the child can be permitted to follow his general inclination. For some children, expression may be subjective with elements of objectivity. For other children, the objective may be suitably tinged with the subjective.

There are many paths to expression. The structure of art education is formed from human differences; it is designed to take into account the many ways in which different children may relate themselves to their environment.

Six

PRECOGNITIVE THINKING

Precognitive thinking is a basic mode of thinking in art activity. The precognitive mode uses all levels of thinking. The cognitive processes serve as a means for controlling the quality and final forms that result from precognitive thinking.

It has already been said in this text that the kind of thinking most useful in art education is precognitive thinking, which has been described as a blend of feeling and thinking; it combines the rational, the emotional, and the cognitive. The emotional is sometimes correlated with the irrational because emotional thinking or behavior is not always limited by reason.

GENERAL CHARACTERISTICS

Cognitive thinking deals with the process of knowing and perceiving. In an art activity, precognitive thinking takes place before conscious knowing or conscious recall becomes part of the process of making an art form. The worker in art, adult or child, makes paintings or sculptures only partly by deliberately placing colors, objects, textures, and arrangements of parts in a thoughtfully planned manner. Many of the things done during the course of an art activity may be intuitive, inspired, or they may just seem like a good idea that ought to be tried. This process of experimenting with ideas does not have to be accompanied by reason. The attitude that permits this kind of thinking and action to take place is best described as an attitude that says, "Let's see what will happen." This manner of working makes use of the precognitive processes. In this sense, the precognitive process combines impulse with a feeling of rightness.

Previous experience that is used to help make an art work, to give more depth to an idea, or to provide more useful detail in thinking may be thought of as a constellation. A child, for example, sees a fire engine rushing to a fire. When the child makes a drawing about this sight, he may include many things he did not see. He may draw the fire and the firemen who make heroic gestures and do wonderful, heroic things. Added to the picture the child makes might be a gigantic building from which black smoke is seen stream-

ing in a mighty cascade toward an overcast sky. Firemen climbing high ladders and policemen holding back vast mobs of people who have become excited or curious about the fire might also be included. It is important to note that although most of these additions are recalled from other experiences, the child suggests that they were all actually part of his experience of seeing the fire engine. The experience of hearing the noise made by the fire engine and of seeing its speed, its brilliant color, and the firemen becomes the center or core experience around which other associated experiences cluster to form a constellation. The core experience is the motivating force in the formation of the constellation. The rest of the experiences spring spontaneously into being or they are deliberately recalled.

When a child draws a picture of a particular experience, the completed drawing will probably consist of selections from the whole constellation of experiences associated with the core experience

6-1. FIRE FIGHTERS
Crayon. *Author's collection.*

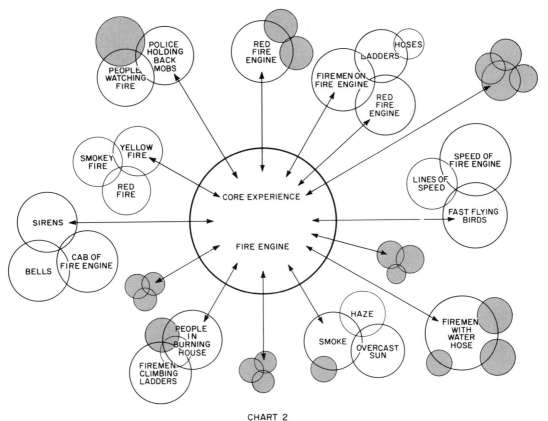

CHART 2

A PRECOGNITION CONSTELLATION BASED ON FIGURE 5–1 AND 6–1.

that originally motivated the art activity. The making of such selections from the whole constellation is accomplished by the process of precognitive experience.

The word "constellation" is useful because it implies a relation between the many facets of children's daily living. A constellation is a group of related things; in art activity, the related things are grouped around a central nucleus. The central nucleus, the basic reality in art education, is the child.

The use of precognitions have to be considered in the light of classroom reality. In this situation, precognitive concepts probably seem more real than they would in a society of adults. Children are more easily subject to imaginative flights of fancy than are older people. Impulse and imagination are important parts of the precognitive processes. If the logical, the purely rational, and the entirely conscious were to dominate thinking, precognitive concepts could not function as an important part of the process of thinking and doing. We have already seen, from the discussion in Part One, that a purpose of the art education process is to give a direction and purpose to the

impulsiveness and natural vitality of children. Imaginative thinking must be respected and permitted to grow as a legitimate part of the thinking and performing processes of constructive work. From this point of view the imaginings, fancies, and spontaneous responses of children must be used as elements in the learning processes. To accomplish this purpose, we have to find a means for giving these modes of response a purpose and direction. The teacher can encourage the use of precognitive processes in the children's art activity by involving the children in group discussions that will result in a pooling of the experiences of all of the children in the group. The relation of the logical to the illogical, the rational to the irrational, or the emotional to the reasonable is a part of the precognitive process. The relationship between these opposites is a necessary part of the formation of the poetic image in painting, sculpture, or other art forms.

The young child who fears airplane travel because the airplane and people in it get very small as the airplane recedes toward a faraway horizon is being completely illogical. The child's fear would be removed if he could learn that it is visual perspective that makes the airplane *appear* to grow smaller. It is this kind of irrationality that often makes adults think children are being charming. In actuality the child has formed a type of metaphor. This metaphor is illogical because it is formed from a lack of understanding. However, children can make logical, useful metaphors such as the one made in Figure 5-1 by the child who likened the speed of a fire engine to the speed of a bird. The relationship between speed, the fire engine, and the bird may have been consciously arrived at. If the child is given the opportunity to look for other relationships, he may discover many possibilities. The overcast sun, in the same illustration, is the kind of sun one might expect to find on a day when the smoke of a great fire hangs over the town. This effect was discovered through experimentation with materials. The child's spontaneous recognition that an atmosphere suitable to his expressional purpose could be thus achieved was at least, in part, the product of precognition. After the child had discovered how to express the quality of an overcast sun and the relationship between the speed of the fire engine and the flying bird, he had to apply reason to his discovery. With the aid of a critical eye the child had to determine if this was the best kind of expressional technique. Were there better ways in which the idea could be expressed? Did this discovery suggest other ways in which the expressional purpose could be achieved? This process of thinking is a vital aspect of the precognitive process. In this way the critical consciously evaluating mind judges the results of a spontaneous subconscious action. Children may respond to "What is the best way to do this?" with a quick idea, a sudden inspiration. The teacher should then say, "Yes, that is one way to do it. Do you have other ideas?" or "What other kinds of things do you think will do it as well or better?"

What should the teacher do if the children will not respond with ideas? The teacher will then have to change the frame of reference to find things that are part of the interests and real life of the children.

The teacher must realize that the process of recall, inspiration, or the whole process of precognition does not necessarily take place before art activity begins. Precognition may be motivated by discussion and by the process of art activity. The very process of working with materials, of forming images into symbols, may cause precognition to function.

With these general understandings regarding the function of precognition in the processes of art education, we can describe the relation of the precognitive to the cognitive, the functional structure of precognitive processes, the nature of precognitive thinking, and the precognitive processes as they operate in the art education activities of very young children.

RELATION OF PRECOGNITIVE AND COGNITIVE THINKING

Cognitive thinking is the means for operating precognitive thinking; it acts as a brake, a control, a device for scrutinizing and partially evaluating the images and symbols called forth, sorted, selected, and formed by the processes of precognition. Cognitive thinking serves as a means for adding quality to the images and symbols of precognition. Experiences filed in the subconscious are most useful if they are refined by the rational or cognitive processes. The scrutiny of the rational mind is one of the important means for preventing unhealthy or malformed images from being promiscuously filed in the subconscious. If such useless and possibly harmful images emerge during the processes of recall, the rational mind is able to destroy them. This is an analytical process that is essential to the precognitive processes.

FUNCTIONAL STRUCTURE OF PRECOGNITIVE PROCESSES

The processes of precognition provide a rich source of experience because the subconscious can scrutinize more rapidly and effectively than can the conscious mind. This fact raises a problem of understanding. If the cognitive processes are the instruments of selection and scrutiny, how can the precognitive processes perform similar functions? The answer lies in our understanding of the interrelatedness of the rational and the irrational. In a large sense, the two factors are combined in the processes of precognition. Precognitive processes, which are in part a result of previous cognitive activity, can perform a process of selection and scrutiny below the level of awareness. Most conscious scrutiny takes place before the precognitive processes come into existence. Consciously scrutinized perceptions provide raw material for the precognitive processes.

Precognitive processes operate most effectively when children learn through manipulation of visual forms and plastic materials.

FUNCTION OF COGNITIVE THINKING

Purely conscious thinking is not entirely satisfactory for art activity because of the danger that rationality may exclude qualitative emotional feeling. The concepts children form are not always purely logical. The meanings we find in child art are important because they are blends of thoughts and feelings. By means of the process of art activity, we hope children will learn to use emotions in order to give meaning, truth, and reality to experience and expression. Through the art activity, we hope to help children communicate their ideas and concepts. These ideas and concepts will be rich in texture and meaning if they are associated with a qualitative emotional and experiential background.

The richness of expression in art depends to a great extent on the richness of the child's precognitive constellation. However, the fact that a child possesses a rich constellation is no assurance that he will make rich and meaningful art forms. The teacher may have to find a means for helping the child uncover this constellation. This can be done by helping the child make useful associations. The teacher should point out the fact that things can be described in many ways and that ideas can be related to other ideas in order to make them vivid. This is the process of forming metaphors, making similes, and establishing analogies. This understanding of the nature of the precognitive process is closely related to the most elementary aspects of the contribution of art activity to the education of children. From this point of view, the educational purposes of art education are largely achieved through the "free use of analogy and allegory, superimposing dissimilar ingredients into new perceptual and conceptual patterns, thus reshuffling experience to achieve that fantastic degree of condensation without which creativity in any field of activity would be impossible." [1]

PRECOGNITION IN ART ACTIVITY OF EARLY CHILDHOOD

In practice, the youngest children must draw from a limited constellation of experience. Because of this incomplete constellation of experience, too great a dependence on a yet incompletely developed consciousness, and an inability to properly correlate emotional responses with images of perception, the conclusions of very young children often seem to be completely devoid of reason.

Figure 6-2 illustrates this understanding. If the lion in this drawing is considered in objective terms, it is not very lionlike. This type of representation is a natural phenomenon in early childhood formations of image-symbols. The children may not be completely aware that this lion is not a lion of objective experience or a lion that might be formulated by mature persons who can more readily separate the consciously perceived objective lion from the lion of imagination, which results from the stimulation of a constellation of subconscious images and symbols associated with lions. The child's lion is the product of a constellation of awe-inspiring beasts. The lion's physical bulk is a generalization that depicts a lion's most obvious characteristics and their associations with human qualities. Because of the child's constellation of experience, the lion appears gentle; it is not represented as an untamed nature, a terrible force, or an unconquered enemy of man. The lion's characteristics fall within the peculiar limitations of childhood experience. Its environment is the illogical environment of an imagined jungle, which is the product of stories the child has been told. The child's associations for the lion and jungle are derived from cats and images of culturally inspired beliefs in the amiable and friendly nature of animals.

The child's original perception of the lion may have begun with a visit to a zoo, a movie about jungle creatures, a story, a play, or a bit of role playing. These experiences form the constellation,

[1] Kubie, *Neurotic Distortion of the Creative Process,* p. 34.

6-2. LION
Detail from mural, *The Jungle. Teaneck, New Jersey, Public Schools.*

the preconscious and subconscious ingredients of the precognitive processes that may take place simultaneously or in some erratic pattern depending upon unique personality formations, situations, and qualities of situational motivation. Added to these processes are the nature of the materials in which the symbols are formed, the exchange of ideas between the children, and scores of other factors that may vary from one situation to another.

The special interest of the teacher in this portrayal of a lion must be to know which parts of the process are in action, which are slighted, and which are not present at all. The teacher should diagnose the process; then, she must provide techniques for adding the missing elements and strengthening those that are weak.

If the process is truly a precognitive process, it can not result in an objective image of lions in general. The lion will be the product of the unique qualities of each level of the individual's experience, maturity, and intellect.

Seven

PRODUCTIVE THINKING

In art education, productive thinking is the process of integrating think-ing with the act of producing physical forms that are expressive of the purposes and processes of art activity. Productive thinking differs from abstract thinking because it deals with combining thinking with physi-cal materials. This combination of thinking and materials may result in an art object.

RELATION OF PRODUCTIVE AND PRECOGNITIVE THINKING

Productive thinking results from the processes of precognitive think-ing. "Productive thinking" is the name we have invented to denote the transition from the precognitive thinking processes to the processes of acting upon physical materials in order to make symbolic and meaning-ful structures. Productive thinking makes possible the transformation of plastic materials into images that have origins in precognitive thought. Through the processes of productive thinking, precognitive thought processes become organized and tangible.

7-1. PORTRAIT
Painting by eighth-grade student. *East Orange, New Jersey, Public Schools.*

FROM SYMBOL TO METAPHOR: INTEGRATION OF PRECOGNITIVE WITH PRODUCTIVE THINKING

Productive thinking is the convenient term for the interactive relationship between thinking and making. The process of causing thinking to direct the transformation of material in terms of images formed in precognitive processes must result in a new form. To this new form we give the name "metaphor." A metaphor in art is a formation of materials that may suggest ideas and meanings that enrich experience. In this sense the metaphor is not the original experience. It is the transformation of experience in terms of related images and the forming of relationships with other experiences. This forming of relationships with other and possibly diverse experiences is a function of the precognitive processes. It is during this process that a rich, diverse, and unique form of metaphor evolves. The metaphor, in this case, is a plastic image, a physically formed symbol. The metaphor is a plastic figure of speech.

The richest and most useful plastic metaphors are not mere reproductions of experience; they are commentaries on experience enriched by the store of images an individual is able to associate with a particular experience. For example, in literature, the poet creates a metaphor when he says, "The iron tongue of midnight hath told twelve."

In Figure 7-1 we have a plastic metaphor for the portrait of a girl. This painting by an eighth grade child does not represent a girl; it is a plastic figure of speech. A metaphor has been made for large eyes framed by full lashes and brows. The sign for the nose is an image, a symbol that has become a metaphor for a nose. In the same way, the mouth is a sign of the relation of a mouth to the other features. Similarly, the structure of the face framed by the full hair, the neck tapering toward the head, and the sweep of the black collar beneath the neck all develop a figure that is a commentary on a person. This commentary becomes a unique form; it is rich in its configurations and its pleasing relationships provide an element of surprise. This is the kind of surprise we find in such simple yet poetic statements as this one from Shakespeare's *King Lear*, "Let not women's weapons, water-drops/Stain my man's cheeks!" The visual-plastic form delivers this same kind of surprise, which is the essence of the metaphoric, through the quality of paint, the rhythms of painting, the suggestion in a symbol of an eye, the shape of hair framing a head, or the flush in the face made from a semi-dry brush stroke.

Figure 7-2, a painting by a kindergarten child, is a more elementary kind of metaphor. This metaphor depends to a large extent on the simple kinaesthetic sensation of a movement associated with the expressional purpose. The expressional purpose of this painting is to convey ideas about cleaning. The picture was painted as part of learning involved in a cleanup campaign. The large sweeping line is the rhythm of actively throwing away refuse. The teacher provided the purpose; the emotional experiences of kinaesthesia and painting contribute to forming the metaphor. The relation to the actual images of original perception is indistinct because the child does not yet know how to describe. However, the metaphor emerges from concepts formed from the images and symbols associated with the purposes.

Figures 7-1 and 7-2 are evidence of the exist- ence of processes of productive thinking. In each case, the paintings are reformations of experience rather than literal descriptions. This reformation results from the interaction of perceptions, bio- logical activities, motor movement, plastic ma- terials, and concepts.

A child's development in terms of emotional, intellectual, and physical maturation may be known by the way his processes of productive thinking become increasingly effective. The plas- tic metaphor, which is the end result of the processes of productive thought, becomes increas- ingly rich, expressive, economical, and varied in its inventiveness as the child matures. During the earliest stages of child development, the metaphor is simple and in large part the result of physical and emotional elements that make it possible for us to predict the kinds of metaphors that will re- sult from the child's processes of productive think- ing. More mature children, especially children in the intermediate grades, may produce metaphors that are surprising in their uniqueness and effec- tiveness. However, we are always able to predict the kinds of metaphors that will be made by very young children. Uniqueness or the shock of sur- prise may often be evidenced in the work of primary-grade children.

The method the teacher uses to achieve meta- phoric effectiveness is of special importance. There is a distinct relation between the method used in teaching and the character of the productive thinking processes.

If a teacher proposes to a class that each child paint a portrait of a friend, the emphasis is im- mediately on the object. The object is the por- trait. On the other hand, if the teacher proposes that the class use materials to suggest the charac- teristics of a friend, the emphasis is somewhat different.

The processes of productive thinking require that the teacher plan a procedure that will en- courage the children to explore materials. The purpose of this exploration will be to find ma- terials and working techniques suitable to the special kind of portrait to be painted. It is per- fectly possible that certain kinds of hair, char- acteristic of certain kinds of persons, might be best expressed by pasting colored yarn in the place where hair should be. Or perhaps steel wool or fabric could be used to suggest a particular quality that is desirable to represent the unique character of a unique personality. In another in- stance, the textural quality of paint may be most satisfactory if the paint is applied with a sponge rather than a brush. Regardless of the productive techniques used, the teacher is responsible for motivating the children to explore materials in

7-2. I THREW OUT THE GARBAGE Kindergarten painting. *East Orange, New Jersey, Public Schools.*

order to achieve the ability to express the uniqueness of the person painted.

The kind of rhythm that expresses cleaning a dirty basement in the painting entitled "I Threw Out the Garbage" (Figure 7-2) resulted from classroom dramatization of the subject of the painting.

In the cases of the portrait painting lesson and the painting based on a cleanup campaign, the emphasis is not on predetermined techniques for representing the experience. The emphasis is on exploration to discover productive processes that will give depth of meaning to the purpose of the art activity. This can happen if the teacher is able to lead dicussions and study to help the children learn as much as possible about their subject. This period of becoming acquainted with the subject should be the first phase of the art activity. The second phase should be concerned with the productive thinking processes. Although some discussion may be useful during this phase, it is most helpful if the children can immediately begin to work with materials. The initial choices of materials may be tentative; however, thinking about the subject in terms of forming expressive metaphors from physical materials must be done by working with the materials themselves. The best aid to the productive thinking processes is active involvement with materials and ideas. The teacher should encourage the children to hold open-minded attitudes toward materials and their relation to ideas. The children should also be encouraged to explore and to discover what materials can do to help them express their purposes. To do this, the children must be willing to continuously evaluate their own progress. In this way, the productive thinking processes will be given a direction, and new directions and ideas may be discovered.

SENSE EXPERIENCE AND THE PROCESSES OF PRODUCTIVE THINKING

Our earlier reference to the German Bauhaus took note of the interest among art educators in the training of the human senses. In elementary-school curricula, there is a need to help children make good use of their sensitivities. The teacher will find that through the productive thinking process of art activity, children's sensitivities can be cultivated, educated, and developed. This process is very important because sense perception is one of our major means of knowing and learning.

In art activity, we have said that the visual experience is very important. We have also said that children differ in the ways in which they use their senses. Some children are more visual, some are more haptic. The productive processes of each type of child will result in different kinds of art forms. The ways in which the two general types of children use their senses will determine much about what they can learn from the processes of art education.

There are other senses besides the common senses of seeing, hearing, smelling, and touching. In our description of Figure 7-2 reference was made to the importance of the kinaesthetic sense, the sensation of movement. In addition to the kinaesthetic, another sense of special importance in art activity is the sensation of sympathetic understanding.

This sensation is also known as empathy. Sympathetic understanding is what a physician often needs in order to know what is troubling a patient who doesn't feel well. This aspect of medical diagnosis may be one of the reasons why the work of the physician is often described as an art. Sympathetic understanding is very important to all artists—the painter, the sculptor, the musician, the actor, the dancer, the poet, and the novelist. The arts are unique because they are concerned with projecting understandings that cannot be known by any other means.

Each one of us has sensations deep within our body that are difficult to describe without the use of parallels. For this reason we often describe a sensation as being "like" something else.

Sensations that originate deep within our body are referred to as the enteroceptive. The enteroceptive is one of the neglected areas of sense experience in education. It is one of the important kinds of sense experience that we all constantly undergo. When we can not know the sensations of the enteroceptive or can not make these sensations known to others, we are forced to live in an isolated world; our bodies become islands.

Productive thinking involves a projection that makes possible two important things with regard to the enteroceptive: during the course of art activity the child is able to create appropriate symbols, with visual means, to describe the choices he makes from enteroceptive experience. The second significant aspect of productive thinking is that it aids in the creation of a sensitivity to the enteroceptive experiences of others.

Sensitivity to the enteroceptive experiences of others is a mark of the artist. Sympathy with others and enteroceptive understanding is a faculty every human being is known to possess in some degree. The artist, with his highly developed level of sensitivity, is able to project himself. In this way, the artist can describe the condition of man and the sensations of other people. The successful novelist, the sensitive playwright, the painter, the sculptor, the musician, and the poet must possess this faculty at a highly developed level. In art, feelings of empathy can lead to the development of a social intelligence.

The second type of sense perception is commonly known as the kinaesthetic sense, which can be most easily described if we refer to its existence as being made possible by the activity of the proprioceptors. The proprioceptors provide for responses made as the result of the action of sensory end organs in the muscles, joints, tendons, and the deeper layers of the skin. The proprioceptors respond to stimuli originating in these parts of the body as a result of body movement. The proprioceptive mechanism has long been known as an important sensory factor in the processes of art activity. It is usually referred to in the literature of art education as kinaesthesia.

The sensation of body movement has been a well-known aspect of art activity because it serves as a bridge between the processes of forming perceptions into symbolic structures and the action of the biological human upon ideas and materials. In its purest form, it develops symbolic structures through patterns of body movement. Such patterns are best known as the art of the dance.

The art work of children reflects the response of physical movements to stimuli. Children respond easily and quickly with rhythmical body movements to sounds that are rhythmical. It may be possible to relate such natural body responses to expression in art activities.

Descriptive movements are characterized as gestures intended to define or represent perceptions of various types. The efficiency of the de-scriptive movement is determined by a combination of growth in motor control and in forming power, which is the ability to organize symbols into forms that will adequately represent or express a conception.

The proprioceptive mechanisms are of special interest to art education because they represent a means that provides for direct transfer of sensation into visual-plastic form. This is most evident, at elementary levels of development, in the child's first attempts to make drawings or to model objects with pliable materials. We have reason to believe that forms made at the earliest stages of development are often the result of pleasure in the sensation of movement. From this beginning stage, the child must develop the ability to establish a connection between the sensations of kinaesthesia and their graphic representation. This connection involves a translation of the sensations of physical movement into objective symbolic structures.

Figure 7-2 is an excellent example of this kind of translation of movement into an effective symbol. The sweeping line of the painting forms an objective structure, which becomes a metaphor to communicate the sensation of throwing.

Kinaesthesia represents an almost involuntary muscular participation in art experiences. Figure 7-3, the sculpture by Henry Moore is an example of this. In Moore's work (Figure 7-3), there is a sensation of moving around and through the sculpture. If the open spaces were not part of the design, the sense of movement through space and of a three-dimensional rhythm would be lacking. This kind of movement sensation has led to the construction of forms through which children really can move. Playground equipment has been made that permits children to climb through and around the forms.

In the work of very young children, this kind of movement sensation dominates art work in a raw form. It is a raw form because none of the more complex, and therefore more qualitative, forces of the precognitive processes are acting upon the processes of productive thinking. In the art forms of early childhood, as in Figures 7-2 and 7-4, the rhythm of lines and shapes are organized in terms of the paint used and possibly in terms of earlier experiences with materials and pictorial forming processes.

7-3. RECLINING FIGURE
(1938) by Henry Moore. *Collection of the Museum of Modern Art, New York City.*

Figure 7-4 is a scribble drawing. No control is evident in the arrangement of its forms. Although an attempt has been made to make the line movements follow a rhythmical pattern, the pattern is not under control; it loses force before the rhythmic phrase is completed. Before he completed the rhythmic phrase, the child's attention may have wandered to wonder about the chalk or about the colors; or it may have been suddenly directed toward the work of a classmate. The level of productive thought used in creating this drawing was at a low level of development. The limitations evident in this drawing are caused by sparse experience. The child has not yet developed skill in relating his experiences to the productive thinking processes. This drawing is an example of the typical art work of early childhood. The main emphasis is on the manipulation of materials and the image-symbols are either primitive or lacking in clarity. Precognitive thinking has little influence on the productive processes involved in this type of art activity.

Figure 7-5 is an example of how the processes of productive thought evolve into a more meaningful arrangement of image-symbols, concepts, physical materials, and working processes. Figure 7-4 is dominated by the child's attempts to control the materials and by his sensations, most of

which are body sensations. Image-symbols and concepts play a very small part in this picture. In Figure 7-5, there is still strong evidence of the sensation of arm movements and the struggle with rhythms that grow out of body sensations. However, there is evidence that symbols concerned with portraying a specific image are also present. There is a fair degree of correlation between movement sensations, image-symbols, and the control of materials. The significance of this painting lies in the fact that in it the movement sensations and the control of materials are becoming coordinated with a concept. The concept, derived from the child's own sensations, is purely personal. A higher level of productive thinking would have made it possible for the child to correlate his body sensations with the materials to create a sense of rhythmic or structural organization that would have been derived as much from the image-symbols and their unique characteristics as from the child's own inner sensations. In other words, the child will reach a higher level of productive thinking when he is able to bring to the expression of an image-symbol structure, such as clowns, a rich store of body sensations, previous experience, and a developed understanding of how these can be correlated and integrated with the physical materials. In the case of Figure

7-4. SCRIBBLE
Chalk. *Author's collection.*

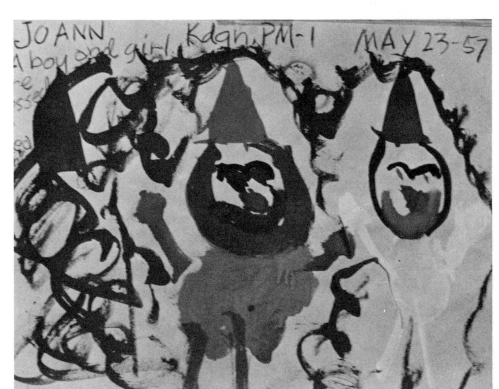

7-5. CLOWNS
Collection of Theodore Lynch.

7-5, the physical materials are opaque paints on paper. Figures 7-4 and 7-5 show that child art begins with limited amounts of productive thinking. The earliest work of children is most often almost purely involved with a sense of movement and the pleasure of manipulating materials. The children with whom we will be concerned, beginning with the earliest days of the kindergarten experience, will show evidences of using some measure of precognitive thought in their work. Productive thinking, or the process of giving form to precognitive thinking, develops as the child matures. The quality of this particular kind of maturation depends upon the teacher's ability to help the child and to guide his working and thinking. The teacher can provide this kind of guidance if, on the basis of the work the children do, she knows what they are able to accomplish. If the teacher can understand the work the children do, she will know what they still need to do in order to achieve some valid educational goal through their art activity.

Figure 7-5 can be used as an example of how the teacher can find guidelines in a child's work that will indicate how she can best help the child. In this painting, there is evidence of the many different elements that combine to form a new symbol. The symbol is a composite, made up of many different kinds of symbols. This combination of parts is the metaphor, the expression formed from the processes of productive thinking. The circular and scribble-like lines on the left side of the painting seem to be ready to change into a clown. This change from rhythmical lines to the metaphor of a clown involves a change in the child's thinking as well as a change in the character of the painting. The child's recognition of rhythmical lines and colors that suggest clowns can lead him to deliberately guide his rhythms to form his own notions of what a clown is like. In Figure 7-5, the clown that is about to emerge from the scribble lines is related to movements the child must have made with his own body. These movements might be body sensations related to the child's idea of the way a clown must feel. In a sense, this is a manner of internalizing the sensations of a clown. The child thinks of how it must feel to be a clown, and then translates the sensations of "clown" movements into line and color. This movement, shown

in the painting as a brush line made with one fully loaded paintbrush, moves across the top of the paper to the right and on the extreme right begins to take the shape of a clown. At this point, there is some evidence of a new element intruding into the productive thinking processes. Up to now thinking was almost entirely concerned with movements and the manipulation of materials. At the moment lines and shapes suggest a specific form, the child becomes aware of inspiration. Intuition and impulse begin to operate and, for the child, an image—in this case an image of a clown—becomes joined to the rhythmical movement. At first this image is formed in terms that the teacher might not easily understand. The child himself may have only a glimmering of the form, but this glimmering is enough to add impetus to the arrival of inspiration. As soon as the child sees an image being suggested in his rhythmical scribble, his conscious mind begins to direct the forming processes. On the extreme right of the picture a dark egg shape is painted. This shape suggests a head. At this point, the child stopped to consciously examine his image-symbol of a clown. The very fact that the child paused in his painting, that he stopped to study his work, caused a break in the rhythmical action of painting. For this reason we can see a break in the painting's rhythmical continuity. This break may be described as a loss of contact between the concept of a clown and the body sensation of movement. This kind of break in rhythm also occurs when the child has to pause in his work to dip his brush in paint. Whatever the cause, it will be noted that the intrusion of conscious thinking is marked by irregularities in the expressive power of the painting.

From the time the child begins to paint the center clown, the painting shows evidences of undergoing a variety of major changes because the nature of the art activity is changing. As the child paints the center clown, his processes of precognitive thinking become hopelessly involved and confused. This happens because the child is not yet able to make good use of critical thinking. Since the child is unable to correlate conscious and unconscious thinking, he becomes frustrated. Frustration begins to dominate the process because the child's thinking is no longer uninhibited. As thinking becomes more inhibited, it loses its earlier rapid and rhythmical fluidity, and the paint becomes a clumsy hindrance to the development of a metaphor for a clown.

The problem in classroom teaching is to maintain a good relationship between fluid rhythm and critical thinking in art activity. One of the best ways to accomplish this purpose is to give the children opportunities to act out the parts of the painting they are making. For example, if the child who painted the clown had the opportunity to talk about clowns, to try to perform as clowns do, and to discuss clowns with his teacher and classmates, he would have a greater knowledge of clowns, of how they look and behave. The child's increased familiarity with his subject helps him avoid awkward pauses during the development of expressive rhythms into effectively expressive metaphors.

Dramatization and role playing in the case of the clown painting would have given increased depth and breadth to the precognitive and productive processes. Role playing, discussion, and dramatization would have helped the child make stronger associations between the clown, the feelings we may have about clowns, the senses we use to enjoy clowns, and the senses—such as the sense of rhythm—that help us paint pictures about clowns.

PRIMARY GOALS OF PRODUCTIVE THINKING

The significance of productive thinking is that it produces a real condition that is educationally valid. The process of productive thinking during art activity is an integral part of the process of human growing. The art objects made by children during this process become the sign of the quality of the process. These art forms become the signs of the existence of art education, the material evidence of the process. It must also be noted that because the process is concerned with education, the art objects that result from productive action are milestones. The forms resulting from the action of productive thinking are gateways to new achievements. The process itself is never-ending. It follows that a goal of productive thinking must be to provide understanding of directions for growth, for newer and superior modes of productivity. The act of productive thinking results in an open-ended sym-

bolic structure. Conventional assumptions that the work of art is a complete whole and that its very completeness is necessary for the existence of beauty or aesthetic value, are not held in art education. Productive thinking, in terms of the purposes of art education, finds aesthetic value in flux. A purpose and goal of productive thought is to achieve a continuity of process rather than the sterility of closure. Perfection in this light is the achievement of a process that points to new directions.

The result of productive thinking, the open-ended symbolic structure, represents the interaction of the human creature with his experiences. The symbolic structure becomes the objectivization of concepts in a form that represents the individual's integration with the flux of living and with his intellectual and cultural environment.

A goal of productive thinking is growth. The art forms that result from productive thinking and the art activity of which it is an integral part, should represent an ever-increasing maturity.

The nature of the growth, the maturation, that we hope will result from productive thinking is described by Lewis Mumford [1] as the ultimate stage in the person's development of his relation to the world. This is the occasion when the art object no longer represents the immaturities of selfish purposes and exhibitionism. In this final stage, the artist is one who expresses a kinship with people and seeks no reward except the satisfaction of performing a socially worthwhile act. The work of art then takes on the burden of the human purpose. The art form acquires a life that continues to aid in the evolution of values that were originally intrinsic to the results of productive thinking.

CHILD ENGAGEMENT IN PRODUCTIVE THINKING

A child is engaged in productive thought when he becomes involved in the process of forming workable metaphors from the image-symbols of perception. If a child has a paintbrush, he must correlate the working characteristics of the paintbrush with the requirements of transforming sym-

[1] "Art and the Symbol," pp. 28-29.

bols into concrete images and metaphors. He will learn that the paintbrush can be dipped into paint and that it becomes a flexible tool for arranging paint on paper according to the demands of the image to be formed from mentally-formed symbols of experience. However, it must be noted that a child does not always begin to perform an inventive image-making action as a result of motivations from an idea. The correlation of materials with the processes of art activity makes it just as possible for motivation to be derived from materials as from experiences of perception. The art activity and the processes of productive thinking that are basic to art education may begin from the simple act of placing a brush in paint and from the simple pleasure of watching the paint take random form on paper, even if the resulting form is a doodle made by absent-mindedly moving the hand that holds the brush.

The pleasure of movement sensations and the relationship of muscular movement to the formation of visual images on paper can become a dead end if the teacher is not able to provide the kind of guidance that will lead to productive thinking. In this case, productive thinking means the process of correlating the activity of image making with the symbols of experience. It is exactly at this point that the processes of art activity, thinking, and growth begin.

The question of which comes first, motivation from materials or motivation from perceived experience, is not of much importance. It usually happens that one or the other form of motivation exists. This is a characteristic of ordinary experience. Inspired experience of an unusually high order, which generally results in a natural correlation between image formulation and materials, may be rare in the case of young children; usually the materials must be present before the transfer of concepts into visible and concrete structures is possible. The teacher should decide which form of motivation is most useful in terms of a particular child's interests.

In very young children drawing or painting is a doodling process that results from pure pleasure in working with art materials. The function of the teacher must be to find an adequate means for relating this kind of activity to productive thinking. The engagement in painting processes without productive thinking is pure imaginative play.

It may also involve irrationality without the control of rational means; or it may be nothing more than the employment of subconscious thought processes, which might be undesirable because the subconscious may become involved in the development of unsatisfactory habits.

RELATION OF PLAY TO PRODUCTIVE THINKING

Children often use materials to form images without direction from a teacher or a more experienced peer. Usually, materials that are close at hand will be selected for this purpose. Thus, scrap materials and bits of natural materials such as stones, sand, earth, and scraps of wood or twigs may be selected. Most often this selection is made without much conscious direction. When a child selects materials, he is often motivated by a spirit of play. The child may become intrigued with the qualities of particular materials. His curiosity about materials causes him to manipulate them; this manipulation is described as play and is a process that involves pleasure. Impulse may direct the forming processes, and intuition sometimes suggests to the child that certain kinds of manipulations are more desirable than others. Impulse is directed by the child's natural energy. Intuition may be the beginning of thought and may come into being as a result of suggestions for forming that can be derived from the manipulative characteristics of the materials.

Playful manipulation of materials is a natural activity for children. Children enjoy playing with sand on a beach, drawing with a stick in soft ground, or absent-mindedly drawing or making familiar signs with chalk on a cement pavement or on the wall of a building. This absent-minded, undirected process of shaping materials is not the goal of art education. However, we have reason to believe that this process of play can provide educational advantages. In our discussions about art activity we have indicated that play can lead to the forming of purposes and to the creation of valid directions for work. Play is a means for uncovering educationally useful impulses and for finding directions for working that may not reveal themselves in any other way.

In the classroom, children should be provided

with a variety of materials that might suggest ideas. The kinds of materials that will encourage children to want to play with them are materials that arouse curiosity, are colorful, and are texturally unusual or inviting. For example, beach sand invites the child's curiosity because it can be shaped and will retain the form the child gives it. Certain kinds of plastics are appealing because of their color, their smoothness, or their transparency.

The classroom teacher should encourage children to bring various kinds of materials to class. Such materials will be those about which the children express curiosity. This is a good way for the teacher to know how different kinds of materials affect children and to become acquainted with the kinds of materials that interest them.

Since the classroom teacher needs to be able to show children what they can do with different kinds of materials, she, too, should play with materials in order to discover how different materials lend themselves to particular expressive purposes. For example, a flashbulb that is painted red might become the red nose of a puppet or marionette. If the same flashbulb is painted white with a dark circle in the center, it could become a puppet's bulging eye or the terrible eye of the giant Cyclops. Ordinary gravel might become a decorative element in a diorama, a painting, or a three-dimensional mural. Clay can retain the impress of a thumbprint or a hand. Paper can assume unexpected expressional power when it is bent, folded, twisted, torn, cut, or creased.

The productive thinking process becomes a rich and useful experience if the teacher can cause the children to stop at appropriate times to evaluate the things they have done with materials. This evaluation process takes place when there is evidence that ideas are being suggested even though the children may not be aware of them. The purpose of evaluation is to point out possible directions. Such directions can be indicated by some of the things the teacher or children begin to observe emerging from the play activity.

The evaluation aspect of the play activity provides opportunity for the teacher to indicate directions of which the children may not be aware. It also provides the children with the opportunity to pool their ideas and to learn from each other. This is the most useful kind of planning process because it comes from the children themselves. In this way, directions for work are not imposed; instead, they are recognized by the children as useful and purposeful directions.

Since children are not always able to formulate directions themselves, the teacher must be able to provide the spark that will cause them to recognize possibilities for art expression in their play with materials. The teacher can do this by studying the results of the children's play and by helping the children recognize these results as suggestions for formulating directions and purposes.

Play as a means for initiating the processes of productive thinking need not be considered too childish for children in the upper grades. Play with materials is natural in the early primary period, when habits of exploring materials become developed as a pleasurable experience. For older children, this same process of play becomes pleasure in exploration and experimentation with materials. Older children should become increasingly critical of the results of their explorations. The evaluation sessions should increase in depth as the children mature.

Play that promotes the productive thinking processes is best encouraged if the children, regardless of age level, begin the productive process with an open mind toward materials. No material should be considered to have specific limitations or to be good for some predetermined purpose. The purpose of the process of play is to seek out unknown potentials. Materials may be found to have a surprising number of possibilities for expression. The processes of play may indicate that exploration of materials need not be the first concern of productive thinking; concepts may exist before materials are investigated. In such a case, the purpose of play with materials would be to find materials that would serve a particular expressive purpose.

In most cases, the processes of art activity will be used to develop and enrich a specific, clearly defined purpose. For example, it may happen that the children are concerned with dental hygiene. In teaching the children good dental habits, the teacher can use the art activity as a means for enriching her lessons. For example, the teacher can require that the children make posters to illustrate the importance of brushing their teeth.

If a decision is made to use poster board and opaque water paints before the children begin to work, limitations are immediately imposed on the children's thinking. If children are allowed to select their own materials, they will have the opportunity to experiment and to seek out materials that may dramatize or more effectively communicate the object of their study. In order to encourage play with materials, the teacher may ask the children to look for materials, shapes, colors, and textures that will describe how decay begins. In this way, the teacher provides questions rather than answers. Could colored construction paper be used for the lettering? Or would this purpose be better served by making the letters from some fabric? Perhaps clay, plaster, or a white plastic could be used to form a three-dimensional illustration to achieve added emphasis or increased reality. A group of children in a primary-grade class emphasized an important understanding when they used a large piece of porcelain to represent a human tooth. On this porcelain tooth, the children represented decay starkly and dramatically with melted black and blue wax crayon remnants.

TECHNIQUES FOR MOTIVATING PRODUCTIVE THINKING

It is of special interest to note that the quality of play and the use of materials and their manipulation as a part of the play activity often result in a curious derivation of symbols from the nature of the material itself. This kind of symbol formation is seldom directly related to symbols that are transformations of images perceived during the processes of visual experience.

Since symbols formed from materials are not always simple manifestations of play with materials and concoction of shapes from the materials, such symbol formations are not always possible during the earliest stages of manipulative play when the experiences of visual activity are seldom easily separated from image making. Instances in which symbols are formed from the qualities of materials as the result of sensual pleasure derived from manipulation of the materials form a high order of separation of activity from sense experience. There is even some question regarding the desirability of creating such

a separation. However, there is no reason to believe that the making of forms that derive their symbol structures from the character of the materials employed is not a good activity. It should be noted that productive thinking involves a development of sensual understanding and pleasure, coupled with a rational understanding of the character of a material, its possibilities, its plastic limitations, and the symbol formulations or plastic metaphors to which it lends itself with the greatest naturalness.

We have reason to believe that the process of using materials in the spirit of experimentation and discovery is wise, but that the process is most conducive to productive thinking when rationality is used to evaluate the results of an intuitive, manipulative, and experimental process. Productive thinking also requires that possible relationships be sought between the natural formations to which a material lends itself and the suggestions these formations provide in relation to perceptual experience. This procedure offers opportunity to discover the appropriateness of a material for the expression of symbol formulations from the images of experience.

At the more highly developed levels of art experience there is some reason to believe that the discovery of symbol formations natural to particular materials is a desirable process. Productive thinking may be possible in such cases because of the unusually highly developed sensing and perceptive apparatus of the individual artist.

Productive thinking that is directed toward forming symbols from manipulative play with materials and creating symbols in terms of the characteristics of materials is a process with which the professional artist has much experience. In an essay on the life and work of the twentieth century Swiss painter Paul Klee, Daniel-Henry Kahnweiler describes Klee as an artist who sees the world as being in a state of perpetual flux. For Klee, painting is a world and a life unto itself; for him, there is no finished world. Klee felt that the created symbolic structure should never be a mere representation of things just as they are—he said that the drawing of a man "just as he is" will result only in a tangle of lines. We have, here, a statement of the multiple characteristics of productive thought. Most interesting is the correlation Klee establishes between materials and concept. Klee never creates an image that is a replica of experience. To him, such a replica would be a raw kind of production that could have very little to do with art. He feels that art must be a transformation from the raw images of experience to aesthetically satisfying, formed, meaningful symbols composed in a symbolic structure that is the work of art. To Klee, the essential reality of a symbol is not an image of perception, but the material of which the symbol is formed, the character of the formation, and the effect of manipulative processes that take place in the light of perceptual experience.

The relation of material to experience and to the character of created symbols varies quantitatively. In some works of art, the character of the perceived images strongly reflects on the formations given to the materials and on the resulting character of the created symbols. In other cases, the symbols are not the result of sense perceptions, such as sight, hearing, touch, smell, and sound. They might result from the kinaesthetic sense or simply from sensations that arise from within the physical organism. In the last case, created symbols may result from purely personal formations or from formations made possible because of the harmony resulting from human muscular contact with the sensual qualities of a particular plastic material.

It must be understood that although the result of productive thinking with materials is frequently associated with images of perceived experience, the perceived image should not completely dominate the material. Such domination would result in a completely illogical situation because the material is the reality with which the artist or child deals during the process of productive thinking. Productive thought is required to give the forms meaning, but the validity of the forms created from a material depends to a large extent upon whether or not the material is manipulated in a manner suitable to its character.

In actual practice, very young children will manipulate a material in terms of their own sensations. In the egocentric world of children, perceptual experience may play very little part in the manipulation of materials. In the case of the youngest children, roughly preschool children, plastic material becomes an extension of physical movement. There is little reason to believe that a correlation is made by the child, during the earliest stages, between his action upon a material and the possible satisfactions to be derived from the formations he gives the material. Because of this lack of correlation, some teachers advocate that the very youngest children be given large pieces of paper and a single large crayon, which the child can easily hold. By the same token easily manipulated materials, such as mud, clay, and sand, are most satisfactory at this stage. In other words, materials should be selected that are most conducive to the development of processes of productive thought.

During the next stage of child growth, the child becomes more aware of the formations that are possible with particular materials; consequently, productive thinking is more likely to become a significant factor in his work, and the processes of art activity will become educationally valid. However, the scope and depth of the child's productive thought processes are still not equal to that of the older children. During its earliest phases, productive thinking is significant insofar as it is able to provide understandings of broad relationships between visual symbols and the elements of the art form. Productive thinking among primary-grade children can reach a level of quality similar to that found in the work of older children, or even equal to that which may exist in professional art activity. The work of the younger children, however, will lack the depth of the more advanced work.

STRUCTURE OF VISUAL-PLASTIC METAPHORS

In Chart 3, the main stem of the process of art activity is the heavy arrow labeled precognitive thinking, which is shown to have its source in experience. Precognitive thinking is formed from the raw images of experience, which are shown to become image-symbols. The processes of productive thinking, which are the means for manipulating physical materials to form the visual-plastic metaphor, are considered to be dynamic unending processes. Once the metaphor has been formed, processes of evaluation lead to increasingly richer understandings that provide for the enrichment of experience and the development of more sophisticated precognitive, productive, and forming processes.

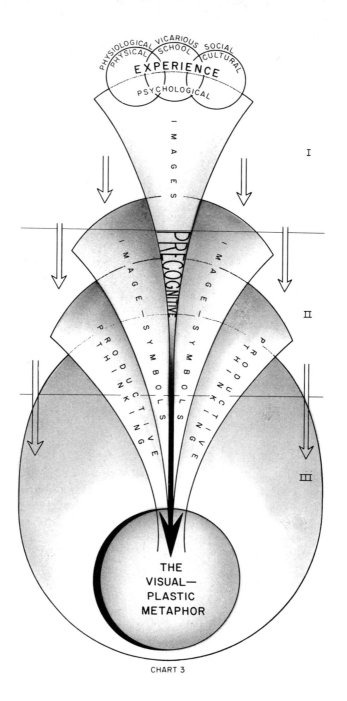

EXPERIENCE

PHYSIOLOGICAL VICARIOUS SOCIAL
PHYSICAL SCHOOL CULTURAL
PSYCHOLOGICAL

IMAGES

PRE-COGNITIVE

IMAGES

IMAGE—SYMBOLS

PRODUCTIVE THINKING

THE
VISUAL—
PLASTIC
METAPHOR

I

II

III

CHART 3

The section of the chart labeled I is the part of the process that usually comprises the total activity of preschool and kindergarten children. The more mature children in the kindergarten are likely to become involved with processes that gradually move through section II. By the time children reach the first grade they should be moving easily through section III. Because of the lack of developed productive thinking processes in section I—when aimless scribbling is usually the main art form—children will often resort to giving names or verbal descriptions to the things they make. Children do this when their ability to express their experiences in their art activities is very limited. Children in the second phase, part II of the chart, are still not able to express as much as they experience; in this section, the metaphor is still meager. Section III of the chart is one that the primary-grade child should be able to achieve. Processes of evaluation should be designed to help the child achieve this ability to form metaphors from his experiences.

Eight

LEARNING IN THE ART PROCESS

Learning in art activity is a general form of learning that can emerge from the process of art education. Learning will take place if emphasis is placed on experience, concept formation, pleasure in the art activity, completeness of experience, imaginative thinking, and creative action. Learning through art activities takes place partly as a result of inter-action of the child with precognitive and productive thinking processes. The unique contribution of art to the learning process is largely a result of the process of giving a physical form to images and symbols. The process of forming concepts, in terms of image-symbols, into visual structures, pictures, sculptures, or other kinds of crafted forms becomes an effective process for improving and increasing understandings.

ROLE OF SUBLIMINAL PROCESSES

According to Lawrence Kubie,[1] we learn mainly through subliminal processes. The discussion in this text has placed a large emphasis on the role of precognitive processes. Although such processes are not identical to subliminal processes, they do make extensive use of knowledge and perceptions that exist below the level of consciousness. Kubie takes this understanding to another level when he says that understandings ac-

[1] In an unpublished lecture, "Research on Protecting Preconscious Functions in Education." By courtesy of the author.

quired at subliminal levels are more varied and more extensive than those acquired during states of consciousness. During periods of sleep, he says, sensory experience is mainly of the sort that takes place deep within our bodies. This kind of sensory experience is called enteroceptive. At the same time, another kind of experience occurs that is known as the result of activity of the proprioceptors. Proprioceptive sensations are received in the tissues of the body. These sensations act as stimuli that cause the muscles and tendons to respond in a sympathetic manner. A small amount of learning may result from the senses of sight, smell, taste, hearing, and the sense of movement. But it is obvious that these senses, known as the exteroceptive senses, play a very unimportant role in any learning that takes place below the level of consciousness. This understanding regarding the role of the subliminal processes in learning has important implications for teaching methods in art education. The use of subliminal learning and the more general characteristics of the precognitive thinking processes provides a direction for the planning of elementary-school art activities.

The definition of precognitive processes refers to the use of experiences that have been stored below the level of consciousness. The problem in teaching is to insure the richness of this precognitive store and to develop a means for helping children make use of this form of thinking in the process of learning. The teacher who understands the need for enriching the precognitive store will want to use a means to help children broaden, modify, and enrich their experiences by relating them to other experiences. If children are able to enrich their art activities with their experiences, the metaphors they create with art materials will show increased quality, depth, and breadth. Precognitive experiences will be most useful if they have been subjected to many different kinds of sensory conditioning. This sensory conditioning of experience is not unlike the method children naturally use to discover what a thing is like. They will touch, feel, or smell an object with which they are trying to become acquainted. In much the same way, we rarely accept a fabric before we feel it with our hands. In this way, our experience of knowing becomes more profound and perhaps more qualitative.

In classroom practice, it is most useful if children can learn to explore experiences in much the same way they learn to explore materials during the processes of productive thinking. Playing with experiences is just as valid for learning as playing with materials. Children need opportunity to talk about their experiences, to exchange experiences, and to dramatize their experiences. The familiar kindergarten and primary-grade "show and tell" is an example of how experiences can be explored.

The teacher's job must be to help the children know and acquire experience through many senses. To accomplish this, children should explore many materials and many different ways of knowing. During the process of exploring materials, they need help from the teacher in relating experience to the results of their productive thinking processes. An important part of this process is the transfer of experience to a variety of sensory levels. Children will know experiences better if they can explore many different ways of knowing. For example, a sound can be described as a rhythm made up of blue and red colors. Textures can be formed from paints, chalks, or crayons. The speed of a fire engine, as in Figure 5-1, can be likened to the speed of a bird; the sound of the sirens can be associated with bright red colors that shoot out in many directions from the noise-making instrument. This experience could be dramatized with rhythmical patterns of words as in poetry, explored in body movements as in a dance, or likened to patterns of sounds made with a rhythm band. Children play and invent in many different ways. Part of their play and invention finds expression in picture making, which is a free, inventive, imaginative, and descriptive mode of expression.

The process of relating the many sensations through which we gather experience and knowledge to expression in art materials is a form of projection. Projection takes place when the blend of precognitive thinking and an immediate conscious purpose is given a form in paint, clay, paper, crayon, chalk, or any other plastic material. In this way, the precognitive and productive thinking processes blend to form the beginning of a learning process.

SPOT-SAMPLING: PROVIDING A BASIS FOR LEARNING

Preliminary to the learning process, we spot-sample our experiences, whether they be on the enteroceptive, the proprioceptive, or the extero-ceptive level.[2] This sampling process involves the use of precognitions; it is done with the memory images we store in our subconscious and pre-conscious minds. Thus, much of this sampling is done below the level of awareness. This process is notable for its rapidity. We can sample with great speed because we use simple and fragmen-tary symbols of visual memories that can repre-sent many things at the same time. This is the same kind of imagery that, in primitive form, comprises most of our dreams. This process is valuable in learning because it allows us to project such imagery in a manner that our conscious mind can study and understand.

PROJECTION OF IMAGERY

The process of sampling afterimages, since it generally occurs below the level of awareness, does not involve conscious learning or thinking. The first step from sampling to the use of the process for learning takes place when we employ a projec-tive device in order to study the images. During the process of projection, we give the fragments of sensory experience symbolic structures. It is at this point that the processes of precognitive thinking become necessary for the formation of a learning process.

Learning begins to take place when a child projects the fragmentary afterimages he selects from his subconscious mind and makes them con-form to a purpose formulated partly during the process of spot sampling, partly during the proc-ess of projection, and partly as a result of es-tablished requirements, imposed directions, or some previously agreed upon objective.

During the earliest stages of elementary-school experience, the child will usually relate his projec-tive experience to active involvement in art work. This early part of the process can involve forming of concepts only in the mind; however, the most effective learning takes place when the projective processes involve the manipulation of tools and materials. The manipulative processes will give tangible structure to the processes of projection; the images selected during the processes of pre-cognition will be given life in a material form and relations will be established within the limita-

[2] See Chapter Seven for a discussion of these modes of perception.

tions imposed by the child's experience. In other words, learning will take place after the institution of successful precognitive and productive thinking processes.

STRUCTURING: ESTABLISHING RELATIONSHIPS BETWEEN SYMBOLS AND MATERIALS

During the first stage of development, when art activity is used for the inauguration of a learning process, the child must be helped to establish relationships between symbols and to understand how these relationships can be manipulated through means of a plastic material to achieve a meaningful design.

The learning value of the establishment of relations between concretely formed symbols is slowly increased when the teacher can help the child associate immediately perceived experiences with experiences stored in his memory.

During the period of development of a useful learning process, children lack the ability to relate specific images to previously acquired experiences. They are not always able to consider a broad range of possibilities or to evaluate the possibility that some image or images from previous ex-perience might help to reinforce and to make more vivid the picture, sculpture, or other con-struction they happen to be creating. Although this ability may exist in a fragmentary sense, children are not always able to use it in a planned or organized and purposeful manner. Because children, during the earliest stages of elementary school, do not use logic in the way that older children do, a goal of learning must be to help the children learn to use systematic and purpose-ful relationships.

An example of this kind of pre-learning process is easily found in most primary-school art activities. The typical kindergarten experience is a good example. A child may be given clay. He begins to make a form. Someone tells him to make a dog. The child struggles with the shapes. The result will be called a "dog" because the child has worked upon it in terms of his images of a dog. In verbal descriptions, the child may tell you that this is his dog, or a friend's dog. The legs may fall off while he is talking; this fact will not bother the very youngest child, but the more mature child will be distressed. This is so because the youngest child cannot anticipate

8-1. BUS TRIP
Author's collection.

what happens when he tries to turn "clay" into "dog." Clay and dog as material, symbol, and concept are not integrated; in the child's mind, the clay is a poor symbol for dog. For the older child, the clay can be made into a good symbol for a specific kind of dog. The older child will be embarrassed by the structural faults of his clay construction.

An example in painting might be found in the work of the child who has had a vivid experience. A kindergarten class went on a field trip. The children were excited and intrigued by the bus in which they rode. The teacher asked the group to make pictures of the trip. Some of the children talked about the bus, telling how much fun they had had and how much they liked the bus. Figure 8-1 is an example of one of the paintings produced by a member of this group. The child's first job in making this painting was to describe how the children looked when they were riding in the bus. However, the visual experience is not always of primary importance to a child. The feelings the children had, their excitement, the strangeness or newness of the experience, and the thirst they felt because there was no water fountain were all integral parts of their experience.

The process of making such a painting causes the child to be faced with a multitude of problems. His immaturity causes a combination of confusions. He makes an effort to project images, but is bewildered by the problem of controlling paint. The problem confronting the child about to paint a picture of an experience involves the achievement of techniques for projecting ideas about the experience on paper. The nature of the material and the problems of representation cause the child to resort to forms that, in his thinking, represent aspects of the experience. These forms are the child's symbols for his experience. It must be noted that the concepts regarding the bus experience and the effort to translate these concepts into images made from paint must cause a reformation of image-symbols, which will result in the visual-plastic metaphor. The child must find his own way; he must develop and seek a means to portray his experience. Relationships between paint, body movements, and images inevitably govern this process of discovery. A learning process must exist before we can hope that the child will achieve a solution. As in the case of the clay image of a dog, the material presents a new problem. The processes of working with the material, the processes of productive thinking growing from and merging with pre-cognitive thinking, provide the elements of the learning process.

In Figure 8-1, it is evident that the painting was begun without the child knowing for certain just how the image-symbols would be formed from the paint. Beginning from the bottom left of the painting, there are several large masses of paint. These masses begin to suggest the structure of the bus which finally emerges from the left to right, right to left, and upward and downward curving strokes of the brush. It is this pattern of arm and brush movement that finally achieves the symbol of "bus," which apears as a half-round shape made with a thin line of paint. This line occurs in the right upper middle of the painting. This form, a metaphor for bus, is given completeness when the child paints a rectangle below the half circle or bus symbol. The bus symbol is then given completeness by placing within it the children who rode in the bus. The child's uncertainty regarding methods for forming the variety of symbols that were part of his experience is evidenced by the image in the upper left of the painting. This, in the child's opinion, was the bus driver.

The painting of the bus trip shows evidence that the child had difficulty relating his experiences to materials. This painting is the start of a learning process because the child is being made aware of a need for relationships between image-symbols and materials. In this process of painting, a search for a means to express the child's multitude of feelings about the experience takes place. It is during the process of projection —that is, during the process of forming concepts with paint and brush—that a recognition of this need comes into being. The need for expression places emphasis on the need for thinking about how expression can be accomplished.

INITIATION OF LEARNING THROUGH DISCOVERY

The process of seeking a means for creating the picture of the bus experience is curiously expressed through a metamorphosis from purely rhythmical brush strokes to images. The child's act of discovery took place during this process of metamorphosis, when the child became aware that the movement of his brush could be translated into a symbol for the bus. This discovery became a basic element in the process of learning.

Jerome Bruner describes the act of discovery as being comprised of four advantages: 1. An increase in intellectual potency takes place. 2. There is a shift from extrinsic to intrinsic rewards. 3. A process of learning occurs through the acts of discovery. 4. Discovery is an aid to conserving memory.[3]

If the child who made the painting of the bus began with a desire to experiment with materials in order to discover how they could be made to form a suitable expression of the experience, there is reason to believe that his work involved learning. The person who develops the attitude of "let's see what will happen" is the person who will devise a means, who will construct meanings, and whose curiosity will lead to fruitful rewards. If a child gains satisfaction from his accomplishment, he will be led to attempt newer investigations and expressions. In this case, the reward is intrinsic, and the child is aware of the value of his exploratory methods because through them discovery becames possible. This is evident in the painting of the bus because the emergence of the bus image from purely rhythmical lines is a sign of a moment of discovery. We know that the child was aware of this moment of discovery because

[3] Jerome S. Bruner, *On Knowing, Essays for the Left Hand* (Cambridge: Harvard University Press, 1962), p. 83.

he exploited it by placing the images of children in his symbol for "bus." In terms of the kindergarten child's level of development, his finished painting represented a satisfactory metaphor that expressed his experience.

The experience of painting the picture of the bus involved a process of becoming acquainted with relationships that could be made between materials and the elements of experience. The parts of this process were placed in a relationship by the child who sought and discovered a solution to the problems of representation and expression. This kind of experimentation and discovery becomes learning that is stored in memory. Such learning is useful because it has been constructed by the child. This fact makes the learning available for future use because the child experienced the process, contrived the means for reaching solutions, and realized the emotional satisfaction of accomplishment.

STRUCTURE OF LEARNING THROUGH ART

In essence, the process of learning through art activity is a process that includes perception, projection, forming, relating, and conscious scrutiny and evaluation of the results.

In his book, *The Process of Education,* Jerome Bruner lists three processes that may take place "almost simultaneouly." These processes include: the acquisition of new knowledge, the manipulation of knowledge to make it fit new tasks, and evaluation.[4]

The process of learning described by Bruner is suitable as a beginning for understanding the learning process in art activities. Our discussion of the process of spot-sampling of afterimages, the process of projecting these images, and the association of these images with related experience may correspond to the process of securing information for the development of an art activity. This process involves the acquisition of knowledge about observations, experiences regarding visual phenomena, and sensory perceptions. This perceptive process involves a process of making comparisons with concepts previously held, the development of patterns of relationships between images and sensations, and the develop-

[4] Pp. 48-49.

ment of an awareness of the effect of one perception upon another. In short, the initial step in the process of learning is the achievement of understandings regarding the structure of an experience. This structure is made up of the factors that give each experience its unique qualities. This process also involves association of observations, participation in experiences, and confirmation of previous and related experiences. The coupling of these diverse processes usually results in the development of newer, revised, or richer understandings.

FUNCTIONS OF IMAGE-SYMBOLS

The parts of the processes of art activity, perception, motivations to activity, thinking, feeling, conception, and evaluation, are parallel to the processes of learning listed by Bruner. The major difference is that in art activity, perception must be of a visual form. Learning in art activity is concerned with the development of thinking in terms of physical image-symbols that are translations of the images of perception. These symbols are the raw material of the art processes; they are the source of knowledge needed for the development of a process of art activity. The use of this knowledge requires the action of thinking and feeling in order to make possible the evolution of purposeful or expressive forms in a plastic material. The final phase of the process, evaluation, makes the art process a learning process because it makes the children aware of problems that still need to be solved. Evaluation indicates solutions that have been found and solutions that still need to be found; it offers directions for future work.

The flexibility of the process of art activity and the student's understanding of its structure and implications are of special interest in terms of the development of a learning process. Bruner is not only concerned with the manipulation of knowledge; he is also concerned with the ways in which the manipulative processes can be made to fit new tasks.

DEVELOPMENT OF LEARNING PROCESSES

The first part of the learning processes, the acquisition of new knowledge, is related in many respects to the Bauhaus method of developing the exteroceptive or distance sensors. Such development was accomplished by having the student participate in sensory exercises. One activity that constituted such an exercise was the making of charts illustrating textural differences between materials, the effects produced when these differences were associated or related in a variety of ways, and the manner in which ideas and concepts could be formed from these relationships. It should be noted that these were texture exercises in which the student learned through a process of drill. The drill involved practice in sensing the textures by feeling them with the fingers. In a similar manner, studies were made of volume and space, of mass and its relationships to space, of the unique qualities of materials, and of the effect on these materials of various tools and different kinds of working processes. Such studies were intended to provide students with opportunities to replace inexact knowledge, to refine knowledge, and to gain understandings and information of the various techniques useful in working with materials, associating particular materials, associating particular materials with particular categories of expression, and knowing the structural characteristics of materials that make them suitable for broad categories of designing.

The second part of the learning processes involves the development of a means for manipulating symbols and materials in order to achieve a meaningful symbolic structure and to discover the qualities of materials that suit them for expected or unexpected expressional or utilitarian purposes. In the education of young children, this is a fairly simple procedure. Through exploration, children can become familiar with the qualities of paint, clay, fabrics, wood and metals. With a proper approach to this kind of information, it is possible to provide children with open-ended understandings about possibilities for forming and manipulating various kinds of materials; the children should be able to become capable of making their own selections of materials that are most suitable for particular art jobs. An activity concerned with the development of visual forms for the expression of a house, child, parents, or family might require color, pattern, house, and landscape symbols. A child aware of the working advantages of paint or crayon might select one of these ma-

terials because it possesses qualities most suitable to his purpose. It might happen that a child will know that each material possesses qualities uniquely suited to the expression of particular details in the picture. The result will be a painting in which two materials are used. Or, to extend the idea, pictures might contain three, four or five different materials. It is not unreasonable to suppose that a good learning process might involve the selection of sand pasted on paper, sections of fabric, newspaper, sandpaper, or any other material that might be useful as a means for achieving a particular purpose. This phase of the learning process involves a willingness on the part of the child to experiment with materials, to improvise, to observe, and to evaluate. In the words used by Bruner, this is a ". . . process of manipulating knowledge to make it fit new tasks." We are extending this idea for art education and we are placing it on a concrete level by saying that this manipulation of knowledge is correlated with a process of manipulating physical materials. The processes of learning involve seeking relationships between perceptions, seeking associations of perceptions, establishing meaningful relationships between images and symbols of perceptions, forming concepts, and relating all of these processes to plastic materials.

The key aspect of the processes of learning is the process of evaluation, which is a process of examination, of looking, thinking, and projecting future directions from past accomplishments. Evaluation is the means we use to guarantee the effectiveness of the learning process and to insure its most effective continuation.

USE OF GENERAL UNDERSTANDINGS IN ART EDUCATION

Jerome Bruner has said that general understandings are more valuable in the processes of education than specific knowledges.[5] This assertion is based upon the belief that we can apply and use knowledge when we have general understandings about how a thing works. This is an important concept for the teacher who wants to plan art activities that will encourage creative action and inventive thinking. Children will find

[5] *The Process of Education*, Chapter 2.

pleasure in learning through art activity if they are able to combine knowledge with materials in order to make rich expressive metaphors. Children need to learn how to make knowledge work for them.

In art activity, students are engaged in a process of making discoveries. The processes of art activity are not routine; neither the teacher nor the children are always sure of what kinds of forms will be made. The process of finding solutions to art problems requires that the children have understandings regarding the techniques for working with tools, for manipulating materials, and for making the kinds of forms that seem indicated for a particular purpose. General understandings relate as much to techniques for developing processes as to knowledge about the subject being expressed.

The teacher helps children achieve general understandings by helping them become familiar with materials. The teacher may first have to demonstrate the properties and creative possibilities of materials. The children should be helped to establish purposes and to formulate directions for working with ideas and materials. Such learning experiences result in general knowledges that can be applied to special situations. These general understandings provide the framework within which the unique functions of art in the learning process can operate.

Almost any educationally valid art activity will illustrate the way in which general understandings are used as a context for the art processes. For example, a portrait of a particular person can not be painted in the same way as any other portrait. Each portrait will have a different expressional purpose because every person is different and the purpose of a portrait is to communicate the unique personality characteristics of a particular individual. In the same way, if a child is making a puppet of a clown, he will have to evolve techniques suitable for forming the particular things that make his clown an unusual being. Some clowns would be effective if the child used red yarn to make a shock of red hair and black buttons to make large black eyes. Another child could make a wonderful clown with a nose made from a burnt-out flashbulb that had been painted red. Such activity involves the combining of precognitive and productive thinking. The effective combination of these two

processes will lead to useful exploratory techniques.

General understandings are defined here as a principle. The specifics of teaching may be another matter. For example, in teaching paper sculpture it may be possible to tell the children that to make a sculpture it would be best to begin by making a cylinder. Then, the children might be told to paint eyes, nose, and mouth on the cylinder. The difficulty here is that we are describing the specifics of a technique. The children are being told what to do and when to do it. Nothing is being done to indicate that this is a process that might lead to other and different kinds of paper sculptures.

In order that the children be able to learn the general processes necessary in working with paper sculpture, the teacher must show the children what paper is like by demonstrating the working characteristics of a great many different kinds of paper. Cutting, folding, rolling, twisting, bending, pasting, stapling, and other processes must be investigated. Then, the children should be given opportunities to explore the materials, to compare notes with each other, and to evaluate their findings. When useful discoveries have been made, the teacher should show them to the class. From general understandings about these processes, application to the forming of particular objects will take place. For example, if one child set out to make a sculpture of an elephant, the teacher would place emphasis on the characteristics of an elephant. Then the problem would be to determine the paper sculpture techniques that could be used to make forms to express the characteristics of this particular kind of elephant. (Figures 5-1 and 5-2 are good examples of this process of applying general understandings about materials and objects to the creation of successful expressive symbols for specific objects.)

For the youngest children, the use of feeling and emotion will be more important than established techniques in applying rational understandings. If children are allowed to "feel" their way to the solution of problems, they will develop the confidence they need for the experimental seeking attitude that is used by even professional artists. If this process is guided by a knowing teacher, it will eventually lead to the coupling of reason with "feeling."

The process of permitting feelings to serve as a

guide to thinking and doing may be the kind of technique useful in the objective areas of the school program. This process of thinking motivated by feeling and the excitement of discovery will provide an energy and a self-motivating force that will make children want to seek and find. Bruner notes that excitement, the compelling incentive of discovery, is the element of learning all children need for everything they do.[6]

The making of any art object requires the development of techniques that may never before have been known to exist. This is as true for the professional artist as it is for the child. Each art activity will involve new and unexpected problems that will have to be solved in new ways. The establishment of procedures, predetermined techniques, and formulas simply does not work in art activity. A stereotyped procedure will result only in a stereotyped result. When this happens the process of learning through art activity loses potency because many of the necessary parts of the process are bypassed.

The need in art activity for techniques that are developed for each unique situation requires that our emphasis in teaching art must be on the general character of the process of art activity, the general modes of observation and thinking, and only those specifics needed at a particular time.

IMPLICATIONS FOR CURRICULUM PLANNING

This understanding of how thinking and learning take place in the process of art activity has broad implications for the organization of art curricula in elementary school. The emphasis on broad structure or general principles means that a curricular program designed only to provide increasingly difficult work as children progress through elementary school is no longer valid. Determinations regarding the year in which watercolor will be taught, or figure drawing, or composition and design are not major problems. The major problem in curriculum planning is the development of a means for providing experiences that will make possible an increasingly useful participation in the processes of art activity and the planning of means for transferring the valuable learning techniques provided by art to other areas of the school program in which they can

[6] *The Process of Education*, p. 20.

be used. Art education requires a curricular organization based upon thinking and learning techniques that are useful for all phases of living. Art education is uniquely suited to this task. Art can act as a base for all learning because it demands that emphasis be placed on general principles and on concepts formed from experience, which are to be worked out with concrete, tangible materials.

Contrary to older and more primitive forms of curricular organization, learning in art proceeds from the general to the specific. The general principle always takes precedence over the specific, thus providing for a continuous flexibility of approach to each new art experience. The working techniques are known in a general way, but the precise working procedure is sought out and devised according to the requirements of the particular situation.

Art education programs organized around specific how-to-do-it techniques, such as how to draw a face or a figure, how to harmonize colors, or how to design an arrangement for violent movement or peaceful rhythms will be a failure before they even get started. Such procedures make it impossible for children to relate their art activity to the uniqueness of each experience or to the unique quality of their own memories of past events. Specifics of this sort destroy the excitement of discovery, which is a prime motivational force to learning.

When specifics, formulas, or stereotypes are taught as art, they are easily forgotten if they are not continuously used. Purely informational learnings are not easily applied to new situations and unexpected events or happenings. Use by a child of specific techniques or inflexible data makes it extremely difficult for him to contend with the ever new problems that continuously confront him during the course of routine living. Unusually superior children may be capable of understanding the general characteristics of a subject or a technique, but even they may have to struggle too hard for success when they must work only with knowledge of parts, with little or no understanding of the structure of a whole.

THINKING AND LEARNING WITH IMAGES

We have talked a great deal about the importance of images to thinking. One of the things we need to emphasize is that much of our experience, our perceptions, consist of images. Effective thinking is done when we supply symbols for these images. Images in their original form, as we perceive them, are too clumsy to manipulate in the thinking processes. It is for this reason that in mathematics we use signs to stand for concepts, qualities, and quantities. Similarly, language is a means for handling complex abstractions that could not easily be handled with images alone. We should also note that images and the symbols we form from perceived images are a quick and direct means for form making and the accompanying process of thinking and learning in art activities. The symbols we form from the images of perception in art are very real and rich; however, they may exist only in our minds. The value of these symbols is not known until they are combined with a physical material. The act of combining symbols with materials is the process of learning how to express thinking and experience.

We speak of symbols as signs of experience. It should be noted that the symbols themselves are images; however, they are not identical to the objects we see. It is to be expected that the image-symbol will be of a somewhat different nature from the images of direct perception. The symbol will be richer and more ordered because during its formation it will have undergone processes of elimination of extraneous features, it will have been associated with other previously experienced image-symbols that exist in the subconscious, and it will have been scrutinized by the rational mind. These symbols or image-symbols will be efficient instruments of thought. If they remained as the original images of perception they would not be efficient.

Excellent evidence of the effectiveness of symbol or image-symbol thinking is found in a letter written by Albert Einstein to the mathematician Hadamard. "The words of the language, as they are written or spoken, [writes Einstein,] do not seem to play any role in my mechanism of thought. The psychical entities which serve as elements in thought are certain signs and more or less clear images which can be 'voluntarily' reproduced and combined. . . . this combinatory play seems to be the essential feature in productive thought before there is any connection with log-

ical construction in words or other kinds of signs which can be communicated to others. The above mentioned elements are, in my case, of visual and some of muscular type. Conventional words or other signs have to be sought for laboriously only in a secondary stage, when the above mentioned associative play is sufficiently established and can be reproduced at will." [7]

THE ARTIST AND LEARNING PROCESSES

The traditional working methods of the artist provide us with clues as to how children can learn through art activities and still avoid the pitfalls of an education program based on "facts." For the artist, problems are ever new, unexpected, and unpredictable. Each time the artist paints a picture, carves a statue, or designs some object, he expects to be faced with problems never before encountered. Each set of problems will be as unique as the experience he expects to express through the media of art. Prepared formulas, modes of working, recipes, and how-to-do-it techniques may provide clues, but they seldom provide answers.

The artist must depend on his general knowledge of the techniques of his craft and of the techniques for conveying feeling and ideas through plastic materials. He has certain concepts regarding the general "structure" of art forms, which form the crux of his working habits. The artist must use methods of productive thinking, which involve awareness of the characteristics of materials, of their potential for expressions of particular types and of their uses for making general classes of forms that will become organized, formed, symbolic structures. For example, the artist knows that watercolor used on white paper is capable of giving great purity to a color; this purity can be accomplished because of the brilliance of the transparent watercolor through which shines the gleaming white of the paper. He also knows that certain materials, such as oil, can combine the shimmer of transparent glazes of color with the sharpness of opacity. He knows that metals can give a lightness and openness of form to sculpture and that stone can give sculpture mass and

[7] Jacques Hadamard, *The Psychology of Invention in the Mathematical Field* (Princeton: Princeton University Press, 1949), Appendix II, p. 142.

solidity. These are just a few of the general ideas with which the artist works. The artist places his faith in these understandings because he knows that although the acquisition of drawing skills, modeling skills, skills in mixing and harmonizing colors, techniques for brush manipulations, and a multitude of other tricks of the trade are useful, they are not of themselves sufficient for the making of a work of art.

The artist has been stereotyped as a creature of passion. We have much evidence from the lives of artists, from their writings, and from the comments of biographers that the artist works as much from intuitive as from rational levels of thinking. Central to the artist's method of working has been a sense of independence, a self-confidence, and a willingness to experiment. Pleasure in discovery becomes part of the foundation of the aesthetic experience. When the artist engages in an act of producing a work of art, he is searching for this aesthetic experience.

The aesthetic experience is accompanied by the establishing of relationships between ideas, images, concepts, and materials, and by an intuitive sense of the properness of these relationships. Following this initial phase of art production a rational comprehension evolves, a process of inspired or labored correcting. These two general phases are the vertebrae of the structure of art activity.

THE INFLUENCE OF CULTURE ON CHILD ART

The psychological human grows in a cultural soil. The child is the product of his cultural environment. If art made by children is an expression of child understanding, it, too, will be shaped by cultural forces.

CULTURAL BASIS OF ART

The history of art is a history of the different ways of seeing and thinking that have characterized different human societies. The art forms of ancient Greece are more notable for their differences, when compared to the art forms of the old Egyptian kingdoms, than for their similarities. We know that these two cultures borrowed from each other although they were strikingly different in social and political organization and in their cultural traits. The extent of these differences are evident in their art forms. The most notable and typical examples might be exhibited in the fluidity and flexibility of the carving on the typical classical Greek statues. These carvings are rich in fluid movements and in their emphasis on the grace and rhythms of living creatures. Even in comparatively archaic works, which are strongly influenced by Egyptian techniques, a smile impishly breaks through the

coldness of frozen nobility that is the mark of the Egyptian influence.

The despotic and formal government of the Egyptians with their emphasis on unchanging social forms and the stratification of social classes reflects itself in a formal, monolithic, and static art form.

A completely new cultural emphasis comes into being with the rise of the modern capitalist society. This new kind of social force finds expression in the humanist art of merchant-dominated Florence, Italy in the fifteenth and sixteenth centuries. The concern of the Florentines with the condition of man, with the aspiration of man to a dignified and politically free status, is expressed in the lifelike paintings of Giotto and the profoundly humanist visions of such men as Cimabue. This art is a far cry from the tortured hell on earth of the medievalist artists. Such a contrast helps clarify the effect of culture on the art forms. For example, the cultist representations of Christ, the stock in trade of the artists

of feudal Europe, can not be the product of a society for whom man is considered the measure of all things. The suffering nude Christ of the icon makers is as much a symbol of bondage and medieval serfdom as it is a sign of the emergence of Christian ideology. The detailed symbols of Christ's torture are structured in a manner that conforms to the cultural concepts of the period. As society changed and as feudal Christianity gave way to the middle-class Christianity of the early sixteenth century, interest in the grotesque, the bloody, and the tortured ordeal gradually declined in popularity. With an increase of upper-middle-class patronage of the arts of painting and sculpture, the older ferocity in representation was subdued. This change is characterized in Renaissance style by a rationalization of the figure; as evidence of the increasing interest in the mortal body of man, artists began to paint the nude Christ as an excuse for making anatomical studies.

The influence of social ideals, concepts, habits, and attitudes is evidenced by the typical Renais-

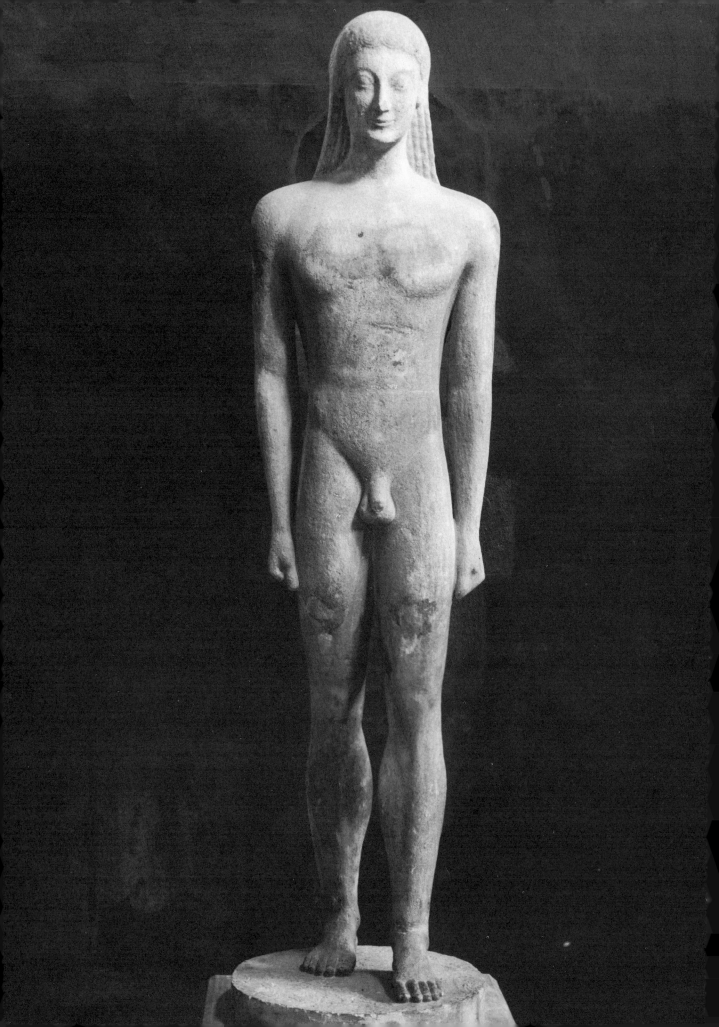

9-3. MYCERINUS AND
HIS QUEEN
(c. 2575 B.C.). Slate, from Giza.
*Courtesy of the Museum of
Fine Arts, Boston.*

9-4. CRUCIFIXION
(Detail). By Master of San
Francesco. Italian, North Um-
bria. *Philadelphia Museum of
Art, the W. P. Wilstach Collec-
tion.*

sance art form, which indicates a concern with a personal protective God. In accordance with the tone of the then prevailing culture, a new theme was introduced into the painting of religious subjects, the theme of the guardian angel. According to this approach, even the role of the Virgin Mary was reinterpreted and she became a Madonna of Mercy.

CULTURAL INFLUENCES IN CHILDREN'S ART

Just as the professional art form takes its purpose and character from the culture that it expresses, the art forms made by children express the cultural environment in which children live. Paintings by boys and girls, for example, tend to mirror the social attitudes toward the sexes. This becomes evident when we note that very young children, regardless of sex, show an interest in home, flowers, sky, earth, animals, self, parents, and friends. As the children grow up, however, we find distinctions being made. The girls, if left to their own devices, select feminine subjects; the boys select subjects, such as war and masculine

9-5. PORTRAIT OF MARCIA BY MARCIA
Author's collection.

sports, which are socially condoned as the proper province of males.

When we consider social attitudes in a culture that makes clear distinctions between the role of male and female, it is important that we understand that these roles are described in the art form, not merely in the selection of subject matter, but also in the line, tone, color, textures, and form of the art objects.

Figures 9-5 and 9-6 are simple drawings, one by a girl and one by a boy. It would not take any special skill for anyone to know that the soldier was drawn by the boy and the portrait of a girl by the girl. The line and color treatment of the girl's portrait have a delicacy that is distinctly feminine. Even the emphasis on the barrette and on the carefully drawn bow lips is evidence of a second-grade girl's interest in the care of hair and of a typically feminine interest in lips. The latter interest finds some expression in the drawing's emphasis on the distinctly sexual connotation of female lips.

The boy's portrait of a soldier is evidence that even in this advanced age of space exploration and scientific achievement, our cultural inclination is to consider war the supreme masculine objective. This soldier is done with the hard, sharp line and the dynamic rhythms of a modern boy's admiration for the military personality.

The contrast between the portrait of a girl and the portrait of a soldier is startling. We must not take this kind of difference too lightly. Here we have evidence of a cultural expression that extends far beyond the simple selection of subject matter. In each case, the delicacy or strength and the rhythm of the line serve to produce an image-symbol. Out of a process of precognitive thinking and productive thought, the delicate curve and grace of a girl and the sharp, hard, strong masculinity of a young male have emerged in accordance with their cultural environment.

ORIGINS OF CULTURAL INFLUENCES

According to our discussion so far we have reason to believe that the children who participate

9-6. PORTRAIT BY MARTIN
Author's collection.

in art activities are a complex of psychological and cultural forces. The way a child participates in an art activity and the art forms he makes result from his organic make-up as much as from the fact that he or she is a member of a group of people. The child's major influences may come from his peers and from his teachers and parents. But these persons are also the products of a society and a culture; consequently, they pass on to the child the cultural concepts, attitudes, and modes of behaving by which they have been bred and by which they live.

The human creature, as a biological entity, responds to environmental stimuli. These environmental stimuli are a complex of forces, but we can group them under the broad name of culture. Culture in this sense means many things; it is a product of tradition and geographical location. Cultural characteristics are products of geographical location because the traditions we hold to be part of our heritage are products of our climate and of the contour of our land, which make certain kinds of dress and behavior necessary for the preservation of body and health. From these understandings, it follows that our children have certain tendencies in their precognitive or productive thinking, in their mode of working, and in the subject matter they select for an art activity mainly because of their cultural environment, rather than because of their psychological make-up.

Leslie A. White describes the differences among peoples as "differences of external cultural stimulation." He claims that what we take to be human nature is not a natural manifestation of human behavior at all; instead, it is a cultural manifestation. "Much of what is commonly called 'human nature' is merely *culture* thrown against a screen of nerves, glands, sense organs, muscles, etc." [1] People around the world behave in different ways because different people belong to different cultures. People who are members of the same culture have standards in common.

There is much evidence available to indicate that what we may take to be normal human behavior may very well be considered abnormal, sometimes even subnormal, by people of other cultures. White notes that even forms of behavior that we have long considered explained by psychological factors are actually culturally inspired. For example, it was once thought that a boy's love for his mother and his hostility toward his father were expressions of his biological nature. It has been demonstrated that attitudes such as these vary with different types of family organizations. What we might refer to as an Oedipus complex is a natural form of behavior in some societies. However, there are cultures in which the sister, instead of the mother, becomes the object of incestuous desire. In other societies, where the mother's brother is the head of the household and the father is simply a friend and companion, the boy's attitude will not be the same toward his mother as it is in Freud's patriarchal home. Even our conscience is not purely a psychological manifestation. Concepts of "right" and "wrong" vary from one culture to another.

INFLUENCE OF THE GROUP ON PERCEPTION

Children are not merely biological organisms whose behavior can be understood if we know how the organism works. It was noted earlier in this text that psychological behavior grows in a cultural soil. We have also noted that one of the goals of art education is the cultivation of uniqueness, that is, the development of a rich individualism among children. It was also noted that this individualism is desirable to the extent that each individual contributes his uniqueness to the group in such a manner that the society to which the child belongs, and under whose influence he or she grows and lives, will profit from each person's uniqueness. Individual uniquenesses combine to enrich the fabric of the social group. Conformity among members of the group can only lead to a weakening of the social fabric, the establishment of a leavening conformity, and a resulting static and lifeless society. Strict conformity would make the contributions of individuals nonexistent, and the social group would settle down to a monotonous and routine existence.

In every society there is a constant tendency for group norms to come into being. These norms exist without much conscious awareness of their influence by and upon the members of the social group. One of the purposes of an educational

[1] *The Science of Culture* (New York: Farrar, Straus & Company, 1949), p. 149.

process is to develop means for establishing a balance between the tendency for group norms to function and for individual uniqueness to contribute to the well-being of the group.

TENDENCIES TOWARD GROUP CONFORMITY

The fact that group norms tend to exert an almost unnoticed effect on group behavior is made evident by some fairly recent research. One example of such a study is the study of autokinetic movements. The studies of autokinetic movement were concerned with an analysis of the reactions of individuals to a moving light. Note was made of the kind of reactions individuals had when they responded to the moving light in isolation compared with their responses while in group situations.

In the study of autokinetic movement, individuals were placed in a room with a moving light and were asked to estimate the distance the light moved. First the individuals made the judgments when they were alone in the room, then, they judged the distance again when they were in the room with a group. At the time that studies were being made of the first group of individuals, another group made the same kind of judgments. In the second group, the judgments were first made in a group and then in isolation.

Judgments made by the first group differed somewhat from judgments made by the second group. When alone, each individual in the first group had to establish his own norms of movement. One individual might see large amounts of movement, another might see very little movement. But when these same persons entered the

9-7. THE JUNGLE
Mural. *Teaneck, New Jersey, Public Schools.*

group situation, they tended to modify their first judgment in the light of the group judgment. In this case, a group norm was observed to develop after at least four sessions. In the second situation individuals, who begin by making judgments in a group situation, showed uniformity of judgment almost from the very beginning.[2]

In art activity, we have noted that group influence is always important. Figure 9-7 represents a larger section of the painting from which the detail of a lion, Figure 6-2, was taken. This is a painting made by a group of four first-grade children. Like most group paintings, it is homogeneous. There is little evidence of divisive individualism. On the contrary, the whole painting is very well unified. It shows a greater degree of unity than we find in Figure 7-5, the circus clowns by a kindergarten child.

In spite of visual evidence that the children conformed to a plan, there is uniqueness in the painting of the lion and other animals. The lion is drawn differently from the other creatures. A study of the details reveals differences in the way each detail is executed. On the other hand, the clowns in Figure 7-5, although done by one child, show changes in treatment from the left to the right side of the picture. The group painting demonstrates differences between individuals, but it is unified. The clowns in Figure 7-5 show variation in one individual's productive thinking from one part of the painting to another. The combination of many personalities working together, each making its unique contribution, results in a strength of expression as exhibited in Figure 9-7.

It could reasonably be objected that in most group art activities, in which the group cooperates on a single project, there is a large amount of agreement regarding the nature of the design and the details of the pictorial organization. This fact, it may be argued, will lead to a useless conformity. The obvious answer to this objection is that in Figure 9-7 the details of individualism are agreeably coordinated within the total design structure. There are evidences of varying levels of child development, but they do not detract from the total design. For example, the lion is much more

[2] From a study reported by Muzafer Sherif, *The Psychology of Social Norms* (New York: Harper & Row, Publishers, 1936).

skillfully drawn than the creature immediately above it or directly to the left of it. The lion is well defined and is immediately recognizable as a lion. The species of the other creatures is debatable. On the other hand, the expressiveness of the lion is no greater than that of the creature in the upper-left-hand corner.

The group painting of the jungle is important in terms of what happened while it was being painted. The behavior of the four children and their relations to each other must concern us, as well as the painting itself. We have reason to believe that the most proficient of the four children was the child who painted the lion. This child also painted and arranged many details of the flowers and symbols for jungle growth. In terms of this particular kind of activity, the proficient child became the group leader and exerted the strongest influence in the group. This child became the individual to whom the other three members of the group came for help. The child who painted the animal at the top left may have conceived his animal as a lion. His painting has four legs, a lion's mane, and the ferocious look lions are supposed to have. Ferocity is accomplished by making the mouth a red oval with two large and supposedly fearful teeth painted across it. The child who painted the lion on the bottom right did the same kind of thing, but with greater subtlety. In both cases, the lions have the facial characteristics of children. It seems almost as if the children were placing themselves in the role of the animals they were painting. In the same manner, the beast on the left side of the painting, half way between the top and bottom, owes its fearfulness to its impression of great size. The stripes of color are vaguely associated with a zebra, but the head appears to have begun to conform to the pattern established by the lion. An attempt seems to have been made to save the day by giving the ungainly head a pair of horse (or zebra) ears.

The painting of the jungle is an excellent example of the healthful blend of individual uniqueness and group unity. Included in this understanding is the nature of the conformity that we know is a natural by-product of any group association. We see evidences of this kind of conformity in the drawing of the eyes of the lion in the lower right of the painting and the eyes of the creature in the left center. We may also note that the efforts of the child to make this beast into a zebra had repercussions in the creature located in the center, midway between the lion and the semi-zebra or striped-lion beast. In the center creature, the stripes have become elaborated into a criss-cross pattern.

Evidence of the healthful relationship between members of the group of children involved in the jungle painting is found in the painting's profuse detail. The painting is rich in details of foliage and plant growth. The plants are of special interest because they are mostly flowers, which were made by cutting bits of colored fabric into flower shapes and pasting them in appropriate locations. Other details were developed by putting paint on sponges and then making sponge impressions across the surface of the paper. The richness of this kind of detail is possible because the four children worked together to develop ideas for flowers, foliage, and modes for the representation of these images. Because this is a first-grade group, the teacher did not consider it necessary to tell the children that their images were fanciful and that the flowers were more closely related to their own immediate environment than to an African jungle. The children created an image of a jungle in terms of their own experiences.

The opposite of this kind of group activity, in which the individual interacts with the group, is the case of the child who pursues his uniqueness in isolation. In such a case, there are usually factors within our cultural life that make such a child a special problem.

Figures 9-8 and 9-9 were done by an eight-year-old boy who lives in the city. For him, the tall buildings form the landscape with which he is most familiar. This child sees tall buildings in isolation. In his daily life, he is without strong family ties; his parents are busy with their work and he is left in the care of hired help. The crayon drawing, Figure 9-8, is a sober expression of loneliness. It is dark in quality with strong emphasis on the lighted windows. This is a strong drawing in the sense that the child knows how to draw the images of the buildings. There is none of the childlike gaiety or uncertainty of the zebra-lion creations in Figure 9-7. Figure 9-8 shows little influence from drawings of other persons. In the strictest sense, this is a private expression.

It is also a unique expression for an eight-year-old child. This kind of uniqueness in isolation may develop in one of two ways. The child, if he is very rich in imagination and drawing skill, may continue to achieve excellent and personally satisfying results. But the time must arrive when frustration will enter into the experience of picture making because his experience is essentially a lonely one. We have reason to believe that the group effort is ultimately the most rewarding, provided the individual is permitted to contribute his uniqueness to the group achievement. From many points of view, this child may not achieve the richness of expression he deserves because his social condition is such that he will retreat into himself; his loneliness will become increasingly burdensome. He will not have opportunity to learn from the other members of his age group as did the children who participated in the painting of the jungle mural. Like all small boys, he yearns to be associated with adventure, which our culture describes as the province of the masculine. This desire for adventure naturally

9-8. BUILDINGS
Crayon. Collection of Theodore Lynch.

World War II

Joshua Littman Burk

leads to some emphasis on the warlike and the violent, Figure 9-9 is a drawing by the same child. The drawing is energetic, imaginative, and vivid. The experience is evidently vicarious, as is the painting of the jungle. This drawing again tells us what we already know from our examination of the crayon drawing by the same child. This is a talented child. But other evidence indicates that he is also a frustrated child. The evidence of frustration begins to appear more strongly in this drawing than in the previous one. Here we find a strong attempt to find adventure that is not immediately apparent in the environment. The mural of the jungle is really a painting of a child's world. In spite of the vicarious nature of the subject matter, there are plentiful evidences of influences of firsthand visual experience. In the case of the war drawing, we are dealing with a concern for pure adventure and with a form of experience that no longer belongs to the world of childhood. The starkness and grimness of the symbols is almost frightening.

The cultural aspect of group activity and its influence on children in our culture is well illustrated by the examples of group and individual expression in art. If the group expression is not merely an activity that encourages conformity, it will provide an educationally useful experience. The healthy group experience must be one in which each child learns from his associations with others of his own age and intellectual level. The opposite kind of situation can be destructive of

educational achievement. Human beings are social creatures, and the best results are usually achieved when people can work together.

IMPACT OF CULTURE ON VISUAL EXPERIENCE

The way in which we see things depends to a very important extent on our cultural and physical environment. A child who lives in India expects people to dress in costumes that are typically Indian. The Indian child considers the sari the typical dress for women, but to the child living in the United States, this will seem a strange dress. The American child draws pictures of girls wearing skirts and men wearing long trousers. Similarly, the Indian child draws pictures of Indian men and women wearing their usual attire. In Figure 9-10, a painting by an Indian child, we have a version of a child dressed in full sari-like gown without the end pulled over her head. The painting of a man, Figure 9-11, is definite in its representation of the cloth wrapped around the body and between the legs in the manner of Indian male attire.

Children in our country would have little problem differentiating between types of automobiles. Children from villages in India might not know much about automobiles and, consequently, would not often think of painting pictures of them. However, the typical Indian child, who does not know as much about cars as his American equiva-

9-10. GIRL
Painting. From an exhibition, "Children's Paintings from India," circulated by the Smithsonian Institution.

9-11. MAN
Painting. From an exhibition, "Children's Paintings from India," circulated by the Smithsonian Institution.

lents, would know a lot about water buffaloes. While the American child might make pictures of automobiles, the Indian child might, with an equal resource of knowledge, make pictures of water buffaloes. Even more significant, the Indian child might, if he were brought to the United States, consider all automobiles to be very much alike. In this respect, he would be different from his American friend. If the American child, who has developed some understanding through the natural process of a natural experience, were to draw automobiles, he would probably be sensitive to subtle differences between cars of different commercial manufacture. The Indian child would only be aware of gross differences. In our illustrations we see the same kind of distinctions being made in the case of dress. To the Indian child, the little girl's skirt reflects the fullness of the adult women's sari; in the painting of a man, the Indian child takes for granted the unique character of Indian male attire. If an American child were to paint these pictures, he would need to exert a special effort of imagination.

CULTURAL EFFECT ON COLOR PERCEPTION

Color perception is also a significant aspect of cultural life. Krech and Crutchfield [3] note that when some Baganda people of Africa were asked to sort pieces of cardboard which varied in size, shape, and color, they sorted them mostly by shape and size and never by color. In some cases these people differentiated by color only because they had previously had some contact with European culture. The reason for this becomes obvious when we learn that the Baganda people have no words for color in their language.

PERCEPTION OF SIZE AND SHAPE

Relationships of size, shape, similarities, and differences in configurations of forms are perceived in terms of an individual's cultural atmosphere. It is not unusual for people in our culture to describe size in terms of well-known objects. An example would be the typical inclination to measure distance in terms of city blocks and heights in terms of buildings.

Relationships are commonly established on the basis of perceptual concepts that are unique to a culture. Certainly, the children of a society existing in the jungles of Africa would not compare size to an amphibious tank. Size, for such children, might be related to the size of an elephant or a lion. For the children of a jungle community, such size relationships are accurate. For the American child, the same kind of relationships become fantasies because they are imagined rather than real.

The anthropologist Malinowski, in his description of the people of the Trobriand Islands, notes that these people do not claim to see any resemblances between children and their mothers. On the other hand, even if there is only a very slight resemblance between a father and his children, the people claim to see very great resemblances.

These unique differences in perception and cultural coloration of the visual elements of everyday life are not the result of differences in the organism's method of perceiving. The differences are sociological or cultural because they are caused by differences in experience, learning, language, religion, or other social institutions or traditional assumptions.

The Rorschach inkblot test has provided us with a rich store of information regarding the manner in which different cultures see and perceive visual forms. In a study reported by Bleuler and Bleuler,[4] it was found that when inkblots were shown to primitive desert tribes of Moroccans, these people were much more aware of the tiny details of the blots than were Europeans. The reason for the concern of the Moroccans with detail might be ascribed to the importance of detail in Moroccan handwork and art. By contrast with the response of the Moroccans to the inkblots, Krech and Crutchfield note that "Samoans differ markedly from typical Europeans and other samples of subjects in giving numerous responses to the *white spaces* in the blots, which they perceive as objects rather than as holes." [5] If Samoans see white in preference to black, it may be because white is a color to which they attach great symbolic value. "All of this does not mean that Moroccans can not see 'wholes,' or

[3] David Krech and Richard S. Crutchfield, *Elements of Psychology* (New York: Alfred A. Knopf, Inc., 1958), p. 44.

[4] M. Bleuler and R. Bleuler, "Rorschach's Ink Blot Tests and Racial Psychology," *Character and Personality*, IV (1935), 97-114.
[5] *Elements of Psychology*, p. 46.

Samoans 'detail.' The point is that given these ink-blots, which are susceptible to many different perceptual organizations, people of different cultures tend to look at them in different ways." [6]

INFLUENCE OF ECONOMICS ON PERCEPTION OF OBJECTS

In American economic society, we have reason to believe that economics, as well as the filtering action of traditions and other cultural inheritances, plays a decisive role in our perception of the world around us and in the forming of our experiences. Economic conditioning and economic position can distort the manner in which we perceive things, their sizes, and their relative values.

In a study conducted by Bruner and Goodman,[7] children ten and eleven years of age were divided into two groups. One group was made up of children from a slum area, the other group was made up of children from economically secure middle-class homes. The children were asked to differentiate between what they remembered about the size of a nickel, a dime, and a half dollar. All the children overestimated the sizes of the coins. This overestimation was greater for the half dollars, less for the dime, and still less for the nickel. But the children from the slums overestimated the sizes of the coins more than did the children from the more prosperous families. From this study we might conclude that the perception of size was directly related to the value of the coins for each group of children. The greater the value, the larger the perceived object was thought to be. Evidently, the children from the poorer homes were more sensitive to these money values than the children from the more prosperous homes.

CULTURAL INFLUENCE ON CONCEPTS OF RELATIONSHIPS

The influence of conceptions of value on the perception of size is not a unique phenomena. In the art forms of almost all cultures, important elements have been given emphasis by making

[6] *Ibid.*
[7] J. S. Bruner and C. C. Goodman, "Value and Need as Organizing Factors in Perception," *Journal of Abnormal Social Psychology*, XIII (1947), 33-44.

9-12. MADONNA ENTHRONED
(c. 1310). By Giotto. *Uffizi Gallery, Florence, Italy.*

them larger than anything else in the picture. An excellent example of the importance of size as a means for establishing a relative sense of value is found in such a sophisticated painting as Giotto's *Madonna Enthroned.*

According to the general cultural attitude of the religious society for which Giotto painted his pictures, the most important subject in a picture such as this would have to be the mother and the child. All other elements are secondary in rank, but nevertheless important. The presence of the saints serves to enhance the importance of the mother and child. To indicate the secondary importance of the saints, they are made much smaller than optical experience tells us they should be. To increase the emphasis on the centrality of the mother, in addition to the size of the figure, the dark mass of the mother's gown gives added emphasis to the contrasting lighter tone of her face, upper torso, and her hand resting on the knee of the child.

We have no reason to believe that the artist was unaware of the disproportionate size of the mother and child in relation to the saints in this painting by Giotto. We know that this method of directing attention to primary figures is a frequently used stereotype in the icons of medieval Christianity. And we know that this method may be found to exist in most cultures where the art form is dominated by concepts rather than by descriptive attempts to communicate optical experience. In the art of the High Renaissance, such as in the work of Raphael, Titian, or Tintoretto, the artist is true to the optical experience of a linear perspective, of relative sizes in deep space. The art forms of the High Renaissance are notable for their expressive power, as well as for their descriptiveness; however, this fact does not by any means imply that the earlier work of Giotto is any less powerful or expressive.

Figure 9-13, a drawing by a kindergarten child, is a far cry from the great masterpieces of pictorial expression we have used so far as examples of distortions of size and space in the interest of a cultural requirement. This drawing lacks the great religious impulses, the monumental emotionalism, and the sweep of intellectual power, but its motivations for coming into existence are, in a general way, of a similar nature.

This drawing of a cow came into being after the children had talked about milk, had been told where it came from, and had visited a dairy farm where they had seen cows being milked. When the children finally had opportunity to express their understanding of cows, they were inevitably subject to the suggestions they had received from their teacher, from their experience on the dairy farm, and from the tradition in our culture that milk is a basic food necessity for all children. Hardly a child in the group had escaped the daily pressure from an anxious parent to drink all of his daily quota of milk. In the mind of the child, combined factors of experience, social and cultural attitudes regarding milk, learnings concerning the sources of milk, and so forth, led finally to this practical expression of what a cow means to a small child. The udder and teats of the cow are given prominence by virtue of size and darkness of tone. But the cow, too, from the point of view of a five-year-old child, who measures the world in terms of his own body size, is a large and fearful, but friendly beast. Here size is a determinant of value. It is also a means for placing emphasis on what is culturally significant. The animal itself is indistinct in terms of the child's motor ability to represent the creature he has seen; however, the child was able to express his feeling about the cow's uses and purposes

9-13. COW
Crayon drawing by a kindergarten child. *Author's collection.*

within the cultural context of the child's world.

This drawing of a cow might be said to be the result of a perceptual distortion. The perceptual distortions, however, are the result of social suggestions and a social attitude toward milk as a prime food for little human beings. It is of interest to note that very young children are subject to suggestions when their own experiences reinforce the suggestions. Notice that the cow in this drawing has a nice long tail with paintbrush-like hairs at the end. The dairy farm was a place with lots of flies, which the children had to keep brushing from their faces and from other exposed parts of their bodies. The children had watched the cow whisk the flies off his own seemingly inaccessible body parts with an effective fly-chasing tail. In the mind of the child who drew the picture, the cow's tail had an important function; thus, it, too, received a special visual emphasis. The drawing is an image-symbol that stands for the child's concept of a cow, which is formed from a combination of visual experience, social and cultural modifications of visual experience, and qualitative shaping of the symbolic structure. The shaping of this image-symbol has been done according to the dictates of various emotional responses to a recent experience with the image from which these composites of symbols have been drawn.

SUMMARY

The traditions of a group, the physical environment, and the relationships that exist between children and the people with whom they have daily contact shape and condition the psychological forces that govern their learning processes. Art activity is enriched by the cultural environment in which children live and grow. The art forms children create are largely the result of their cultural environment, their inherited traditions, and their social relationships. The colors, shapes, sizes, and relationships of parts in an art work should be understood in terms of their origins in the social and cultural environment.

On the basis of what we have discussed, it is possible to develop some guides regarding the use of our understandings of the cultural sources of art activity. We have evidence that individuality finds its most fruitful expression in useful contributions to group understanding. It is important to be wary of conformity, the opposite of individuality, because it may gradually lead to an unnoticed but harmful dulling of individual motivation and expression.

Group activity is useful because children learn from each other. Children may tend to mimic the more proficient members of their group, but we have evidence that they are more likely to find indications in the work of their peers of ways they can solve their own problems. Interaction of this kind is beneficial to the entire learning process.

It is important for the teacher to be able to understand the forces that motivate a child during an art activity. The kind of work in process may serve as a guide to corrective measures that may be taken. It is sufficient for us to know that the way children draw, form, or construct during art activity is often the result of social forces acting upon them to channel their image-symbol formations, to sensitize their perceptive mechanisms, and to create specific attitudes and understandings.

A general conclusion that should be gained from our understanding of the role of cultural forces in child art activity is that child art must obtain its essence from the experiences with which children have their most direct contact. In terms of the processes of art education, direct experience provides the only useful basis for the development of a valid educational program. Children will benefit most from understandings that grow out of their own cultural environment.

Ten

THE NEED FOR BALANCE

IN THINKING AND FEELING

The achievement of a balance between thinking and feeling may make it possible to extend the limits of a child's experience, because coordination of thinking and feeling results in the most effective perception and understanding.

Our discussion of the precognitive and productive processes places much emphasis on the importance of a balanced relationship between thinking and feeling in the processes of art activity. The precognitive processes make it possible for the necessary blend of thinking and feeling to exist in art activity. The emotional factor is more likely to function usefully in art activity and productive processes if it is partially directed by unconscious impulse and if it is sometimes manifested as spontaneous comprehension, which may be defined as inspiration. The relationship between conscious and unconscious thinking is an important part of the process of learning. The unconscious mind is considered to be free of the restraints of analytical and critical thought processes, which are more the province of the conscious mind. Both rational and emotional thought processes are essential to the total process of thinking. We know that ". . . rationality is a built-in need and not just a mask for the irrational. . . ." [1]

Art activity is a learning activity because it makes use of both rational

[1] Murphy, *Freeing Intelligence Through Teaching*, p. 37.

and emotional thought processes; it involves both ". . . the impulse to know and the impulse to gratify the inner needs . . . [which] . . . are two aspects of one reality."[2]

The existence of a tendency to use feelings, intuitions, and instinctive drives for doing the important work of the world is largely dependent upon cultural permissions, sanctions, or habits of work. Cultural permissions affect the art activities of children from the more advanced levels of the primary grades onward. As children mature, they may feel shy and insecure about the kinds of forms they are able to make because they think their mode of expression is considered unacceptable by their parents, friends, or teachers. Cultural permissions operate most incisively when older boys are led to believe that their peers consider certain kinds of expression to be too feminine. Girls, not wanting to appear too masculine, may avoid dealing with masculine subjects or using what they think are masculine tools, such as saws and hammers.

An important function of art activity is to provide children with a means for utilizing their feelings without interference from cultural attitudes. This purpose can be accomplished if cultural problems are considered and are used to help, rather than hinder, the use of feelings in conjunction with thinking. Discussions with children about the subject matter of their art activity, as well as increased understanding among the children of the purposes of art activity, will help to solve this problem.

How a child feels about a thing ought to be considered at least as important as what he knows about a thing. In art activity, children's feelings will color and shape the subjects they express. The feelings children have should be considered important aspects of their understandings. In terms of expression, the importance of the expressive form will be determined only partly by the knowledge the child has of the subject.

During the discussion that follows, we will find that the separation of either thinking or feeling from the aesthetic experience is as impossible as the separation of imaginative and creative thinking. Aesthetic experience can not exist if the art process depends on feeling, only, or thinking,

only. A combination of both is necessary to achieve the balance between reason and emotion that makes the art form a pleasurable experience.

THE NATURE OF FEELING: FEELING AND KNOWING

In art activity, feeling has a number of connotations; one of them is emotional comprehension, which refers to understandings that are felt rather than logically and rationally known. This connotation raises a question: What kind of relation exists between feeling and knowing?

Feeling, as used in this discussion, is a form of perception that is dependent on emotions for its existence. In this context, feeling is similar to intuition; it is knowing or learning something because we sense that it is right or correct. From this interpretation, it might be argued that we are talking about intuition rather than feeling. If we restrict ourselves to intuition, however, we must neglect another important connotation of feeling: perceiving knowledge through emotions that have been shaped and structured by subconscious and conscious experience.

EMOTION AND KNOWLEDGE

In practice, intuition is more closely related to instinctive drives and comprehensions than to emotion. In art activity, emotion provides the drive, the incentive or motivation to engage in processes of forming visual-plastic metaphors from the image-symbols of perception. Emotion is a form of excitation, a feeling that is akin to desire. But emotion is not knowledge.

Intuition is most useful when it is directed and colored by qualitative emotion. A qualitative emotion is one that has been subjected to a process of conscious examination and critical evaluation. Such a process takes place when the teacher and children discuss spontaneous responses to experience that can be visually represented in an art form.

Undirected intuitions may dissipate themselves and become useless expenditures of energy. The emotional impetus to learning in art activity helps children avoid making intuition nothing more than an automatic response to some stimulus. Without emotion and the knowledge emotion

[2] *Ibid.*, p. 41.

can lead to, intuition becomes a curious phenomenon rather than a working tool. A purpose of the art education program is to help children develop understandings about their art work that will help guide their intuitive processes. For example, a child may find that wet paint can be mixed with colored chalk by drawing directly into the paint with the chalk. Experimentation might develop this combination of wet paint and colored chalk as a means of expressing the quality of a rainy day, the surface of a lake or pond, or a landscape composed of rough textures of masses of chalk contrasted with the smooth tones of painted areas. If the child has previously worked with either medium, it is possible that his understandings about the medium will help guide the intuitions that arise from his experiments with chalk and paint. In addition, class discussions about the work in progress will give the child more profound understandings about the nature of the experience being expressed. A cycle of growth occurs. Through examination and evaluation, emotion becomes increasingly qualitative. Critical evaluations that arise from discussions are added to earlier intuitions to help the child know the subject better. Broader understandings or more profound insights will make the child more sensitive to suggestions from intuition for better ways to express concepts related to the subject. Intuition is directed by emotion that has become qualitative through increased understanding providing purpose and drive to the use of intuition in achieving expressional forms. Art activity initiates a chain reaction: the more we feel, the more we learn, the better we express, the more we learn, the more we feel, the more we learn, the better we express. . . .

It is important to notice that emotions or feelings are associated with the intuition of rightness. The child will not always be able to explain why what he has done seems the best way to give visual form to a concept; he will be able to explain only that he feels it is "right." A purpose of art education is to give direction to this kind of feeling by encouraging children to think about what they have done, to analyze the appropriateness of a particular form for the communication of a concept. When the child understands these reasons, he should be encouraged to experiment with, and to evaluate, ideas and materials, to discover other ways in which the concept could be expressed. Here he must learn to suspend judgment. Although his first method may seem right, it is not the only possible method. The teacher understands, too, that everything the child learns must be tested by him and continuously re-examined in the light of changing experience, new information, and his earlier concepts. For example, a child paints a picture of a circus. The acrobats are dressed in white tights. The lions are imprisoned in sturdy cages beneath the area in which the acrobats perform. Is this the best location for the caged animals? Do trapeze acrobats always perform in white tights? Are these colors and these arrangements of the elements of a circus the best ones for this painting? Now, reference may be made to the experience of other children, to stories about circuses, or to other pictures. Then, what about the way in which the acrobats have been drawn? Is this the best means for communicating information about the grace, agility, and skill of the performers? Perhaps the children should go to the gymnasium and try, within the limits of their own skills, to assume some of the characteristic poses of the circus acrobats. In this way additional experience, understandings, emotions, and intuitions about expressive means may be developed.

In the art activities of young children, the relation between emotion and knowing is of special interest. Among the youngest children in the early phases of the primary period, the expression of experience is not always deliberate. The scribbling activities in the kindergarten are examples of this. The inclination of children here is more to play with materials than to seek an effective expressive means, because their expressive purpose is not clearly defined before they begin to work with art materials. Such definition of purpose usually begins to take place in the first and second grades and it should be a characteristic of the working processes in the intermediate and upper grades. In the early kindergarten, however, the purpose of an art activity may be developed after the art object has been made or while it is being made. This is the kind of process that art teachers refer to as an explaining process. While a child is manipulating art materials he may offer explanations of what the emerging forms are supposed to represent. The explanations are often invented, hardly ever really explain the forms that are being made, and can also take place after the forms have been made. But the reason why a form is made will often be something other than what the child apparently thinks it is. He may claim that his painting is a picture of his teacher. A few minutes or hours later, he may cheerfully announce that the painting is a self-portrait. After some questioning, the child may proclaim that the picture is a portrait of his mother. His original reason for painting the picture may have been forgotten because it was not important enough, or he may have had no purpose beyond the pleasure he found in just playing with art materials. Because he could give no reason better than manipulative pleasure, he made up a few, just to satisfy his peers or his teacher. The real source of the difficulty is obvious. Rationality was not related to emotion during the process of his art activity. He enjoyed painting for its own sake. Rationality did not actually influence the forming processes. The lack of influence of rational thought results in incomplete forming processes because rational thought must be present to serve as a means for giving quality to emotion and a direction to the intuitive processes.

When children are asked to explain their work, they are also being asked to evaluate. It is this process of evaluation that gives the child some indication of techniques of thinking and performing in future work. In this way, children are helped to find ways to correlate their thinking with their feelings during the processes of art activity. This correlation evolves into the more detailed and critical thinking used by children in the upper-primary, the intermediate, and the upper grades.

The teacher must be aware of the ways in which the youngest children think during art activity, in order to direct their purposes into useful channels. Knowledge for them may be unconscious or intuitive forming as often as it is a process of discovery that grows out of the manipulative processes. This latter process evolves out of the experiments and improvisations with which children can become involved during art activity. The manipulated art materials, whether they begin as scribbling with paint or crayon or as seemingly purposeless manipulations of clay or similar plastic materials, may suggest relationships to experience as they are given accidental forms. It is during this process of experimentation and improvisation that intuition operates. Children may intuitively recognize unexpected possibilities for forming experiences from the shapes that grow out of the manipulative processes.

Group evaluation processes are a useful means for eliciting knowledge from emotion when the discussion gives added energy to the discovery of forms in materials that have been manipulated. For example, a group of children have been given a variety of materials to experiment with: fabric scraps, wire, colored paper, light bulbs, and paper clips. They might be asked to find out what kinds of things can be done with them to suggest meaningful forms. Such activity should be performed by children who have already had some experience with this kind of experimental process or by children who have been shown examples of the kinds of things that can be done with such scraps. Examples of the possibilities for forming by means of this approach may be seen in Figures 22-10 and 22-14. In Figure 22-10, experimentation with wire and paper clips led to the discovery of a metaphor for a man riding a bicycle. This form was developed from the discovery that wire used in a certain way suggested the exaggerated form of a particular kind of bicycle. The paper clips served to form the details of the expression, as well as to hold the parts of the form together. Knowledge of the forms evolved out of some previous experience. In this case, emotional drive was provided by suggestions arising from the materials themselves, as well as from a process of working, which was essentially a process of improvisation. This process elicited intuitions that were motivated by feelings of amusement based on attitudes toward old-fashioned bicycles.

The ghost shown in Figure 22-14, made by a seventh-grade child, evolved from a recognition that gauze materials suggest a means for the expression of a spooky Halloween subject. Correlated with this manipulation of materials was the child's emotional attitude toward ghosts that finds expression in the form given to the materials.

DANGER OF IMPROPER USE OF INTUITION

An important change in the history of thinking about intuition occurs when Immanuel Kant says intuition transcends reason. In Bunge's [3] opinion, this concept leads to the association of intuition with irrational thought processes. "Whereas Kant fell into intuitionism because he realized the limitation of sensibility and the exaggerations of traditional rationalism, and because he misunderstood the nature of mathematics, intuitionists nowadays do not attempt to solve a single serious *problem* with the help of either intuition or its concepts; rather they are anxious to eliminate intellectual problems, to cut down reason and planned experience, and to fight rationalism, empiricism, and materialism." [4]

Bunge's study points out the dangers involved in the use of intuition. To begin with, intuition may lead to a form of irrationalism that, under certain conditions, is far more dangerous than useful. Intuition must not be thought to be separate from rational thought; intuition is a part of rational thought. Complete reliance on intuition can result in a degeneration into anti-intellectualism. At its worst, it will become a form of charlatanism that, in the history of our century, ". . . reached its highest peak in the Third Reich after a long period of preparation, in which intuitionists of all shades and all European nations . . . took part. . . . Nazi Germany exalted blood, instinct, 'sympathetic understanding,' or empathy, the vision of essences and the intuition of values and norms." [5]

SAFEGUARDS FOR INTUITION

Intuition is a powerful force that may be used for good or evil. The one safeguard that can be employed to protect against the use of intuition for "barbarization and deculturalization" is *criticism*. Constant evaluation of the intuitive process is an absolute requirement if intuition is to be a useful part of the processes of art education.

We are forever destroying intuition in favor of understanding. Intuitions must be refined, analyzed, studied by rational processes, and discarded after their purposes have been accomplished. This guide to the use of intuition is proposed by Bunge

[3] Mario Bunge, *Intuition and Science* (Englewood Cliffs, N. J.: Prentice-Hall, Inc., Spectrum Books, 1962).
[4] *Ibid.*, p. 9.
[5] *Ibid.*

when he advocates the use of criticism. The results of the activity of the intuitive modes, says Bunge, are rough hewn products; the hunch or inspiration is interesting but does not achieve usefulness until it is ". . . converted into formulated concepts and propositions, . . . analyzed, worked out, and logically tied to further conceptual constructions. Fruitful intuitions are those which are incorporated in a body of rational knowledge and thereby *cease* being intuitions." [6]

CRITICISM AS EVALUATION OF THINKING AND FEELING

The function of the process of evaluation is to provide a critical study of the results of emotional perceptions, feelings regarding the correctness of concepts, formulations, and metaphors. Evaluation is the means for providing the processes of feeling with useful understanding, meaningfulness, open-endedness, and the possibility of making of the whole an aesthetic experience. Evaluation is the method for making criticism a means of relating feeling to thinking. Unless this relationship is achieved, neither feeling nor thinking can be useful parts of the art activity.

In the process of art activity, feeling must serve as a means for initiating the development of image-symbols into metaphors. Such metaphors may have living and aesthetic qualities because the life-giving force of human emotion infuses the metaphoric structure. Without feeling, the scope of thinking is limited, and useful metaphoric expressions can not be formed. There must be no confusion between the feelings that infuse the intuitive processes and those that infuse the processes of precognitive thinking. Precognitive thinking follows intuition; it uses feelings and intuitions, but it subjects intuitions and impulses to analyses made possible by the experience of selecting and rejecting. A rich experiential background makes available to intuition a variety of perceptions and the multitudinous symbols and conceptions that constitute a large part of the subconscious mind.

When we try to get children to use intuition to start their thinking and activity, we encourage the use of inspiration or the hunch—taking ad-

[6] *Ibid.*

vantage of the accidental forms that emerge from the processes of manipulating materials. But we have to know how long to encourage this way of working and to recognize the time when we can no longer make good use of intuition. Such a time will occur during the later phases of an art activity. When the art form a child is making has become organized, when the whole of the idea seems to be emerging, the time will have arrived for the child and the teacher to do some objective thinking about the work and its progress. The earlier approach that emphasized "Let's see what will happen." should be replaced by questions such as "Why did you paint the picture in this particular way?" "Is this the kind of color scheme that expresses the ideas you are trying to communicate?" "Would the idea be clearer if this texture were rough, and the one next to it smooth?"

This process of evaluation involves a destruction of the processes of intuitive thinking. Emphasis is now placed on the objective purposes of a particular art activity. Comparisons can be made between what a child has accomplished in his work and what he might accomplish using another technique. If the teacher moves too rapidly into the phase of objectivity, there is danger that the vitality of the children's art work may be destroyed. On the other hand, if the objective evaluation is begun too late, there is a real danger that the children's metaphors may become overwhelmed with emotions and illogical constructions.

FEELING AND LOGIC IN CHILDREN'S ART

In art education, the analysis of intuitions is a process of applying logic to art activity. In the art work of very young children, feelings may dominate expression. A lack of constructive logic is a sign of the expected immaturity of childhood. It is hoped that as children mature and become more capable, they will be helped to apply a useful process of evaluation to their working habits, their accomplishments, and their achievement of metaphoric quality. The ability to use criticism as a part of the process of art activity is a learned ability; it is the teacher's responsibility to help children put their feelings to valuable use by combining them with rational thought. The

teacher must help the children learn to balance thinking with feeling.

From these understandings, it follows that without feeling, the scope of thinking in art activities is limited. Feeling provides the means for the operation of intuitive faculties. Because of the role played by feeling in the initiation of art activity, in its relation to the precognitive processes, and in its capacity to infuse the intuitive processes with force and vitality, feeling must be considered a basic means for the development of art activity. Feeling leads the way in experimentation and exploration of materials and image-concepts. Unique, expressive, and economical metaphors come into being because feeling demands their existence and because feeling guides the explorations, the searchings, and the probings of the precognitive processes.

FEELING AND SPONTANEITY

The process of establishing an effective working relationship among intuition, feeling, and rational thought is designed to help children accomplish (1) effective expressions and (2) a mode of thinking that leads to exciting, meaningful metaphors and turns them into an aesthetic experience. The accomplishment of such a relationship involves a process of exploring materials and experiences and of discovering the unique qualities of materials that make it possible for them to form exciting, vital, and unique metaphors.

The first phase of this process is important because it is so closely related to motivation, and we must investigate how motivation is related to subsequent processes. We know that if we place too much emphasis on conscious thinking, the children's paintings or other art work becomes lifeless. In order to help children retain their natural spontaneity, the teacher guides them in the development of effective metaphors.

During the earliest phases of art activity, the manipulation of materials and the formation of image-symbols is spontaneous. Forms and their metaphors seem to come into being as a result of the manipulative processes. The teacher and children need to know how this vitality can be made to express feelings by means of poetic, plastic metaphors.

The history of art offers many examples of the manner in which a qualitative emotional intuitivism has been exploited in order to achieve a meaningful metaphor. The paintings of the various expressionists are excellent examples. One of the earliest of the modern expressionists, El Greco, is apparently guided to a large extent by emotional responses to ideas. Figure 10-1, the famous portrait of the Cardinal Guevara, is vibrant with a sensitive man's indignation at the excesses of the Spanish Inquisition. In typical fashion, El Greco makes the costume of the Cardinal flowing yet full of tensions that culminate in the tense hands of the figure. Tensions are elaborated in an elongated spiral, like a wound-up spring that begins in the heavily emphasized cir-

10-1. CARDINAL DON FERNANDO NINO DE GUEVARA
By El Greco. *The Metropolitan Museum of Art. Bequest of Mrs. H. O. Havemeyer, 1929. The H. O. Havemeyer Collection.*

cles of the Cardinal's eyeglasses and coils through-out the painting, continuing its tense rhythm through the line of the garment and down into the harsh circles opposed by rectangles at the feet of the figure. This kind of tension in painting and compositional structure conveys strong emotional overtones, a sense of the vital emotional drive that probably caused the artist to find his way through the use of a well-practiced and understood technique. The expressional purpose is violently emotional, but the skill of the artist is manifested in the easily understood metaphoric structure employed to communicate these feelings. This painting is an excellent example of a blend of feeling and thinking of a high order.

Figure 10-2 is an example of the delicacy of the balance between impulse and rational thought. This is a drawing of a head by an intermediate-grade child. The vertical line down the center of the face is the result of a misplaced emphasis on a guide line for the construction of the features. The teacher began this particular drawing activity by demonstrating to the children that the head must be divided into areas and that each part of the face has a specific relationship, a proportional size, within the dimensions of the average human head. She attempted to provide the children with objective guides for drawing the human face.

The child began to draw by making an oval shape for the head. He then drew a line down the center of the oval in order to locate the features "properly" from left to right. With lighter horizontal lines, he located the center of the mouth and the center of the eyes. After these technical requirements had been met, the child proceeded to shape the metaphor. The relation of the metaphor to the mechanical lines presents a real problem. This is a drawing of a child with large lips and eyes and a long nose. The location of the center line for the mouth causes the lips to be too close to the bottom of the chin. The rest of the features of the image-symbol struggle to overcome the preliminary restrictions and obstructions to the development of a suitable plastic metaphor.

To begin with the assumption that a metaphor can be adjusted to a preconception is very much like working backward. In this case, the result of the effort is pleasing, but one wonders what would have happened if the child had first drawn

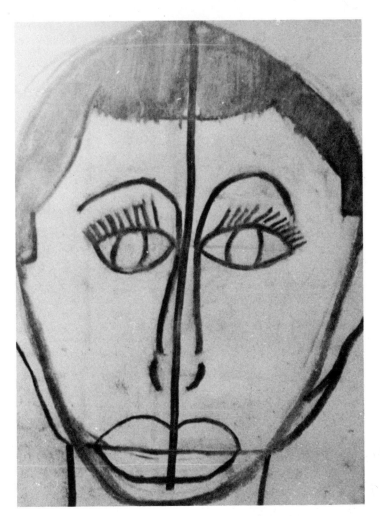

10-2. PORTRAIT
Crayon. *East Orange, New Jersey, Public Schools.*

the head without instruction. Technical or rational adjustments could be made later.

Figure 10-3, the painting of a Chinese girl by an eighth-grade child, is an example of a metaphor that has emerged from the processes of precognition motivated by feeling. This metaphor achieves a level of communicability commensurate with the ability of the child who painted the picture.

It is possible that the child who painted this picture was not immediately aware of the irregularity of the oval shape of the head. The left side of the head forms an approximate forty-five degree angle from the chin and then moves upward in an angular fashion from a high cheekbone toward the hairline. The entire right side of the head is much more vertical with a smoother curve from the chin to a point just above the brow, where it angles inward to meet the hair. The total structure provides the over-all effect of an oriental personality, although the eyes are not

10-3. PORTRAIT
Tempera. *East Orange, New Jersey, Public Schools.*

the stereotype slant. Between the eyes, the brows, and the brushwork pattern of the face, there is a rhythm that extends to the simple inference of a nose. The fullness of the lips contrasts effectively with the implication of an oriental hairdo. Rhythmically related to the face is the collar of the dress. The resulting effect is one that could be achieved only in terms of the characteristics of a particular person, and in terms that had to be devised for this purpose by the child who made the painting. Formulas prepared in advance of the process of painting the picture might have prevented the kind of metaphor that resulted. In effect, this is a successful painting because it is the result of stimulations from a specific experience, because the child who painted it was able to develop the metaphor intuitively, and because evaluation processes during the process of painting helped to strengthen the direction of the expression of this particular concept. The nice

balance of working techniques and the discovery of a suitable metaphoric form serve to express and effectively define a "feeling" for the personality portrayed.

CULTURAL HANDICAPS TO DEVELOPMENT OF FEELING

It is unfortunate that popular over-concern with mechanics and the acquisition of informational data have dominated our century. Artists and scientists have reminded us many times that contemporary cultural attitudes may lead to the destruction of the human spirit. This may happen, some observers believe, because our emotional and intellectual lives have become unbalanced as a result of the increasing specialization of human work. This specialization is described by John Dewey as the "compartmentalization of occupations and interests." [7] Dewey implies that there is a lack of fluid communication between occupations because we have established artificial barriers between areas of work.

The concept of "wholeness" of human effort, thinking, and behavior helps the elementary-school curriculum planner escape the dangers of "compartmentalization of interests." In this sense, the elementary-school program has usually been built on the belief that young people need relationships between the several areas of their school work established for them. Efforts to departmentalize elementary-school programs have often met with failure. But we can not ignore the existing problem because as soon as young people are able to absorb appreciable amounts of information, usually in the intermediate and upper grades, separation of subject areas, departmentalization, and finally compartmentalization begin. The concomitant effect is an alarmingly rapid disintegration of progress. For this reason, we can not ignore the problem at the elementary-school level.[8]

A lack of a balance in thinking and feeling

---

[7] *Art as Experience*, p. 20.
[8] Although specialization presents problems, we must not overlook the work of art education specialists who teach at the elementary-school level. There is always a need for the specialist; however, the work of the specialist must be planned to assure an absolute minimum of compartmentalization.

seems impossible in a world that has given form to human aspiration. Yet, Sigfried Giedion was able to say:

In such a period, [as ours] people no longer expect a scientific discovery to have any repercussions in the realm of feeling. It seems unnatural for a theory in mathematical physics to meet with an equivalent in the arts. But this is to forget that the two are formulated by men living in the same period, exposed to the same general influences, and moved by similar impulses. Thought and feeling could be entirely separated only by cutting men in two.[9]

According to Giedion, the cleavage results in the split personality of our age.

If an educational process emphasizes either thinking or feeling to the partial or complete exclusion of the other, it must follow that intellectual growth will be uneven. "Only very rarely [writes Giedion] do we encounter a master in one field who is capable of recognizing workers of the same stature and tendency in another. Contemporary artists and scientists have lost contact with each other; they speak the language of their time in their work, but they cannot even understand it as it is expressed in work of a different character." [10]

The answer to all this must be that ours is a complex age, in which specialization is unavoidable. But it is not specialization to which Dewey refers; it is compartmentalization. It is not only specialization that brings about a separation of thinking and feeling; this separation is also caused by the ". . . separation of that mode of activity commonly called 'practice' from insight, of imagination from executive doing, of significant purpose from work, of emotion from thought and doing." [11]

Although this is a definite problem of our age, there is an available solution. The methods required by science are not unlike those required for the development of a process of art activity. There is a distinct parallel between the working and thinking procedures of the artist and the scientist. Evidences of these similarities are attested to by mathematicians and scientists, as well as by painters and poets. Henri Poincaré has said that a ". . . mathematical demonstration is not a simple juxtaposition of syllogisms, it is syllogisms *placed in a certain order,* and the order in which these elements are placed is much more important than the elements themselves. If I have the feeling, the intuition . . . of this order . . . I no longer fear lest I forget one of the elements." [12] In this statement, the basic aspects of the processes of art activity are described as involving: the Gestalt (patterns) and the joining of thinking and feeling (intuition) in a unified composite. For Poincaré, understanding is made possible through relationships and logic exists because of feeling or emotional motivation. Without this balance of rational thought and emotion, the processes of art activity might never have existed.

A balance between thinking and feeling is a necessary concern of the teacher. If the work of child art is to be useful in the whole of the process of education, it must represent the ordering of concepts and the forming of feelings and thoughts into meaningful relationships. There should be some evidence in the work and behavior of children that the activities of feeling and thinking enrich each other.

A lack of feeling can result in a routine descriptiveness that lacks the pleasure of the aesthetic experience. Too much unbridled feeling, however, can result in nothing more than an emotional explosion. The processes of art activity can gain little from any kind of highly personal emotional aberration or disturbance. At its most unsophisticated levels, we must expect that child art will express and be an outlet for personal emotion. The danger in this tendency is that if continued, art activity will become more a form of therapy than an aesthetic experience. In the education of children, art activity is not merely a means for "finding an outlet," for "blowing off steam." Such release from tension could be accomplished more easily by just screaming or taking a cold shower, or by doing zestful breathing, vigorous walking, or calisthenics. As growth takes place in child art, we expect growth in the quality of integration of emotion with rational thought and behavior.

[9] *Space, Time and Architecture* (Cambridge: Harvard University Press, 1942), p. 12.
[10] *Ibid.,* p. 13.
[11] *Art as Experience,* p. 130.

[12] Brewster Chiselin, ed., *The Creative Process* (New York: Mentor Books, New American Library, 1955), p. 35.

OBJECTIVE OF CORRELATED THINKING AND FEELING PROCESSES

The way feeling is expressed through the art processes is not necessarily a purely personal thing. Art activities perform their most useful functions, in the area of human expression, when they make it possible for children to become integrated with their world, to understand it, and to express relationships between social and physical phenomena that are important to them and necessary to their emotional and intellectual development.

The objective of an art education program, which successfully aids in the healthful correlation of thinking and feeling, is to help young people learn to give form and meaning to aspects of experience that need forming and objectification.

The professional artist, writes Susanne Langer, does not express his own feelings, but what he knows about human feelings. The symbols and metaphors formed by the artist can extend the limits of a child's experience, just as the creation of a work of art places the artist on the frontiers of human knowledge. "A work of art . . . is a developed metaphor, a non-discursive symbol that articulates what is verbally ineffable—the logic of consciousness itself." [13]

[13] *Problems of Art*, p. 26.

Eleven

THE AESTHETIC

Educational value in art activity is dependent on the development of aesthetic experiences. Because they are aesthetic, such experiences provide incentive for children to infuse art activity with useful enthusiasms, feelings, a zestful desire to make discoveries, and pleasure in the making of expressive visual-plastic metaphors. The aesthetic is the result of a qualitative process of art activity, and it is the sign of a meaningful human experience. In an important sense, the existence of an educationally useful art process requires the presence of aesthetic qualities.

SOURCES OF DEFINITION OF THE AESTHETIC

Since the existence of an aesthetic factor is dependent on a proper balance of thinking and feeling, the presence of the aesthetic implies that a useful precognitive process and a fruitful process of productive thinking have taken place. If these processes are involved in an art activity, the result will be a visual-plastic metaphor that is economical, unique, effective, rich in its implications for interpretation, and strong in its potential for motivating new art activity.

Evidence of the existence of the aesthetic is found in the art work made by children, artists, and nonartists. The metaphor, if it is artistically valid, will indicate some of the characteristics of the processes of creative action that went into its forming. Creative action involves the processes of forming the metaphor and also the effect of these processes on the participant.

The most aesthetically useful metaphors are those which, through the use of efficient processes of precognitive thinking, show evidence of a high degree of selectivity from potentially useful image-symbols. Metaphors that economically and efficiently gain their effectiveness from a prudent, selective, and forceful arrangement of image-symbols are usually the most aesthetically rewarding.

Aesthetic value in the work of children may be deduced from evidence of growth in the ability to select the most useful metaphors and to communicate meanings with increasing economy of image-symbols. This kind of growth indicates increases in ability to construct concepts and to evolve metaphoric structures without becoming overloaded with too many different ideas, images, and symbols. Such overloading often results in overelaboration and redundancy. Skill in the construction of metaphors that gain their effectiveness from an economy of means and from accurate and effective selectivity is referred to as metaphoric economy. Such direct and expressive economy results in aesthetic qualities.

ASPECTS OF MEANING OF THE AESTHETIC

The word "aesthetic" has sometimes been used as a synonym for the "beautiful." If it is used in this way, any conceivable usefulness this designation may have will be completely lost.

In the work of children, concepts of beauty are emotional with strong provincial-cultural implications, which tell us little about the processes with which we are concerned. Dewey disposes of the word in a most explicit manner by saying that when the word "beauty" is used ". . . in theory to designate the total aesthetic quality of an experience, it is surely better to deal with the experience itself. . . ." [1] For our use, in order to gain a better understanding of the nature of the processes of art education, the word "aesthetic" will refer to the ". . . response to that which to

[1] *Art as Experience*, p. 130.

reflection is the consummated movement of matter integrated through its inner relations into a single qualitative whole." [2]

Henri Bergson, the great French philosopher, describes the aesthetic factor as that which is born from intuition. Intuition, in this sense the parent of the aesthetic factor, is that characteristic which leads us to the essences of life itself. For Bergson, intuition and aesthetic experience are the same thing. Intuition, says Bergson, is ". . . instinct that has become disinterested, self-conscious, capable of reflecting upon its object and of enlarging it indefinitely." [3] People can do this because there exists in man ". . . an aesthetic faculty along with normal perception." "If the aesthetic is not present, our eye perceives the features of the living being merely as assembled not as mutually organized." [4] Such perception is seeing without knowing; it lacks the essentials of completeness because intuition is not correlated with what Bergson chooses to call "normal perception." We might call perception without aesthetic awareness a recognition of facts without emotion or understanding of completeness, in short, without a balanced combination of thinking with feeling. The artist, says Bergson, tries to break down the barrier of space between himself and experience. The artist tries to place ". . . himself back within the object by a kind of sympathy . . . by an effort of intuition. . . ." [5] The ability to do this is made possible by the aesthetic faculty.

EMPATHY

The art work of young children illustrates this concept of establishing relations between self and experience. This process is called a process of establishing empathy. All artists must perform this act. The obvious example is found in the playwright or novelist who speaks through the personalities of his characters. Empathy is a process of projecting one's personality into the personality of another person or thing in order to establish better understandings. In this way, the

[2] *Ibid.*
[3] *Creative Evolution* (New York: Modern Library, Inc., 1944), p. 194.
[4] *Ibid.*
[5] *Ibid.*

artist creates metaphors that communicate his feelings and understandings concerning the images to which he gives form.

The way in which empathy serves a useful purpose in art activity is not as easy to understand as the way it serves such a purpose in literature, when a poet or novelist projects his understanding through the personality of another human being. However, in art activity, the visual metaphor serves as a clear example of the function of the empathetic processes.

The art work of children usually illustrates with great clarity the success of the child in projecting himself into the thing to which he is giving a visual-plastic form. Figure 11-1, a painting by a first-grade child, is an example of this kind of projection. In this case, the child has projected himself into his work so completely that the face of the animal takes on the characteristics of a child's face. There can be a variety of reasons for this. It may be that the drawing of the face is simply done according to a stereotype. At this early phase of child growth, there is little reason to believe that much detailed thinking and rationalization regarding techniques for representing an animal will take place. Like most children, this child has painted a generalization of an animal, in which he utilizes techniques previously employed in drawing pictures of people. It is curious that children often draw images that look like children and that they usually have difficulty in making old people really look old. The reason

11-1. ANIMAL
Detail from mural, *The Jungle. Teaneck, New Jersey, Public Schools.*

11-2. PIG
Chalk. *Author's collection.*

11-3. PIG
Chalk. *Author's collection.*

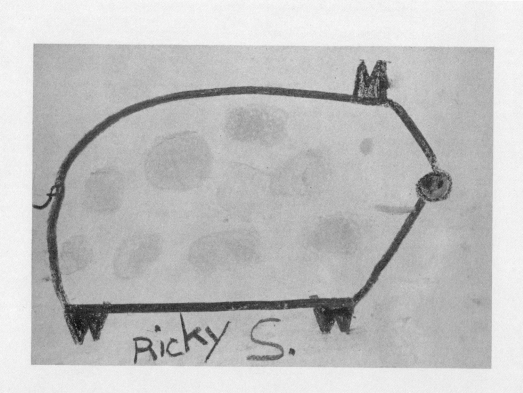

for this tendency could be that the process of empathy makes it easiest for children to place themselves into their drawing and to use themselves as models for everything they do.

The two drawings of pigs, Figures 11-2 and 11-3, are examples of the manner in which children are intuitively able to "sense" the ways in which image-symbols can be structured as effective metaphors. In each case the metaphor possesses the basic elements for the development of aesthetic values; it is economical, direct, and surprising. The sense of great bulk and mass, the image-symbols of pig-like ears, tails, and eyes, and the ridiculously small feet are "felt" images. In each case, the emphasis is on the creation of pig-like image-symbols rather than on the reasoned construction of purely visual forms. These two different metaphors for "pig" are not merely descriptions of the visual image; they are intuitively perceived, empathetic, poetic-visual statements about pigs. The expressions are made in terms of what the children think of pigs according to the standard of body sensation, shape, and size with which they are most familiar. In other words, these metaphors for a pig are made in terms of the children's own bodies and of their feelings about the differences between pigs and people. This latter understanding is obvious in Figure 11-3 in which the pig is given a typical child symbol for smile and in Figure 11-1 in which the animal is given a child's eyes and smiling mouth.

In terms of the relationships established between the experience of "animal" and the projection of self into the experience, we are justified in saying that the child artists have exercised the aesthetic faculty.

Figures 11-1, 11-2, and 11-3 are aesthetic to the degree that the children successfully communicated their feelings for the experiences they were expressing. Aesthetic values are present because the children were able to project themselves into concepts and experiences; they were able to become part of the thing they were expressing and they were able to evolve suitable metaphors.

AESTHETIC EMPHASIS THROUGH METAPHORIC EFFECTIVENESS

The aesthetic value of Figures 11-1, 11-2, and 11-3 may be greater for the sensitive adult than for the average child because the adult will appreciate the child's efforts for their metaphoric novelty, for the effectiveness of the images that comprise the metaphor. For the adult, there is an element of surprise in the child's natural ability to be unhindered by adult inclinations to see parts without seeing the "mutually organized" whole. For the adult, this ability to bypass overly rationalized perceptions and to formulate metaphors that are surprising, as in the bulk of the pig (Figure 11-2) and in the economical linear structure in Figure 11-3, constitutes pleasure in its surprise, in the shock of recognition. Children are inclined to take metaphoric novelty as a matter of routine, but adults are pleasantly surprised by it because they are inclined to seek purely rational relationships. This inclination often results in monochromatic experience, which causes repeated frustration that may discourage adults from trying to achieve the metaphoric freshness and vitality found in the art work of children. Children can achieve metaphoric novelty because they don't pay much attention to the development of rational relationships unless the suggestion to do so is planted in their minds.

Aesthetic value emerges from the process of establishing meaningful relationships between image-symbols and materials. It can exist only when precognitive thinking processes and the scrutinizing functions of cognitive faculties are used. The processes of productive thinking provide the means whereby fruitful relationships can be achieved between materials and image-symbols in order to produce aesthetic metaphors. The establishment of fruitful relationships provides for the discovery of new directions for forming metaphors. This process of discovery involves new and unexpected relationships between materials, image-symbols, and concepts. Stereotypes and clichés destroy possibilities for the development of aesthetic qualities. The achievement of aesthetic value through the development of new relationships involves the extension, completion, or perfection of forms that were previously incomplete or otherwise imperfect. "These forms or wholes are not merely *logical*, or *geometrical*, but more generally . . . aesthetic." [6]

[6] L. L. Whyte, "A Scientific View of the Creative Energy of Man" in *Aesthetics Today*, ed. Morris Philipson (New York: The World Publishing Company, Meridian Books, 1961), p. 360.

11-4. BATTLESHIPS
Chalk. *Author's collection.*

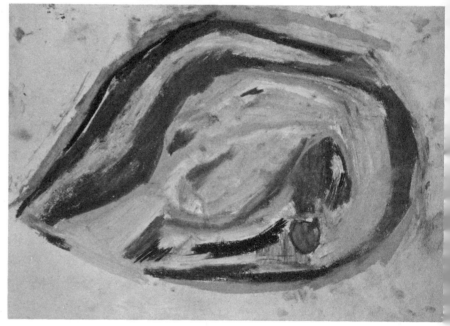

11-5. FISHBOWL
Chalk. *Author's collection.*

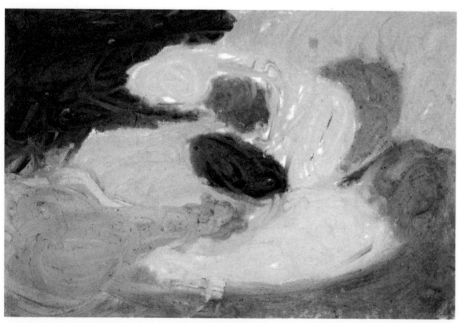

11-6. ABSTRACTION
Chalk. *Author's collection.*

Figure 11-4, a painting of two battleships shooting cannonballs at each other, is a typical example of the expected, ordinary, and obvious relationship. The amount of thought involved in this picture is limited. It is nothing more than a child's painting of naval warfare. Imagination is limited to the actual fact of an aspect of combat. The most that can be said for this painting is that the ships are holding their own; they have been made to look heavy and solid in order that they can more easily stand up to the punishment they receive in combat. This is not a new or novel metaphor; the relationships of the image-symbols add nothing to the knowledge of the "fact." No significant use has been made of materials in order to achieve an effective expression.

By contrast, the painting of a fish in Figure 11-5 is made from a rhythmical flow of wet chalk on wet paper. The rhythm is a felt rhythm; it represents the kind of kinaesthesia involved in the movement of fish in a fishbowl. The quality and structure of this rhythmic organization is the most logical result of the media used. The evolution of this painting should be understood as the result of a recalled experience. It was not possible for the child to stand in front of a fishbowl to paint what he saw. This painting is based on empathetic sensations, resulting kinaesthesia, and the manipulative requirements of the chalk media. The original perception was not a complete experience. The child could not recall all of the details of the experience well enough to reproduce them. The metaphor emerges from the process of productive thinking. The process of forming the metaphor during the art activity results in the evolution of forms that were previously partial, incomplete, or otherwise imperfect. The result is a picture that has aesthetic qualities.

INTEGRATION OF ART PROCESSES AND THE AESTHETIC

The experiences a child uses for the development of an art activity are rarely separated in practice from the art form produced. The separation of any one phase of the processes of art activity would make it difficult for us to recognize the aesthetic.

In order to best understand the aesthetic it is necessary for us to understand the relationship between the processes of experience, perception, precognition, productive thinking, the forming of image-symbols and visual-plastic metaphors, and the interaction of the individual with these processes. It is the interaction of the child with art activity and the resulting sensations that make possible the realization of aesthetic values. If we merely look at a child's painting, we may be pleased with it; we may find aesthetic value in our visual examination and, through an almost vicarious process, we may experience some of the aesthetic sensations that were part of the processes of the art activity. However, the reality of a painting's aesthetic qualities can not be known unless we are thoroughly familiar with the processes of which the painting is only a sign.

Figure 11-6, the chalk painting of abstract and rhythmical forms by a primary-grade child, is a sign of a process of forming. Visual examination of the painting may provide hints regarding the existence of aesthetic qualities; however, appreciation of the aesthetic will be increased through an awareness of the elements of the child's involvement in the process of making the picture. In practice, the child made these rhythmical forms in response to body movements which were in turn motivated by a process of discovery. To the child, these forms are just designs, which resulted from a process of discovering forms in random rhythms made with lines and masses of color. The images that resulted from this process have become living forms because they are deliberately associated with sensations of movement and pleasurable responses to the formations of color and the shaping of the color masses. This experience, which is partly empathetic, involves integration of the child's sensations of color and form with the processes of the activity. The aesthetic exists in the sensation of completeness and in the pleasure of making an organically whole and vibrant form.

Understandings of the significance of the aesthetic values represented by Figure 11-6 may be substantiated by Figure 11-7. This drawing, by a third-grade child, is nothing more than the kind of scribble that emerges from aimless doodling. This scribble differs, however, from the efforts of a pre-school child in that it is characterized by the kind of motor control we normally expect from a third-grade child. After the scribble had

11-7. ABSTRACTION
Chalk. *Author's collection.*

been completed, the child proceeded to color the spaces. The coloring process was mainly cognitive. It involved an element of discovery, for the child was probably curious about how the whole would look after it had been completely colored. This was a routine coloring process, involving shaping and reshaping of forms with the plasticity of chalk. The result is not as good as it might be because it does not involve as much creative shaping and reshaping as did Figure 11-6.

The fact that Figure 11-6 is nonobjective in appearance does not detract from its aesthetic value. Although children frequently draw recognizable objects, such as the fish in a fish bowl (Figure 11-5), aesthetic value does not depend on objectivity in representation. If the teacher places most emphasis on metaphoric construction, the children may also become more concerned with metaphoric construction than with the mere recording of the data of visual experience.

Art forms that merely repeat mundane facts of observation often do not meet all of our requirements for the existence of aesthetic values because they do not make use of precognitive and productive thinking processes.

The youngest children in the primary grades are rarely as concerned with pure visual representation as are older children. Toward the middle of the primary-grade period, there may be an increased emphasis on "logic" and an accumulation

of motor skills for which the children may not be ready. When this happens, emphasis in art activity becomes centered on skill in rendering objective experience. Since the children may not be ready to make a satisfactory relation between skill, objective experience, and precognitive and productive thinking, they may experience frustration. The combination of frustration and poor correlations between objective experience, precognitive thinking, and productive thinking results in a lack of aesthetic quality. Such a result is unfortunate because if all aspects of an art activity provide an aesthetic experience, the resulting pleasure tends to motivate participants to become involved in new, increasingly useful learning experiences.

Paul Klee expressed the purpose of the visual-plastic arts in terms of the methods required for the achievement of aesthetic values when he wrote, ". . . I am not here to reflect the surface (a photographic plate can do that), but must look within. I reflect the innermost heart. My human faces are truer than real ones. If I were to paint a really truthful self-portrait, you would see an odd shell. Inside it, as everyone should be made to understand, would be myself, like the kernel in a nut. Such a work might also be called an allegory of crust formation." [7]

[7] *The Thinking Eye* (New York: George Wittenborn, Inc., 1961), p. 20.

LOGIC OF THE AESTHETIC

Aesthetic value is partly dependent on the logic of metaphoric and visual-plastic relationships. Such relationships do not refer to old dogmas about the need for "design" or composition in child art in order to establish basic requisites for the existence of the aesthetic. Any dependence on "principles" of design or preconceived ideas for establishing rhythm, unity, harmony, diversity, textural control, color, space, and line values does nothing more than provide a basis for the destruction of the aesthetic.

In our discussions regarding the processes of learning in art activity, it was said that some of the most useful learning takes place when the structure of the processes is open-ended and provides a basis for the natural transfer of concepts and understandings to new situations. It was also noted that the element of discovery was part of the essential core of the processes of learning.

Form in art is usually distinguished by its wholeness or completeness. Writers on the subject of aesthetics have long contended that this completeness or wholeness is the basis of the aesthetic, the source of beauty in art. The development of visual-plastic form, the organization of qualitative and expressive metaphoric structures, may be compared with the patterns of growth that characterize biological structures.

AESTHETICS OF FORMING PROCESSES

The forms of living creatures, particularly the human bodies given the status of near godhood by the ancient Greeks, are thought by most of us to be pleasing in appearance because of what we might call their "organic wholeness."

In fact, the contemporary popularity of exercises and reducing diets attest to a common understanding of this kind of aesthetic value. The quality of organic wholeness, which is considered to infer the aesthetic, is indicative of the existence of a purposeful process of growth that relates each new development to all the parts that make the new development possible. The human body grows as a result of a pattern established from certain kinds of activities, biological inclinations, and cultural attitudes toward the actions performed by the body. Thus, the classical Greek attitude toward sports and the development of the physical body was at least partly instrumental in encouraging an appreciation of the functionally formed human figure.

The biological form is distinguished by its appearance of completeness, which results from a process of becoming. At the same time, organic forms are unique; they are individuated. This simply means that each organic form is a recognizable individual whole. Each part of a single biological structure has this quality, but each part can be considered in terms of the completeness of the whole structure. Thus, a bone from a skeleton is not a complete form; but each part of the structure carries implications within itself of its relation to the whole.

It was this sense of wholeness that was described in the painting of clowns, Figure 7-5. The important thing about this painting was the way in which the forms evolved from kinaesthetic rhythms to conscious attempts at descriptive representation. The painting fails to succeed aesthetically the moment the process of rationalization dominates and the relationship between feeling, thinking, and image-symbol concepts is lost. In this case, the parts of the painting show a transition from one aspect of forming to another; however, the completeness of each part in terms of a mature process of precognitive and productive thinking is lacking.

The meaning of aesthetic value is best understood in terms of the evolution of forms related to environment, culture, and physiological and psychological being. It must be realized that the mere functional efficiency of a form does not constitute aesthetic value. Aesthetic value is the result of a complex of forces that go into the forming of organic structures. C. H. Waddington, in his discussion of the character of biological form, says that ". . . man-made forms, such as screws, cogs, propellers, are usually designed for one single function, or at most two or three, and their unity is correspondingly blatant and single minded." [8]

"Organic form [says Waddington] is . . . the resultant of the interaction of many different

[8] "The Character of Biological Form" in *Aspects of Form*, ed. L. L. Whyte (Bloomington: Indiana University Press, Midland Book Edition, 1961), pp. 43-44.

11-8. TREE
Watercolor. *Author's collection.*

forces. The wholeness of the form indicates that this resultant is always in some sense an equilibrium. The internal tensions are balanced against one another into a stable configuration—or rather nearly balanced, since the configuration is destined slowly to change as development proceeds." [9]

AESTHETICS OF RHYTHM

When a sense of growth and a relationship of parts is not adequately developed in a painting, we might say that the wholeness requisite for aesthetic value is not present. In Figure 11-8, a painting of a tree by a primary-grade child, the tree's limbs are literally stuck onto the main trunk. There is no metaphor present for the method of growth that characterizes a tree. The child failed to feel that the tree grows from the inside out and that its parts are rhythmic continuations of ever-changing and developing forming processes. Based upon this understanding, the parts of the metaphor would have been unified and aesthetic value would have been derived from a sense of the completeness of each part and from the delicate balance maintained by the logic of the pattern of organic growth. It must also be noted that this kind of rhythm in growth

[9] *Ibid.*, p. 44.

involves a unity and pattern of relationships that are manifested through the processes of change.

Rhythm is not a repetition of exact parts; it is a pattern that perpetually demonstrates a succession of changes from *being* to *becoming*. This principle can be illustrated by the cellular structure of a plant, which shows a repetition of the cellular forms, with each new form slightly changing its configuration to fit the cellular structure from which it developed and to make minute changes in the configuration of the future cellular pattern. Another example of this principle is the pattern of rings found in a cross section of a tree trunk. As the rings grow ever larger, there is a rhythmic repetition and a rhythmic pattern of change in the size and shape of the cellular patterns that form the rings, as well as in the size and shape of the rings themselves.

In the art work of children, we may observe the development of relationships between the elements of the productive thinking processes and the resultant forms. Figure 11-9, a picture of a child standing in front of a painting done by a child from Southeast Asia, demonstrates the way in which we may kinaesthetically respond to the sensation of holding an umbrella. In the same way, the sense of action of a particular kind of rhythmical activity is illustrated in Figure 11-10, a painting of a group of children playing ice

11-9. PHOTOGRAPH
From an exhibition, "Children's Paintings from Southeast Asia," circulated by the Smithsonian Institution.

11-10. ICE HOCKEY
Painting. *New York City Public Schools.*

11-11. LION
Painting. *New York City Public Schools.*

hockey. In this picture all of the parts become one with the totality of the action because the rhythm of each part is related to the total pattern of action. The movements of each figure grow out of the movements of the other figures in terms of the child's knowledge of the game. Lines, painted on the surface of the ice, trace the skating patterns of the separate players and become a diagram of the rhythmical pattern. The total pattern of action is encompassed, embraced, and contained as a related whole by the sweeping line that is intended to define the edge of the ice pond. The fluidity of the rhythmical visual pattern, and its implications for felt sensations, provides whoever looks at the painting with movement sensations similar to those that must have been felt by the child who painted the picture. If this sensation of relations between parts, of fluid and changing rhythms, and of the development of a purposeful and ever changing pattern is successfully achieved, aesthetic value is also achieved. In other words, the pattern of change and growth and the sensations associated with the painting are felt by the observers and the creator of the picture as much as they are charted by the structure of the total form that comprises the metaphoric structure of the painting.

In Figure 11-11, a painting of a lion by a primary-grade child, there is evidence of the same kind of rhythmical pattern, as well as of a projection of the child's self into the painting. This self-projection is exhibited by the lion's childlike characteristics, which are similar to those we noted in other children's paintings of animals. Other important characteristics are also evident in this painting. It is a metaphoric construction, rather than an attempt to depict a realistic lion by enumerating visual data associated with lions. Emphasis is given to the parts of the lion the child believes are important; for example, the lion's mane is emphasized. The pattern of rhythmical growth and change is largely restricted to the mane, the head, the neck, and the part of the lion's body closest to the head. The tail is vertical, which is in keeping with the concept of "king of beasts." This is a lion formed from current cultural concepts, which the child has absorbed. Aspects of the painting, such as the lion's legs, that don't serve to convey the child's concept of a lion's status, are drawn without the

11-12. PORTRAIT
By Maria des Neves. Colored monotype. *From an exhibition, "Brazilian Children's Art," circulated by the Smithsonian Institution.*

rhythmical sense and the convincing organic relatedness that is so evident in the head of the animal. In terms of the degree to which the child has succeeded in forming a vital metaphoric structure, this is an aesthetically satisfying painting.

The painting of a girl's portrait by a Brazilian child, Figure 11-12, is an interesting and typical example of the manner in which local cultural concepts regarding modes for representing people (for example, local cultural manifestations of hairdo and features) become evidenced in child art. In this painting, the child has painted only the head, neck, and shoulders; however, there is no feeling that the torso is missing or that it needs to be considered a part of this presentation. This painting shows evidence of some of the elements of closure and completeness, which have been discussed previously. This closure is accomplished by squaring off the area below the neckline of the dress and by isolating the whole by providing space around the angular areas. In this way, the concept is concentrated on the rhythmical pattern, the arrangement of the features, and the hair metaphor. The painting is aesthetically satisfying to the extent that the element of completeness was felt by the child and is communicated to the observer.

In Figures 11-10, 11-11, and 11-12, we may not be aesthetically rewarded as we would be if these same pictures were painted by a competent adult artist. Limitations to the child's ability to construct an aesthetically valuable metaphor are to be expected. In the Brazilian child's portrait painting, a professional painter might be troubled by the lack of space around the head of the portrait. Sufficient space has been provided around the lower part of the drawing; but it has not been properly balanced, for a greater sense of aesthetic value, in the upper part of the painting. There is every reason to believe that when the child painted this picture, she was not as aware of the need for space at the top as at the bottom of the painting. The painting of the bottom requires greater rationalization and increased sensitivity to the space arrangements because the procedure is less conventional. Since the top of the head provides its own boundary for completeness, it is considered a lesser problem and is given less attention. As a result, the top of the painting suffers from a lack of planning. In terms of a child's

accomplishment, however, this painting has great aesthetic value.

The treatment of space in Figure 11-12 is unusual for a child. The manner in which the bottom part of the subject is handled with the squared off section below the dress neckline indicates a sense of closure with which most children do not concern themselves. This is a sophisticated kind of closure of the sort a practiced artist would use in order to give completeness to his portrait. We know that many South American artists and some Mexican artists have used such a device. It has become a learned technique, which may have been suggested to the child by an art teacher or by something the child saw in the work of an artist. Through this method of handling space, the child succeeded in accomplishing a rhythmic unity between figure and ground, between the object and the space around it, which contributes to the aesthetic quality of the painting.

CONCLUSION

Aesthetic value is a necessary part of the totality of the processes of art activity. Aesthetic experience must exist from the beginning of the art activity, and it must continue indefinitely. An important function of the program of art education is to perpetuate aesthetic experience.

Educational value is largely dependent on the successful development of aesthetic experiences. Because they are aesthetic, such experiences provide the incentive for children to infuse art activity with useful enthusiasms, with feelings, with zest in the desire for making discoveries, and with pleasure in the formation of expressive visual-plastic metaphors. Educational value in child art activity must be deduced from evidence in the resulting art forms that the child experienced a feeling of the wholeness and completeness of the process of his art activity. This sense of completeness, wholeness, and limited closure may be defined as aesthetic.

The significance of the aesthetic factor as a sign of the existence of educational value is described in terms of the harmoniousness and relatedness of the totality of experience from inception to construction and completion of an art form. This relatedness may form a unified pattern. The pattern is actually a series of related acts that constitute a flux, a structured evolution involving a unity between physical substance, original stimulation or motivation, and perception, which may be defined as a composite of psychological and biological responses. Aesthetic quality may thus be said to be the result of a *Gestalt*. The Gestalt psychologist Koffka defined artistic quality in much the same way when he wrote that as the result of a multitude of stimulations ". . . the nervous system . . . produces processes of organization in such a way that a pattern is produced. . . ." Perception, he continues, ". . . tends toward balance and symmetry." [10] Herbert Read refers to this factor as the " 'feeling' in perception and other mental processes" that we call aesthetic." [11]

In order for the aesthetic experience to come into being, it is necessary for the teacher to become familiar with the processes of re-forming experience in terms of plastic materials to create effective metaphors.

The raw materials of experience are hardly capable of aesthetic qualities. Aesthetic qualities, according to the definition used here, are the result of man-made thinking and forming. The things we see may be subject to redefinition, re-ordering, rearrangement, re-forming, and restructuring; but in their raw state, they can not be works of art. They can not be aesthetic. Raw nature and unselected experience do not constitute a concept, an image-symbol, or a visual-plastic metaphor. The things that exist in experience, in nature, and in our surroundings may inspire emotion in an artist. Such things may motivate the artist to participate in an art process; but only from the processes of art activity can the aesthetic emerge. And the aesthetic can emerge from the processes of art activity only if the involved processes of precognitive and productive thinking are aesthetic.

The existence of the aesthetic is also dependent on two additional factors: a creative process and imagination. According to George Santayana, aesthetic values are derived from ". . . values inherent in imagination, in instant intuition, in sense endowed with form. . . ." [12]

According to this description of the aesthetic, we are faced with a need to understand the factors of imagination and creative action.

[10] Kurt Koffka, "Problems in the Psychology of Art" in *Art: A Bryn Mawr Symposium* (Bryn Mawr: Bryn Mawr College, 1940), pp. 260-61.

[11] *Education Through Art*, p. 60.

[12] *The Philosophy of George Santayana*, ed. Irwin Edman (New York: Modern Library, Inc.), p. 226. Copyright 1936 by Charles Scribner's Sons.

Twelve

IMAGINATION

Imagination is necessary in the processes of art activity because it helps form the processes of creative action. Without imagination, perception and the formation of art objects becomes routine, mechanical, and purposeless. Imagination is descriptive of the processes of a useful creativity. It involves more than just establishing images in the conscious mind; it is a process of sensing relationships and establishing relationships between diverse images in order to form metaphors that are rich in new, unexpected, and useful meanings.

Imaginative thinking provides a means for extending the limits of experience and for enriching experience because it acts as a means for vitalizing the precognitive processes. This vitalization of the precognitive processes takes place because imagination provides the precognitive processes with increased ability to sense useful relationships between image-symbols and to predict the possible results of original combinations of image-symbols and metaphors. In this way, imagination provides a means for increasing the opportunities for the processes of precognition to develop unique and effective metaphors.

Imagination increases the effectiveness of the processes of productive thinking because it helps develop understandings of the relationships between tools, materials, manipulations, image-symbols, concepts, and metaphors.

GENERAL CHARACTERISTICS OF IMAGINATION

From these understandings, we may assume the following to be general characteristics of imagination:

Imagination is a probing faculty that makes it possible for us to discover new relationships.

Imagination is an intelligence that helps us create and give meaning and form to new images by establishing values suggested by unexpected juxtapositions of image-symbols remembered from previous experience.

Imagination helps us form metaphors that are the result of a sensitive and intelligent coupling of unexpected and diverse images and meanings derived from image-symbols.

Imagination, according to the description given here, is a part of creative action. Like creative action, imagination produces new insights and brings into being new experiences and ideas. In actual practice, the creative faculties and the imaginative faculties are inseparable in art activity.

SPECIFIC CHARACTERISTICS OF IMAGINATION

In the processes of art activity, imagination functions in three clearly defined ways, which are specific characteristics of imagination. If the teacher knows and can recognize these characteristics, she will be able to help children use their imaginative faculties to develop useful habits of imaginative thinking.

The specific characteristics of imagination are fantasy, projection, and identification.

A *fantasy* is commonly considered to be separate from reality. It is an unreal mental image, a caprice. Fantasy can be a useless aspect of imagination, but *fantasy is useful if it is self-conscious.*

If fantasy is not self-conscious, the orientation of imagination to reality is a difficult and sometimes impossible process. It is necessary that this need for self-consciousness be understood before fantasy is used in art activity; its use must never exceed the limits of good judgment. Excessive fantasy can lead to disordered thinking and can seriously hinder the effectiveness of imagination in the processes of art activity.

Projection has been discussed in earlier sections as a means for forming the images of perceptual experience into image-symbols and visual-plastic metaphors. Projection may involve a process of mental forming or productive forming through the manipulation of physical and plastic materials. This process is a means for experimenting with diverse relationships, and for seeking out combinations of image-symbols and metaphors, which should be examined mentally or in the process of manipulating materials to produce metaphors that will create new understandings, insights, and experiences.

Identification is the means whereby the individual projects himself into a situation and becomes part of a thing, an experience, an idea, or an image. Identification is *empathy*, which we have already identified as a necessary tool of the artist. This kind of identification makes it possible for the individual to "feel" relationships and to understand intuitively the structure of concepts. It helps individuals establish unique, unexpected, and effective relationships; and it helps them discover suggestions for meanings and values, which can be known because identication makes possible a useful familiarity.

FREE ASSOCIATION: A MEANS FOR DEVELOPING IMAGINATION

Imaginative thinking may be purposeful or it may begin as an aimless process of free association. During the earliest phases of art activity, the processes of free association may be the most effective means for developing a useful application of imagination. Free association may be a potent means for infusing the creative processes with the vitality of constructive imagination. During the early stages of the art processes, the action of free association will usually be autistic. Autistic activity refers to a form of thinking that disregards preconceived concepts, physical reality, and apparently logical relationships.

There is serious question whether autism in a pure form can exist. Pure autism would have to be self contained; it would manifest itself as a form of daydreaming unfettered by experience. This kind of daydreaming could lead to fantasies so pure that they would have no counterpart in reality. For this reason, it is questionable that such autistic and resultingly fantastic thinking could have any worth.

Under certain controlled conditions, autism has a valuable function in the development of imagination. Autistic processes can strengthen the processes of free association. Free association can gain vitality from autistic processes and can thus make imagination a strong ingredient in the processes of creative action. Autistic thinking can free imagination from stereotypes and other limitations that hamper the development of uniqueness. Autism becomes a process of free association that frees the thinking processes from bias and permits the immediate establishment of a clear relation of thinking to feeling.

12-1. FIGURE
(1927) by Andre Masson. *Collection of Professor William Rubin.*

Free association brings into action a spontaneous and natural form of image-symbol. Free association becomes most useful when it matures and takes upon itself the characteristics of the precognitive processes. After the processes of free association have brought image-symbol relationships and new metaphors into conscious awareness, they can be tested, studied, and evaluated. This evaluation process may be an individual or group activity or both.

Free associations are free because they are spontaneous and unhampered by interference from the conscious mind. Their value lies in later application of rational thinking, which provides the means for making selections from the results of the processes of free association.

In essence, free association is closely related to precognitive thinking because it must use image-symbols that are stored in the subconscious mind.

FUNCTION OF IMAGINATION IN ART

In the arts of painting and sculpture, free association has always performed an important function. In this century, the processes of free association have been used in a new way as an important means for forming metaphors that are surprising and original. Specific reference should be made to the work of the surrealists and the automatists in painting. Such artists as Joan Miro and Andre Masson are well known for the effectiveness of the work they accomplished using the technique of free association.

In his "Figure," Masson permitted his lines to develop without conscious effort on his part. The result could have been an indefinable object, a pure fantasy; however, the precognitive processes necessarily caused a scanning of the image and it emerges with specific expressional implications. The artist might insist that his image or metaphor has no definition or verbal parallel and that there is no possible explanation of its meaning. However, the fact remains that the image is definable; a concept emerges from its metaphoric construction.

The painting of the "Dutch Interior" by Miro is an excellent example of a painting that probably began as a random free association and emerged as a composite of forms vaguely associated with image-symbols from prior experience. It is not possible to assume that such images never existed; they did exist. They are imaginative metaphors that come into being because a controlled autism, a process of free association, gives a new form to familiar objects. The associations, in this case, are free to the extent that the resulting metaphors are not hampered by restrictions imposed from images produced by other artists or from images consciously perceived in experience. Apparently, such images are first drawn in either an experimental or a doodling manner. Then autistic processes are scrutinized by an intelligence familiar with the processes of invention. The processes of making selections and of reshaping the constructions and relationships that evolve from autistic and free association processes are highly skilled. Miro is not fearful of the new and different; rather, he seems to take pleasure in the evidence of a highly imaginative metaphoric structure to which he has contributed some consciously guided changes and renovations. These consciously guided renovations can be known only if we observe the artist at work. It is important to understand that a process entirely dependent on autism could result only in a doodle. The forms in Figures 12-1 and 12-2 are inventive, related in surprising ways, and quite different from metaphors ever before created by an artist.

The paintings by Miro and Masson demonstrate that imagination is not just the product of a conscious search. The processes of free association and critical scrutiny produce forms that are related to each other as a result of the interaction of symbol, image, and metaphor. The resulting relationships are not "logical," they do not make expected closures; consequently, they produce psychological shock. This psychological shock results in the general effectiveness of the total metaphor. For example, the Miro painting establishes unexpected relationships such as the dog in the left foreground, the form that suggests a dog just above and to the right, and the line and mass construction that creates a surprising transition from the recognizable animal to the plastically imagined creature. The fantasy in this second creature involves additional unique associations such as an open-ended keyhole from which a cat appears to emerge. The curiously in-

12-2. DUTCH INTERIOR
(1928) by Joan Miro. Oil on canvas, 36⅛ x 28¾ inches. *Collection of the Museum of Modern Art, New York City. Mrs. Simon Guggenheim Fund.*

vented metaphors in this painting place in juxtaposition recognizable and purely invented forms and shapes. In some of these shapes, we can recognize objects or we can invent additional objects ourselves.

The painting by Masson gains its unique effectiveness from the metaphorical distortion of the figure that apparently results from a conscious or unconscious placing of emphasis on the agile brutality or athleticism of the figure. Surprise is manifested and developed in the way the artist formed a symbol for a face from mass and tone rather than from the line that first established the rhythmical pattern of the figure. This transition from line to toned mass provides an additional element of shock. Surprise is also manifested in the location of the large eye at the bottom right of the painting.

In the paintings by both Miro and Masson, the effectiveness of imaginative play in the development of the metaphors can not be overlooked. Imagination provided the means for causing the

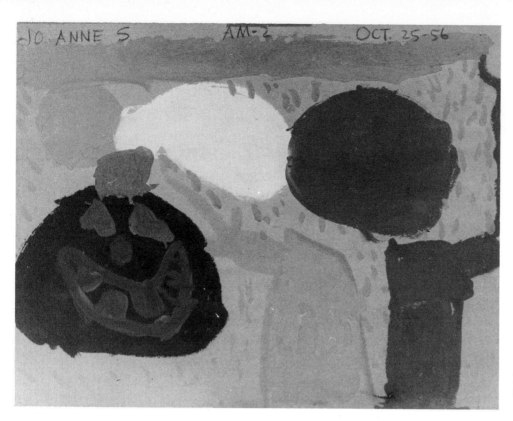

12-3. PUMPKIN
Kindergarten painting. *Collection of Theodore Lynch.*

12-4. FANTASY
Crayon. *Collection of Theodore Lynch.*

metaphor to leap beyond the routine, to become more than a mere repetition of visual perception. Imagination makes it possible for the spectator to participate in the forming processes because the artists' scrutinizing search for meanings in his autistically evolved forms is continued by the persons who look at the pictures. In an important sense, these pictures are not painted for observers; they are invitations to participate in the processes of scrutinizing the products of imaginative play and free association.

Such a combination of free association, discovery, and the resulting creation of imaginative and effective metaphors does not take place easily in the art work of young children. What we may take to be the exercise of imagination in the work of children is often nothing more than the result of typically childish thinking and forming. The development and formation of imaginative metaphors from image-symbols takes place only after children have learned to participate in useful productive processes.

Young children find it difficult to separate themselves from their fantasies. Children tend to be egocentric and incapable of making distinctions between themselves and the environmental forces acting upon them. Thus, the child who has seen an airplane on the ground and in the sky might think of them as two separate things. The airplane on the ground is very large and the airplane in the sky is very small. The child might even believe that the flight of the airplane causes it to shrink. Because of the child's inability to make clear distinctions, he often can not associate his picture with the object he draws. From this point of view, we might consider the very young child to possess an advantage because he knows that the picture he draws is not really the thing it represents. This knowledge, however, is not sufficiently conscious to take on the aspects of profound logic.

The result of the child's egocentricity is an inability to scrutinize the products of free association and to recognize new and unique forms of relationship. The child's ability to recognize, to relate, and to provide meanings is not fully developed. The child's store of prior experience needs to be continuously increased. An increase in experience provides an ever increasing source of raw material for imaginative use. The art

teacher can encourage growth in imagination by helping the child increase and use his experiences to form expressive metaphors. In this way, the child will gain increased opportunities to use his imagination.

Figure 12-3 is a painting by a kindergarten child. In typical fashion, the child has established an illogical relationship between the pumpkin on the left and the forms on the right. The forms on the right side of the painting may have meaning for the child, but their meaning is partly hidden by the child's inability to define the form he attempts to represent. We know that the mass painted at the top of the painting is a sign for the sky and the circular form just below the sky and to the extreme left is a sign for the sun. Imagination has very little to do with the form of these images; the child did not think of them as metaphors. In each case, the images emerge from the child's illogical and egocentric conceptions about Halloween. The results are not imaginative because the child is attempting to describe what he knows Halloween to be; he uses symbols that he has been led to believe are most characteristic of the Halloween celebration. His mode of presentation is limited by uncritical associations between shapes and concepts of pumpkin, sky, sun, and landscape.

Figure 12-4 is a crayon drawing by a sixth-grade child. The subject of this painting, like the painting in Figure 12-1, deals with fantasy. The rhythmical pattern is a felt pattern; there is a well defined rhythmic movement from object to object across the surface of the picture. In a process of free association, which may have involved doodling, images of fantastic structure take form from the linear patterning of the trees. These images emerge from the rhythmical drawing of the tree trunks and their branches; they are the natural extension of forms, like branches of a tree, that grow rhythmically out of a central core. In much the same manner, small figures with the same general fantasy characteristics of the trees are drawn on the ground. The kind of free association that leads to a controlled fantasy is evident here as it was in the Miro painting. Although this drawing lacks the highly developed proficiency of the professional artist's work, the result of the autistic processes involved is an imaginative rendering of something never seen in actual experience. The associations with fantastic forms are drawn from the reality of a tree and a landscape; the metaphor has been developed from this vividly real basis.

Figure 12-4 represents an imaginative drawing because it combines parts into a whole conception. The drawing uses elements of trees, such as the outward-growing branches, and elaborates upon them to form images that are quite different from what one might ordinarily expect to find growing out of a tree. The process of making these metaphors from the trees represents a process of closure. Closure resulted when the child discovered in the rhythmical characteristics of trees a means for expressing his particular brand of fantasy. The process was one of restructuring, of reconstituting forms from more typical forms found in ordinary experience. The processes of discovery, restructuring, and closure comprise an imaginative process. It must be noted that this kind of development does not take place in Figure 12-3, the painting by a kindergarten child.

SUMMARY

Imagination, writes Susanne Langer, is ". . . the source of all insight and true beliefs. Imagination is probably the oldest mental trait that is typically human—older than discursive reason; it is probably the source of dream, reason, religion, and all true general observation. It is this primitive human power—imagination—that engenders the arts and is in turn directly affected by its products." [1]

John Dewey has said that the word "imagination," like "beauty," has caused much confusion because of its use as ". . . the chief theme in aesthetic writing of enthusiastic ignorance." [2]

Jean-Paul Sartre considers imagination to be an active force that searches and finds its object in conscious perception. Imaginative consciousness is different from mere perception. Imagination is ". . . spontaneous and creative; it maintains and sustains the sensible qualities of its object by a continuous creation." Imagination gives clarity to perception. Without imagination, the images we perceive are vague and incomplete.

Imagination provides sharpness of focus. Images perceived without imagination are passive; those perceived with imagination are ". . . shot through and through with a flow of creative will." [3]

Imagination is the opposite of adherence to pre-established modes of doing things; it is opposed by all that is routine. The imaginative faculty provides the ability to find a richness in thought and experience that could not possibly be obtained from forms of mechanical perception, which involve passive biological responses to stimuli. In this sense, imagination becomes a rich inner vision that is deeper, finer, more lushly textured, and more exciting to the mind than any mechanical perception could be.

Intrinsic to the richness of inner vision, which apparently serves to describe the adventurousness of imagination, is the moment when inner vision is confronted by the cold and passive harshness of the outer vision of actual perception. Under the impact of this juncture of imagination with actual perception, inner vision could easily collapse because it does not possess the substance and tangible power of perceived actuality. At this moment, the artist can demonstrate the power of his will and the validity of his processes of cognition, which are derived from the activities of the art processes. "The artist [writes Dewey] is driven to submit himself to the discipline of the objective vision. But the inner vision is not cast out. It remains as an organ, by which outer vision is controlled, and it takes on structure as the latter is absorbed within it. The interaction of the two modes of vision is imagination; as imagination takes form the work of art is born." [4]

Imagination, therefore, does not exist alone; it is not isolated within the mind. Such isolation is impossible. The usefulness of imagination is entirely dependent upon its combining with the elements of ordinary perceptions.

An understanding of the relationship between imagination and the perceptions of experience is critical to our understanding of the processes of art activity. Imagination isolated from perceived experience is fantasy. Fantasy is not objectionable, but it is objectionable in isolation. Fantasy

---

[1] *Problems of Art*, p. 70.
[2] *Art as Experience*, p. 267.

[3] *The Psychology of Imagination* (New York: The Citadel Press, 1961), p. 20.
[4] *Art as Experience*, p. 268.

lacks substance until joined to perception, observation, and participation in live experience. When the juncture of fantasy with experience takes place, we can describe the result as imagination. Imagination, under such conditions, results in structured, formative thinking.

Imagination is a useful aspect of the processes of art activity to the extent that it controls and is controlled by objecive perception. Objective perception without imagination becomes mechanical, dull, and purposeless. Like the philosopher, the child will not surrender his inner vision: ". . . the object just as an object is not his concern. It is placed in the context of ideas and, as it is thus placed, the latter acquire solidity and partake of the nature of the subject." [5]

[5] *Ibid.*

Thirteen

THE PROCESSES OF CREATIVE ACTION

The related activities of thought, feeling, and imagination make possible the existence of an inventive, probing, and seeking process, which is intended to culminate in discovery. Discovery is basic to the child's realization of achievement. The drive toward discovery and the integration of all parts of the structure of art activity involve the processes of creative action, which consist of acting upon materials with selected ideas.

Creativity is probably the most discussed, analyzed, probed, poked, digested, and redigested mode of behavior in any study of the processes of art activity. This interest in creativity is a testimony to its importance in art activity.

From the very first, it must be understood that creativity is not the separate and special province of art and art education. The creative faculty is essential to all aspects of human living and progress. Without creativity, the human race would still be cowering on its collective knees in some dark, dank, and unlivable cave. The faculty of creativity has made it possible for people to gain control, in some measure, over a world that is essentially hostile. It has enabled us to harness forces of nature to work for the benefit, rather than the destruction, of mankind.

The faculty we call creativity is an integral part of all aspects of the processes of art activity that have been discussed in this text, and all major parts of the processes of art activity are necessary to the existence of creativity. Creativity includes the initial processes of perception, as well as modes for forming unique and effective metaphors.

Jean-Paul Sartre indicates that without imagination, perception is passive; in combination with imagination, perception is caused to pulsate with a strong surge of *creative energy*.[1]

In the traditional literature of religions, creative energy is considered a divine force. In the Hebraic Genesis, it is the force that orders the universe, separates the heavens from the earth, brings order out of chaos, and breathes the spark of existence into inert matter. Creativity is thus synonymous with power, force, change, relation, organization, purpose, and meaning. It is life-giving, rhythmic, constructive, clarifying, flexible, and progressive. Such a description is correct in terms of our understanding of process, thinking, emotion, the aesthetic and imagination.

FUNCTIONS OF CREATIVE ACTION IN ART ACTIVITY

In a study, conducted by Eindhoven and Vinacke, of the creative habits of professional and nonprofessional artists, it was determined that there is a difference between the modes of creative activity among artists and persons who are not artists. The results of the study are summarized as follows: [2]

1. Artists have more control then non-artists; they have greater flexibility in their ability to handle media, concepts, images, and visual forms during the processes of art activity. The professional artist tends to use more media and to produce a greater variety of techniques and approaches to an idea because he has had more training and has acquired a greater understanding of the processes of art activity than the nonprofessional artist.
2. The artist's approaches to the problems of art activity are different from the non-artist's.

[1] *The Psychology of Imagination.*
[2] Jan E. Eindhoven and W. Edgar Vinacke, "Creative Processes in Painting," *Journal of General Psychology*, XLVII (1952), 140-69.

3. The artist does not immediately produce his final result. The work of the artist involves constant changes and evolves over a period of time. During the first stages of productive work, the artist appears to be able to develop a general visual-plastic idea; later, he selects, modifies, and reorganizes. During the early stages of his work, the artist experiments; he tries images and ideas for "fit."

The results of this study, as summarized by the two investigators, indicate that there is no real separation between the elements of the creative processes, but that all the aspects of the processes form a continuum; ". . . they blend together in an intricate manner."

In the study, the problem of describing the process of creative work in art activity was made difficult because of variations in the details of the process as they were manifested by different individuals. Consequently, it was decided that ". . . it is impossible to understand meaningfully the nature of creative processes without giving proper attention to individual differences. . . ."

The process of creating a painting, in terms of the description provided by Eindhoven and Vinacke, is illustrated in the excellent record we have available of the development of Picasso's "Guernica." "Guernica" is a mural, a large wall painting, eleven and a half feet high and twenty-five feet, eight inches long. The mural was painted in 1937 at the request of the then existing government of Spain. During that year, Spain was embroiled in a civil war; a military group led by Francisco Franco was attempting to overthrow the Spanish Republican government. Franco was aided by the military forces of Nazi Germany and Fascist Italy. Many anti-Fascist and anti-Nazi people in other countries were strongly opposed to a Franco victory. Among these people was the Spanish artist Pablo Picasso, who was, by choice, a resident of France.

During this civil war, Picasso was asked to paint a mural for the Spanish government building at the Paris World's Fair. Shortly after he received this commission, word was released about the Nazi or Fascist bombing and complete destruction of the civilian population of the Spanish Basque town of Guernica. Picasso selected this event as the subject of his mural.

Two days after the bombing of Guernica took place, Picasso produced a sketch (Figure 13-1)

13-1. COMPOSITION STUDY
(1937) by Pablo Picasso. Pencil on gesso, 21⅛ x 25½ inches. *Extended loan to the Museum of Modern Art, New York City, from the artist, M. Picasso.*

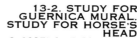

13-2. STUDY FOR GUERNICA MURAL. STUDY FOR HORSE'S HEAD
(May 2, 1937) by Pablo Picasso. Pencil on blue paper, 8¼ x 6 inches. *Extended loan to the Museum of Modern Art, New York City, from the artist, M. Picasso.*

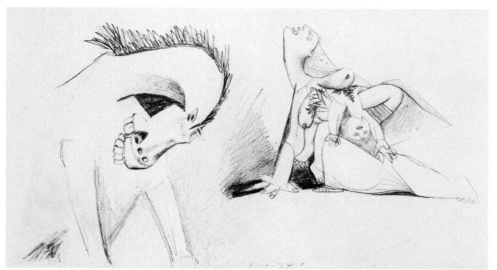

13-3. STUDY FOR GUERNICA MURAL. HORSE AND WOMAN WITH DEAD CHILD
By Pablo Picasso. Pencil on white paper, 9½ x 17⅞ inches. *Extended loan to the Museum of Modern Art, New York City, from the artist, M. Picasso.*

13-4. STUDY FOR GUERNICA MURAL. WOMAN WITH DEAD CHILD ON LADDER
(May 9, 1937) by Pablo Picasso. Pencil on white paper, 17⅞ x 9½ inches. *Extended loan to the Museum of Modern Art, New York City, from the artist, M. Picasso.*

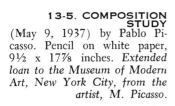

13-5. COMPOSITION STUDY
(May 9, 1937) by Pablo Picasso. Pencil on white paper, 9½ x 17⅞ inches. *Extended loan to the Museum of Modern Art, New York City, from the artist, M. Picasso.*

13-6. GUERNICA.
(1937) by Pablo Picasso. Finished mural, 11 feet 6 inches x 25 feet 8 inches. Extended loan to the Museum of Modern Art, New York City, from the artist, M. Picasso.

for the mural. This sketch, dated May 1, 1937, indicates the general idea for the mural: a dying horse in the center of the composition, a person holding a lamp emerging from the indication of a window on the right, an animal form on the left, and a dead figure in the foreground. In his first sketches, the artist establishes the outlines of the general concept that emerges in the detailed metaphoric structure of the final work.

The following day, May 2, 1937, Picasso painted his study of the horse's head, Figure 13-2. The artist had in mind some general image-symbol of the horse as a friend of man, a concept he probably associated with the function of the horse in the bull ring. The animal in this drawing, however, is not a horse; it is a metaphor piled on a metaphor. The first metaphor refers to the dying horse, the friend of man, the force between man and brutality. The second metaphor is the metaphor of the shriek emerging from the friend of man. This is a matter of interpretation. Picasso does not offer this explanation. But there is reason to believe that this pointed shape emerging from what is a symbol for a horse's head is the artist's vigorous reference to a wild cry of agony. Instead of what would normally be expected to be a tongue, the artist paints a dagger-like shape emerging from the symbol for the animal's gigantic throat. Thus, the dying shriek is poetically described.

The sketches, dated May 8, 1937 (Figure 13-3), show evidence of a continuation of experimentation with the image-symbols and an attempt to devise new metaphors. The metaphor for the horse is changed; and another metaphor is sketched about a woman struggling to move upward and to carry a child, a symbol of young life and of the woman's own life-giving powers, toward some salvation. It is curious that this struggling woman appears in the final version of the mural (Figure 13-6) as the supplicating woman pleading with brutality (the image-symbol and metaphor of the bull) and as the struggling, upward-moving figure to the right of the horse. This same concept takes form in other ways during the probing process of finding suitable metaphors as in the figure of a woman reeling from a ladder in Figure 13-4. Here Picasso is seeking a metaphor to express the concept of life reeling from a death blow. It is curious that this

metaphor is composed of a complex of metaphors, which emerge as a complete metaphoric structure. The hand of the figure attempting to grasp the rung of the ladder lacks the ability, the flexibility, and the strength to grasp the rung; and the child she clutches to her is a flat, lifeless, manikin-like form.

The process of evolving suitable metaphors continues during the process of forming the whole structure into an effectively organic design. Figure 13-5 indicates that just a little more than a week after the search for suitable metaphors had begun, Picasso was able to sketch the total structure of the mural in substantially the manner it was to assume when completed. However, it should be noted that the completed mural is much more sharply defined than the sketches. The meaning of the lamp held by the figure emerging from the burning building is elaborated in the unique symbol directly to its right, which is often referred to as the "electric eye of night." The horse, dissolving into a newspaper, is perhaps a symbol of a massacre so devastating and so complete that no individual remained alive to describe the horror; this symbol suggests that the only way we could possibly know about the massacre would be secondhand, through the stories we read in the press or through the other media of modern communication. This concept could be expanded to an interpretation of the metaphor as describing the foolishness of mass murder which, in the fashion of murderers, attempts to hide the fact of the deed. This metaphor could be interpreted as an indication that modern man, with his technology, makes the hiding of infamous acts impossible.

The total process of the production of "Guernica" indicates a number of interesting things about the processes of creativity in the visual-plastic arts as shown in the work of a proficient artist. Reference should be made to the assertion, made by Eindhoven and Vinacke, that the artist begins his work with a general idea of what he plans to do and then concerns himself with details of organization, developing concepts and image-symbols, and forming suitable metaphors.

It is doubtful that this kind of elaborate and probing process will dominate the work of young children. On the contrary, the youngest children will produce paintings with speed and with a certainty that their accomplishment is exactly right. Young children make little change in the structure of images or metaphors during their art activity; and they seldom engage in preplanning, such as that done by Picasso. Unfortunately, in some teaching methods, preplanning is considered an unnecessary factor in the art work of children because it is thought to interfere with a desirable spontaneity.

The impact of "Guernica" lies largely in the effectiveness of its metaphoric construction. The picture does not conform to standards generally accepted by visual-minded, enumerative, and factual modes of popular thinking. The artist does not attempt to demonstrate his ability to enumerate the visual characteristics of the objects in his picture. As a metaphoric structure, the mural provides a poetic description of the artist's profound revulsion and horror in reaction to an

act deliberately designed to destroy life. The metaphors are shocking. There is an element of surprise in the uniqueness of the metaphors and in the startlingly clear manner in which the artist has related his metaphors through the simple device of geometrical forms that embrace the whole painting, overlap, and interweave the metaphors in a manner designed to increase their effect.

CONDITIONS OF CREATIVE ACTION

In his essay "The Conditions of Creativity," Jerome Bruner lists as some of his conditions for the existence of creative action, *effective surprise, detachment and commitment, passion and decorum,* and *freedom to be dominated by the object.*

13-7. TWO-HEADED PIG
Chalk. *Author's collection.*

Picasso's "Guernica" meets the first requirement. There is some question regarding the extent to which the work of children can meet this requirement. In the work of young children, there is more evidence of the stereotyped form than of the surprising metaphor. We can almost predict the kind of forms that children will make; and we can usually predict a child's level of development from the forms he makes during productive processes. However, in spite of this general rule, children are capable of producing and often do succeed in producing effective surprise.

Figure 13-7 is a drawing by a third-grade child. The drawing begins in routine fashion as an attempt to draw a picture of a pig. The child begins by making a large uncritical mass that immediately represents the bulk of a pig. A line quickly drawn on the left end of the mass becomes a symbol for "neck." In the same rapid fashion, the child draws a circle with eyes and a mouth to represent a pig's head. At this point, the child pauses in his productive activity because the head he has drawn looks more like a child's than a pig's head. The child tries to think of characteristics or image-symbols that he associates with pigs. He draws the exaggerated ears on top of the pig's head and adds a short tail to the right end of the large mass. To the child, the short line for the tail suggests a metaphor similar to the short line for a neck drawn at the left end of the pig's body; consequently, the child draws another head on the end of the tail. With this second head, the child begins to lose contact with the process of making a pig. The child now thinks irrationally in terms of people, the subjects he knows best, and the pig's face becomes the face of a child. Next, the child draws the feet. The teacher has told the children that pigs have short legs, but has said nothing about their feet. The child draws short lines for legs and longer near-horizontal lines for feet. The feet point to the right in the direction of the child's last thought. To provide light, the child quickly draws a symbol for the sun in the upper left corner of the picture.

It is interesting to note that during this process of drawing the pig, the child drew all of the symbols rapidly, with only a minimum of thought. Any thought involved resulted from environmental disturbances, which were not always directly related to the productive thinking actually taking place.

A comparison between the working method of the child while drawing the pig and of Picasso while drawing "Guernica" is useful. In both cases, there is an effort to represent concepts and feelings about the subject portrayed. The child made such an attempt when he drew the large oval, which became an effective metaphor for the body of the pig. The difference between the artist's and the child's process of developing metaphors is that the purpose and the direction of effort is more emphatic in Picasso's work. The child permitted his thinking to wander during the productive process. The artist knew his goal from the beginning and searched in a highly diverse fashion for the symbols and metaphors that would most effectively develop and express his meanings and feelings. The process employed by Picasso is highly imaginative; he tries a great many different techniques and forms in order to achieve his goal. The child, who is not able to draw from a vast storehouse of visual-plastic experience, limits himself to forms that are closely related to the stereotypes of child art.

Picasso's work is full of what Bruner refers to as "effective surprise." The child's work has some of this quality; but in general, it is the kind of form we expect children to produce. Picasso's work, effectively surprises us because we recognize the forms the artist has used as symbols, but we are shocked by the strange shapes and contortions he has given them. When we become aware of the metaphors the artist has created, we discover a refreshingly new and different poetic statement in the visual-plastic structure. In the child's work, the surprise resulting from the second head growing out of the tail is immediately cushioned by the realization that this is the kind of result that is expected from an immature individual, who is not yet able to maintain a span of interest long enough to develop depth and breadth in expression. The ingredients of expression are present and the child's method of attack is not too different in general character from that of the experienced professional artist; however, the element of immaturity is too evident to make profundity possible. In the child's drawing, the characteristics of imagination, as defined in Chapter Twelve, are present only in rudimentary form.

The work is imaginative only to the extent that the child is led by motor skill, example, and suggestions to make certain kinds of forms. It is the teacher's responsibility to recognize characteristics of imagination and to help the child develop them.

The elements of detachment and commitment are clearly demonstrated in the process of painting "Guernica." Picasso has investigated the subject of his theme and has explored the elements that make his theme an effective expression. For example, the bull, in the cultural traditions of the Spanish people, is a symbol of brutality. In Picasso's painting, the bull serves as an effective metaphor for Fascism. The mural exhibits detachment in the artist's dispassionate recognition that life begins with the mother and is nurtured and sheltered, according to our traditions, by the female of the species. Picasso exploits these cultural understandings in order to best express his own commitment to an ideal of humanity, to a belief in the sacredness of life. The elements of passion and decorum are also present in Picasso's expression of the destruction of Guernica. There is passion in the expression because the artist is guided by a need and desire to find a unique, effective metaphor to communicate his deep convictions. Decorum is apparent in the artist's finished work and also in his experimental sketches in their expression of his love and respect for form and materials. As Bruner has stated, such a feeling for form and materials is evidenced in ". . . an etiquette toward the object of our efforts, a respect for materials."[3]

In the painting of the pig, Figure 13-7, such considerations of passion and decorum never actually enter the child's process of productive thinking. These factors should be understood as the result of an evaluation process. The teacher and the group can note indications of unique metaphoric structures, such as the formation of the pig's ears and the implication of a snout. It might even be that some kind of useful understanding can grow from the symbol of the double head, such as "This is a pig that looks in two directions at once, and can not turn around too easily because he is so big and fat and clumsy."

The artist's "freedom to be dominated by the

[3] *On Knowing*, p. 24.

object," a terminology devised by Bruner, serves to point up a quality in creative work that some artists are fond of referring to as sincerity. The trouble with the word "sincerity" is that it only partly describes the concept of the artist demonstrating integrity in his work by remaining free from "tricks" of representation and the development of optical illusions that are contrived and imposed on the expression. The artist derives his forms, his metaphors, and his total structure from the character of the expression and from intellectual and emotional convictions. Imagination is merely a means that is available to the artist for seeing and sensing forms that grow out of the objects with which he is dealing. Thus, the artist derives concepts—for example, life, brutality, and impotence—from familiar objects, such as those used in Picasso's "Guernica": a woman, a bull, and a clumsy hand.

It is farfetched to expect young children to display this same "freedom to be dominated by the object" in their work. However, it is possible to find examples of this kind of domination in the creative work of children who have been made aware that it is good to seek images, metaphors, and relationships in forms and materials.

Figure 13-8, a landscape by a primary-grade child, is an example of how a child can find forms in common objects, which can be developed to create surprising arrangements or patterns. The painting began as a picture of a tree and a house. As a result of the teacher's effective guidance, the child exploited the patterned arrangement of masses of light that were first painted as sky seen through the foliage of the tree. As a result of this patterning process, the child developed a structured metaphor of sky and tree foliage and then proceeded to use the same form-seeking procedure to complete the development of the whole painting. The result is something more than an inept attempt at enumerative representation of the facts of a remembered visual experience.

ROLE OF INSPIRATION

One of the results of the deliberative experimental process that follows the initial phase of inspiration is the development of unique and effective metaphors. We have illustrated the

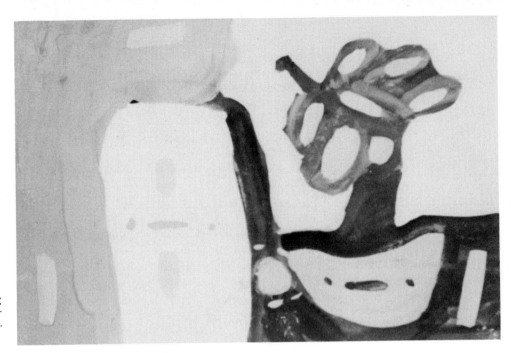

13-8. LANDSCAPE
Painting. *New York City Public Schools.*

manner in which creative action involves an ability to construct metaphors in accordance with the maturity of the participants in the creative process. In order to construct metaphors that are effective and unique, the creative worker must use the elements of imagination, sensitivity, feeling, intuition, knowledge, experience, personal conviction, and understanding of materials and technical processes. The effectiveness of a metaphoric structure may be determined by a kind of thinking, prolonged contemplation, and continued probing that seeks out many different solutions to problems of visual-plastic expression.

There is a need for spontaneity in art activity and in the processes of productive thinking. However, after the initial phase of art activity takes place, a process of deliberation should be brought into existence. We have evidence that the absence of spontaneity is often accompanied by lifelessness, that children can "work a picture to death." After the first burst of inspiration, children may not know what direction to take to perfect their production. It is the responsibility of the teacher to know the potential of the child at each stage of his development, and to help him work effectively within the limits of his potential. An important job of education is to lengthen the child's span of attention, interest, and effort.

One of the characteristic aspects of the creative process is the manner in which inspiration functions. The works we have discussed exhibit little evidence that successful results can be achieved

quickly and spontaneously. The major evidence of immaturity in the art work of children may result from their reluctance to develop their work beyond the first stages of a nearly spontaneous action. The method of drawing the pig (Figure 13-7) is an excellent example of a process of spontaneous inspiration; however, even this drawing shows evidence of a beginning deliberateness.

It is probable that the most instantaneous kind of expression can be found among the efforts of very young preschool or kindergarten children. The work of the mature artist is noteworthy for the spontaneity expressed during the first phase of art activity and for the probing, deliberate, experimental method that follows. From this observation we might assume, as did Eindhoven and Vinacke, that the creative processes in art activity are marked by an initial inspiration—a spontaneous comprehension of the expression and its general characteristics—which is followed by more deliberate experimental phases.

In the work of the non-artist, the creative processes are marked by development from a satisfaction with the first results of spontaneous forming to a gradual increase in concern with experimentation and study of the initial concepts. Immediately following the first burst of inspiration, it is imperative that a deeper and more detailed probing of relationships and ideas take place. For children, as for professional artists, this probing involves references to experience; it is an aspect of precognition, but it includes reference to culture. This probing may be one of the first and most useful methods for helping children extend their metaphors beyond the first stages. And in cases when the first stages involve no initial burst of inspiration, such probing can often provide a basis for inspiration.

Inspiration may be slow and labored or it may be a rapid explosive understanding. The order of thinking is not fixed in this respect. Creative action may begin at any one of a multitude of starting points; there is no precise way to predict where the starting point will be.

INTEGRATION OF CULTURAL FORCES WITH CREATIVE ACTION

Picasso's "Guernica" is the product of a deep-rooted cultural tradition. Several of the most critical metaphors used are based on Spanish cultural tradition. The bull represents brutality, and becomes a metaphor for Fascism; the horse represents the faithful friend of man, and motherhood is symbolic of the essence of life. Picasso's use of the bull as a symbolic metaphor is interesting. In the context of his mural, the bull becomes a symbol of hope and faith because in Spanish cultural tradition, the bull is usually defeated in the bull ring. In the mural, the bull is depicted as insolent; however, his brutal victory is fated to be temporary, in spite of the fact that the warrior lies dead in the picture's foreground.

Above the entire scene is the penetrating electric eye of night, a symbol of modern technology, which will permit no refuge for the political scoundrel.

Figures 13-7 and 13-8 also contain obvious cultural implications that have served as the pivot of the creative processes. One child's concept of a pig and another child's understanding of the relationship of trees to houses govern the structure of the pictures. The metaphoric effectiveness of these pictures is limited, but it does exist. We know from our previous discussion of productive thinking that the nature of the materials used, in addition to the image-symbols brought into active use by the precognitive processes, interact with and serve to control and to help evolve the effectiveness of the total metaphoric structure. During creative action, this interaction of materials with thinking processes serves to enhance and vitalize the creative processes. The interaction of cultural forces completes the creative action by establishing a total pattern of cultural, psychological, biological, and physical characteristics of materials and manipulations as the sources of the action of creative forming.

INTERACTION OF CULTURAL FORCES WITH PLASTIC MATERIALS

The clay figure (Figure 13-9) and the stone snake (Figure 13-10) are primarily cultural in origin. We have no way of knowing to what

13-9. VESSEL IN FORM OF SEATED MAN
Clay. Colima, Western Mexico (middle). *Philadelphia Museum of Art, the Louise and Walter Arensberg Collection.*

13-10. SERPENT
Green igneous rock. Aztec, Central Mexico (terminal?). *Philadelphia Museum of Art, the Louise and Walter Arensberg Collection.*

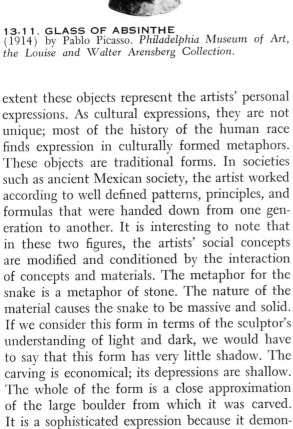

13-11. GLASS OF ABSINTHE
(1914) by Pablo Picasso. *Philadelphia Museum of Art, the Louise and Walter Arensberg Collection.*

13-12. CONSTRUCTION
Scrap material sculpture. *East Orange, New Jersey, Public Schools.*

extent these objects represent the artists' personal expressions. As cultural expressions, they are not unique; most of the history of the human race finds expression in culturally formed metaphors. These objects are traditional forms. In societies such as ancient Mexican society, the artist worked according to well defined patterns, principles, and formulas that were handed down from one generation to another. It is interesting to note that in these two figures, the artists' social concepts are modified and conditioned by the interaction of concepts and materials. The metaphor for the snake is a metaphor of stone. The nature of the material causes the snake to be massive and solid. If we consider this form in terms of the sculptor's understanding of light and dark, we would have to say that this form has very little shadow. The carving is economical; its depressions are shallow. The whole of the form is a close approximation of the large boulder from which it was carved. It is a sophisticated expression because it demonstrates a sensitive appreciation for the material. Within the limitations of the material, in this case a green igneous rock, the sculptor has evolved a form that, for his social group, has profound emotional and religious significance.

Although this figure is a traditional form, it could not be identically represented each time a sculptor carved a similar snake. In each instance, the sculptor would have to make his figure conform to the shape of the rock with which he worked. The kind of creativity displayed in Figure 13-9 evolves out of group consciousness. The idiosyncrasies of the individual artist may

be partially expressed, but the integration of the social concept and the physical material is a fact.

The same principle of a culturally inspired form operates in Figure 13-10, a vessel in the form of a man. This is a clay figure made by members of an ancient Mexican civilization for utilitarian purposes. Again, the metaphoric structure is integrated with the materials. This might be a traditional shape, one developed and perfected over a long period of time, but the nature of the clay from which it is formed strongly affects its character and structure. Unlike the snake, this form has deeply shadowed areas because the nature of clay permits the formation of wide openings and deep depressions.

The two sculptured forms, Figures 13-9 and 13-10, are fine results of creative effort. However, they are not results of the creative effort of an individual; they are the creative achievement of a culture. The two sculptures contrast in an interesting manner with the achievement of Picasso. "Guernica" is a creative achievement because it results from one man's exploration and search for ideas and materials.

Actually, individual expression through metaphoric construction is a modern phenomenon. It is a credit to our democratic tradition that the individual in our society is considered important enough to express uniqueness in creative work.

Our modern approach to creativity is illustrated in Figure 13-11, "Glass of Absinthe" by Picasso and in Figure 13-12, an intermediate-grade child's construction of a unique head.

Picasso's "Glass of Absinthe," although not one

of his major works, is typical of the inventive, surprising, and effective metaphors that are characteristic of his best work. As his expressive purpose in this sculpture, the artist adopts a general cultural attitude toward absinthe. Absinthe is an alcoholic beverage that is noted for producing an effect not unlike the one so wittily described by the artist. Like the Aztec artists, Picasso is not representing a thing he has seen. Instead, he is forming a metaphor that describes a feeling, the feeling that results from drinking too generously from a glass of absinthe. In this metaphor, the glass serves as a container for the beverage and as an appropriate metaphor for the effect of absinthe upon the individual. If a metaphor is to be expressive, it must be made from materials closely associated with the concept described. The ability to recognize and to make use of relationships between concepts and materials is the essence of creative activity.

Figure 13-12, a sculpture by an intermediate-grade child, has much in common with Picasso's sculpture. The child explored a variety of materials and succeeded in developing an effective and unique metaphoric structure, which seems to evolve naturally from the materials used. This form is the result of the child's own exploration and discovery; it is the most personally creative and the least self-conscious of the four sculptures just discussed (Figures 13-9, 13-10, 13-11, and 13-12).

METAPHORIC EFFECTIVENESS THROUGH CREATIVE ACTION

The twentieth century artist, like the child artist, expresses his own sensitive responses to experience through processes of creative action. "The Fish" (Figure 13-13), by the twentieth-century artist Constantin Brancusi, is representative of the work of the modern artist who experiments with materials and techniques to discover their potential for expression. This figure is not a fish nor is it an enumerative description of a particular fish; it is a commentary, and a poetic metaphor. We know that fish are sleek streamlined creatures that move easily through water, which is transparent and mirrorlike. Brancusi has represented this understanding with glass and polished marble. Unlike the child's work, Figure 13-12, this sculpture takes its cues from nature. The result provides a new experience for the

13-13. THE FISH
(1922) by Constantin Brancusi. *Philadelphia Museum of Art, the Louise and Walter Arensberg Collection.*

13-14. ABSTRACTION
(1932) by Jacques Villon. *Philadelphia Museum of Art, the Louise and Walter Arensberg Collection.*

observer. By contrasting the opacity and changing curves of the marble fish with the transparent reflective quality of the circular mirror, Brancusi has succeeded in creating a pleasing, unique, and effective metaphor. Aesthetic value emerges from the perfection of Brancusi's creative process. This perfection becomes continuous as the observer, sensing the qualities developed by the artist, continues to participate in the feelings the artist has succeeded in expressing.

Although the child's sculpture (Figure 13-12) is not as economical, clear, or logical as Brancusi's, the creative processes involved in the formation of both sculptures have much in common. Both the child and Brancusi engaged in a process of creative search and discovery that involved concepts, feelings, imagination, and the development of effective metaphors associated with the sensations and feelings that grow out of perception.

The process of creative search is not necessarily a purely visual and tactile experience. Figure 13-14, a painting by Jacques Villon entitled "Abstraction," illustrates the way in which visual concepts can be related to almost pure or abstract sensations such as movement. In this picture, the artist succeeds in defining a slow undulating rhythm by the simple expedient of a line painted

to indicate the direction of the movement. Emphasis is given to the sensation of rhythm by contrasting the leisurely grace of the line against a relatively static space. The contrast of the thin line against massive forms, defining a deep perspective, serves to emphasize the line's movement. In this simple and direct manner, the artist creates an effective and surprising metaphor. The process of search and discovery, which is the heart of creative action, is most satisfactorily realized when an artist is able to include more than purely visual sensations in his work. Villon, like Picasso, has correlated several sensations in his visual-plastic metaphor.

In the work of children, this combining of many categories of sensation becomes an increasingly effective process as the child's awareness and sensitivity to experience and the manipulation of ideas and materials increase. In the earliest work of children, as in the first stages of graphic representation, the drawing is made up almost entirely of movement sensations with little attention given to the development of metaphors that are related to experience. At later stages, the child may draw pictures that are meant to embody experiences; however, the child's desire to describe often overpowers and destroys his metaphoric expression.

13-15. DRAWING
Chalk. *Author's collection.*

13-16. CIRCUS
Mural. *Teaneck, New Jersey, Public Schools.*

Figure 13-15 is a drawing by a child who is still too young to know how to explore sensation and materials to find a means for relating experience to materials. The child tries to express a concept about an experience, but fails to create an effective metaphor; the result is a static drawing.

Figure 13-16, a detail from the circus painting (Figure 5-2) made by four first-grade children, succeeds in combining movement sensations, concepts of a circus, and imaginative elements associated with the festive experience of a circus. The successful communication of the feeling of a circus is accomplished by the flowers on the right, by the lilting and rhythmic movement of the trapeze artist (who is conceived as a girl in typical child's clothing rather than as an appropriately attired adult acrobat) on the left, and by the clown in the foreground. The effect of excitement in dynamic movement is achieved through the pattern of spattered paint. This last innovation may have been suggested by the teacher as an inventive way to handle materials in order to achieve some of the sensations associated with the experience of a circus.

From this discussion it should be clear that details of the creative processes can not be predicted. The closest we can come to such predictions is in the art work of old cultures, where work was directed mainly by cultural forces or traditions. The processes of creative action, like the processes of art education, can flourish only in the atmosphere of a balanced relationship between reason, emotion, and the precognitive and productive processes. The main concerns of art education, invention and discovery within the context of a child's world, also provide the basis for the function of the creative processes.

AESTHETIC COMPONENTS
OF CREATIVE ACTION

The processes of creative action can result in an aesthetic experience when they involve the individual in processes of precognitive and productive thinking, which lead to the transformation of image-symbols into ordered and related metaphors. Creative action is possible when an effort is made to establish a unity of experience from inception to completion of an art activity.

The aesthetic value of an art activity is increased if the individual can recognize directions for future work in the results of his completed art activity. All processes of art activity should be developed in a creative manner. Without creativity there can be no ordering and directing of the imagination; and without imagination there can be no search, which is guided by qualitative emotional drives.

(Creative action itself is not aesthetic, but it can produce the aesthetic. The aesthetic can come into being if creative search results from an understood need to order the disorder of perceived phenomena. Creative search is motivated by a need to make satisfactory adjustments to experiences in order to form, control, and give meaning to the interaction of self with the environment. Environment is an important part of creative action. The cultural, social, and natural environment can influence the character of metaphors, which represent the transformation of human experience.

RELATION OF CREATIVE ACTION
TO SELF-EXPRESSION

A severe problem that tends to obscure understanding of the creative aspects of art is the frequent confusion between originality and the expression of a distortion of the creative processes.

A large emphasis on creative self-expression may do nothing more than encourage distortions of experience caused by undiagnosed neuroticism.

Self-expression can be "a confessional [or] a frozen tantrum." In the art work of very young children, this kind of self-expression is much less common than in the art work of intermediate and upper-grade children. When this kind of "frozen tantrum" is all that the processes of creative action can evolve, satisfactory art activity does not take place. The difference between neurotic self-expression and aesthetically valid creative processes in art is clearly described by Susanne Langer as a distinction between the expression of feeling by an artist and a mere emotional explosion such as that which takes place when a baby laughs or cries or when a politician blows off steam. The artist "formulates that elusive aspect of reality that is commonly taken to be amorphous and chaotic; that is, he objectifies the subjective realm. What he expresses is, therefore, not his own actual feeling, but what he knows about human feeling. Once he is in possession of a rich symbolism, that knowledge may actually exceed his entire personal experience." [4]

Art teachers should be aware of the uses made of creative self-expression in art activity. Most of these uses are involuntary. Clinical workers have found that self-expression in art may be useful as a means for draining off unhealthy mental energies; however, it is not a main function of art education. If emphasis in art activity is placed on this kind of purgation, the role of art education processes will easily be misunderstood.

FREE ASSOCIATION AS A BASIS FOR CREATIVE ACTION

How can the creative search function on a level that will result in useful learning processes and successful art achievement?

Lawrence Kubie recommends that the processes of creative action grow out of a process of free association. In our discussion of imagination (see Chapter Twelve), free association was described as a form of autism. Autism was defined as a form of imagination that is free from stereotypes and, therefore, capable of freeing the thinking processes from bias.

According to Kubie, the processes of free association are valid as a means for developing creative action if they are ". . . subjected to a process of retrospective, conscious, self-critical scrutiny for a necessary secondary process of checking and testing." [5] If used in this way, the processes of free association will be more than just an exhuming of neuroticisms and an evaporation of mental irregularities. When the creative processes and free association are used as therapy, the program should be directed by a person specifically trained in such work. This kind of work is not the function of the average teacher, whose major responsibility is for the development of healthy young people.

Free association is useful in the processes of creative action because it permits the individual

to ". . . roam freely from mental highways to its byways, unhampered by conscious restrictions, gathering analogous but seemingly unrelated ideas and impressions, putting them together in varying combinations until new relationships and new patterns come into view." [6]

The processes of free association are hindered in their development of creative activity if the scrutinizing function of the conscious mind is employed from the very beginning of the activity. In the work of young children, the processes of free association dominate; the main shortcomings in such work result from the lack of a conscious scrutiny of the initial phases of the activity. The participant in creative action must know when to permit cognitive thinking to study the products of free association. It is often very difficult for the individual involved in an experience to make free associations and to remember the details of the experience. For this reason, many creative people keep a notebook with them at all times. In this way, they are able to record the details of an experience and can later subject their free associations to rational analysis.

The sketches made in the development of "Guernica" represent a refinement of concepts and visual-plastic images. The sketches were used as building blocks and the details of the final conception were refined from the images and metaphors that developed successively from sketch to sketch.

Metaphoric effectiveness does not develop rapidly; and although free association is a rapid process, the products of free association need time to incubate and ripen. The artist often records his first inspirations and then sets them aside, after which he can return to his productions ". . . with lessened identification and less personalized defense of them, than is possible at the moment of creating or immediately thereafter." [7]

The characteristics of the processes of free association must be defined and their relation to the processes of creative action must be understood. Free associations are the opposite of anything predictable; they are the opposite of conditioned responses. Free associations do not achieve efficiency through repetition or drill. They

---

[4] *Problems of Art*, p. 26.
[5] *Neurotic Distortion of the Creative Process*, p. 54.
[6] *Ibid.*, p. 53.
[7] *Ibid.*, p. 55.

come into being as the result of precognitive activity. Their effectiveness, therefore, is dependent on a rich store of prior experience. The products of free associations are related in ways that can only be felt during the precognitive processes. During the processes of productive thinking, meaningful relationships are made as the result of manipulative and scrutinizing processes.

The rapidity of the processes of free association makes them useful in creative action. We have previously noted that precognitive processes are rapid. For example, in his sketches of "Guernica," Picasso used rapidly drawn lines in order to record his initial inspirations with the speed required by the associational processes, which served to initiate the development of the painting.

Free association involves a learning experience to the extent that it serves as a device for sampling the elements of subconscious experience. From this point of view, free association is a means for providing the precognitive processes with energy. The samples secured by free association are later subjected to the critical scrutiny of the conscious mind, which checks the samples for usefulness and relatedness. In this way, relationships are "tightened" and associations are "polished."

According to Kubie, free associations carry their own implications of danger to the healthy development of people participating in the processes of creative action. Some people do not easily engage in the processes of making free associations. For many people, such processes become a "leap in the dark." Because free association may result in a dredging up of feelings of guilt and terror, some people confine themselves to stereotypes and clichés. Well known forms provide the fearful with security, which acts as a shield against unknown fears. In addition to stereotypes and clichés, people who are fearful of free association processes rely too heavily on cognitive thinking. Rationality, logic, and a definable sequence of thoughts and images become a net in which such persons bind themselves and prohibit themselves from achieving creative processes that will be aesthetically rewarding.

Anxiety in the face of the venturousness of the free association processes may also limit the creative work of persons who are not outwardly fearful of uncharted thinking, new concepts, and the shock of an effectively expressive metaphor. Painful emotions and fears may limit the creative act for the adventurous as well as for the fearful individual. Kubie notes that the influence of painful feelings and emotions on the conscious, preconscious, and unconscious levels of the mind plays an important role in determining the freedom with which even the most inventive artist can function in creative work. A person may be adventurous and guilt free in one aspect of creative action and restricted in others.

There is some evidence that a lack of venturousness in one area of creative action operating on an unconscious level, tends to interfere with the effectiveness of creative action in other areas. This interference tends to hinder the flow of all free and creative associations. However, if such restrictions operate on a precognitive level (or on the level Kubie refers to as preconscious, which is similar to our precognitive level) ". . . their influence will be more selective, with the result that they will be inhibitory in certain directions and overdriving in other compensatory areas." [8]

FUNCTION OF EVALUATION DURING FREE, CREATIVE ASSOCIATION PROCESSES

The processes of creative action require a careful analytical and critical study. This study must be dispassionate and, if possible, should involve group evaluation.

Group evaluations may help overcome the individual's inclination to use free association to create unsatisfactory private expressions. Purely free or private expressions may result in the creation of forms that are nothing more than a means for driving the ". . . creative zeal blindly in an effort to resolve some ancient dilemma, to pay an old debt or to settle an old grudge, to achieve the unattainable goal of a childhood fantasy, or to lift the curse from something which in childhood had been an overwhelming source of pain, humiliation and terror." [9]

It is imperative that the teacher recognize the shortcomings of an uncontrolled creative process. An educationally useful creative action requires a proper blending of free associations and criticism.

[8] *Ibid.*, p. 59.
[9] *Ibid.*, p. 61.

We have referred to criticism as the means for guiding the processes of imaginative thinking. Thus, criticism may be used as the means for providing the processes of creative action with the benefits of correctly utilized processes of creative imagination.

SUMMARY

Available understandings of the functions and operating characteristics of the processes of creative action enable us to formulate fairly specific guides for the achievement of valid creative activity. According to our understanding of the processes most useful in art activity, creative action involves the construction of metaphors that are effective expressional devices. Such metaphors should demonstrate the creator's understanding of his purposes, of the concepts he is expressing, and of pertinent processes of technical production.

Children can succeed in creating effective metaphors if they are able to develop flexible habits of thinking.

Flexibility means the ability to explore new areas, to evaluate new directions of thought, and to work without the restrictions of unhealthy neuroticisms. Flexibility requires that the processes of creative action be guided by inclinations to think fluently in order to devise effective new forms.

Fluent thinking means the ability to make use of rich experiential background in the processes of creative action to insure a strong process of precognitive thinking. Such fluency provides an awareness of the many possibilities for forming particular ideas and concepts. Fluent thinking also helps develop the ability to arrange and organize metaphors in a way that will increase the effectiveness of their expression.

Creative imagination does not exist because it is directed to exist. Creative action can not be legislated. Creative action and imagination are effective to the extent that they operate freely with the help of flexible and fluent thought processes.

The processes of creative action must utilize the materials of perception in a unique manner. By means of such utilization, the brain and the mind—the biological central nervous system and the intellect—form a "plastic record," which is colored by the uniqueness of individuality.

In several studies conducted by J. P. Guilford,[10] it was concluded that creative people are sensitive to problems, that they have adaptive and spontaneous flexibility (the ability to adjust quickly and easily to strange situations), that they are original, that they can redefine problems in new and increasingly useful terms, that they have ideational fluency (the ability to express ideas in a multitude of ways), that they have associational fluency (the ability to make associations between diverse ideas and things), and that they are capable of closure (the comprehension of totalities).

Studies of creativity[11] seem to indicate that all people are creative to some degree. The more fluent a thinker a person is, the more creative he may be. Fluency, in this context, refers to richness and variety of thought. The greater the profusion of ideas, the more likely it is that a larger proportion of the ideas will be good. High quantity does not mean that low quality will follow; the opposite is more likely to be the case.

Flexibility of thinking is a necessary attribute. Spontaneous flexibility refers to the ability to see things from many points of view and to apply a multiplicity of thoughts, colorations, ideas, associations, relationships, and understandings to perceived experience. Adaptive flexibility refers to the ability to redefine and reinterpret, to transform familiar things, ideas, and concepts into new relationships and structures.

The creative thinker, according to the requirements for flexibility, is an elaborate thinker. He sees all kinds of implications in observations, perceptions, and ideas.

Basic to all processes of creativity is the ability to evaluate what is done. This ability might come under the heading of selectivity. The ability to evaluate is the ability to select and reject and to critically determine the value of what has been done. Evaluation is a motivating force in the proc-

[10] See especially "Psychology of Creativity," *Teachers College Record*, LXIII, No. 5 (February 1962), 380-92.
[11] For example, the National Science Foundation study of creativity, conducted by the Department of Art Education, Pennsylvania State University.

esses of art activity; it is the intellectual aspect that enables us to progress from idea to idea, through the creation of multiple numbers of art forms and a series of forming processes, in which each form and each forming process is an outgrowth of its predecessors.

One of the most significant aspects of the work done by Guilford is the discovery that aptitude for creative thinking does not have fixed limits of achievement for each individual. Heredity may establish a ceiling, but individuals rarely reach this ceiling. The development of creativity is something over which we can exercise a large measure of control.

Our knowledge of imagination, creativity, and the kinds of thinking that are involved in the forming processes of art activity provides us with specific implications for the guidance of young people. The following statements will serve as a short summary of these implications and as a guide to your own thinking.

1. Adventurousness is a prerequisite for art activity. The art processes require a spirit of "let's see what will happen." Some of the strangest possibilities may offer some of the best solutions to a variety of problems. Concepts, ideas, and experiences need not be rejected simply because they are unusual or seemingly irrational. Although at first glance, some materials or combinations of materials may appear unlikely candidates for the embodiment of a concept, the materials should be tried anyway. The best initial advice is "be adventurous."

2. Fearlessness is the mark of the artist. Fearfulness is the one quality that will most quickly kill adventurousness and take the fun out of living. Fearfulness may take many forms. Its most common apparition is the mistake. It is important to remember that in the processes of art activity, a mistake is not a crime; it is just a false lead and a signal to try something else.

3. Tolerance of your own ideas is essential. Intolerance results in the destruction of hope. The spirit of inquiry is elemental; if there is no willingness to be curious about the unfamiliar and the strange, there can be little hope for effective art activity.

4. Ideas should not be immediately disposed of just because they happen to look like questionable prospects or mistakes. All ideas should be given a chance to develop. Final judgments should be delayed. New relationships may suggest themselves as the result of other experiences that may be added to those already considered. Incubation and slow growth are often intrinsic to the creation of value. Some of the most beautiful forms in nature come about without perceptible changes. We don't always see growth; but we become aware of growth as new relationships intrude.

PART THREE

GENERAL CHARACTERISTICS OF CHILD ART

Fourteen

THINKING AND WORKING PROCESSES

IN PRIMARY-GRADE ART

The natural development of child art indicates a basis for the construction of curricula for primary-grade art education programs.

The development of the forms of child art is the history of the growth of important interactions and relationships between precognitive and productive thinking.

During the earliest stages of the primary-grade period, the interaction between precognitive and productive thinking is only partly developed. This partial development is illustrated by a typical tendency among children to manipulate materials simply because the manipulative processes give them pleasure. The painting, sculpture, or other art form resulting from such manipulative play is nothing more than a playful arrangement of art materials. Scribble paintings, unrecognizable clay structures, or arrangements of colored paper are the usual result of this kind of play.

Early evidence of the child's attempt to relate thinking to the products of manipulative play is the child's inclination to name the products of his play. Children will often name their work without prompting. When this happens, it may mean that the child has become aware of a need to relate his work to some aspect of his own experience. This awareness can become an important step toward the child's understanding of a need to relate thinking to his manipulations of art materials. The first step toward combining thinking with feeling in art activity can be achieved if the teacher encourages the children to talk about their work.

FROM SCRIBBLE TO STRUCTURED FORM

The first important stage in the achievement of interactions between thinking and doing takes place when the scribble is made at the same time the child decides what it will be. When naming and doing work together in this way, the final result may be a visual-plastic metaphor.

Children may sometimes formulate purposes before they begin to draw. In such cases, any one of the following results may occur:

1. There will be a successful interaction between concept and material, and the result, as far as the child is concerned, will be exactly what he intended.
2. The result will have nothing in common with the expressed intention, but the child will have forgotten his stated purpose and will revert to the naming of a scribble.
3. The result will be different from the expressed intention because the child will develop other purposes as a result of suggestions made by other persons or by the natural evolution of forms from the materials with which he works.
4. The result will be different from the child's intention and he will become discouraged and give up.

FRAGMENTATION OF EXPRESSION

Some of the first pictures and sculptures made by very young primary-grade children appear to adults to be masses of confusion because adults have no fixed standards or formulas to guide them in making judgments about child art. The teacher should know that in order to judge the art work of a child, it is first necessary to know the child. The teacher must realize that a child is not always aware of what he is trying to communicate in his art work. Children often make pictures without purpose. Such purposeless art activity sometimes leads to discoveries if it involves experimentation and search. However, purposeless art activity that is devoid of search easily leads to disorganization and fragmentation. This kind of fragmentation takes place because the child is not searching for relationships. Some

relationships may result from activity that is purely intuitive, but we have previously noted that intuition without rational thinking does not usually result in satisfactory art expression among children.

As a result of a natural and understandable enthusiasm, children will sometimes try to put too many ideas in a single expression. The result is similar to that which occurs when too many ideas are put in one sentence: the central idea is likely to become obscured and lost. This will often happen when ideas are not clearly worked out and understood. It is also childlike to try to express too many things all at once.

One of the most common causes of unclear expression and communication is an inability to find a form that expresses ideas adequately. This type of shortcoming is most typical in the work of the more advanced primary-grade child. The less advanced child tends to want to express simple ideas that are easily formed in the gesture-like drawing typical of the early primary-grade group. Lack of clarity is sometimes caused by inadequate motor skills. Again, this is a quality that is most common among the more advanced primary group. The younger primary children, who seem to be less concerned about manual skills, feel less handicapped by limited motor skill than do the older children.

The lack of meaningful relationships between the parts of a single drawing or sculpture is probably one of the most common causes of fragmented expression. The tendency among the youngest children to permit their art forms to be dominated by kinaesthetic movements generally prevents fragmentation. However, fragmentation may occur if the kinaesthetic movement is not continuous. A continuous kinaesthetic movement is related to a gesture intended to define a single idea. Interruptions in this movement can lead to fragmentation caused by a breaking off of expression. When the expressive rhythm of the kinaesthetic gesture is broken, children often have difficulty in forming a related movement from the point where the previous expressional movement stopped. This kind of interruption in the rhythmical movement of the productive thinking processes was explained in the discussion about the painting of clowns, Figure 7-5. Fragmentation may also result when several separate normally unrelated things are brought together in one picture. This happens when the child has only a partial understanding of the thing he is symbolizing. In this situation, the child's thinking causes him to move rapidly from one part of the paper to the other, without pausing to consider that he is actually making a number of unrelated pictures on one sheet of paper.

EVOLUTION FROM SYMBOLS TO CONCEPTS[1]

Another important stage in child art is the strange evolution from symbols to concepts. In child art, symbols often evolve out of manipulative activities. During the course of these activities, the child recognizes configurations that remind him of familiar experiences. A configuration may become a symbol for a face, a man, the sun, a tree, a house. The symbol appears to come into being before the concept is formed. Ideas, concepts, and symbols play an almost amusing "shell game." Out of this interplay more complex configurations may emerge and assume the status of poetic metaphors. Because of the interplay between manipulation, the formation of symbols, and the act of relating manipulated forms to ideas and experiences, it is difficult to say that the concept comes before conceptual forming or that conceptual forming leads to the invention of symbols and metaphors.

The teacher must be sensitive to this interaction of symbols, manipulations of materials, experiences, ideas, and concepts. Because of this interaction, many teachers have felt that too much discussion in preparation for an art activity is not a very good idea. More successful results may be achieved if children are immediately allowed to become involved in working with art materials. Discussions about the art activity should be held after the processes of working with materials have started and the children have begun to explore, invent, and discover things about the materials with which they are working. According to this procedure, directions for an art activity grow out of the activity itself and are directly related to the manipulative processes. In this way, needs, understandings, art processes, and experiences are related.

[1] See Chart 3, *Structure of the Visual-Plastic Metaphor.*

CONCEPTS AND DIFFERENTIATION

The development of qualitative concepts is usually evidenced through an increasing differentiation in the forms of children's productive work. This increasing differentiation parallels the children's realization that all animals are not dogs and that all people are not necessarily mothers and fathers. Concepts become increasingly differentiated as ideas about things and experiences become greater in number and detail.

ACCELERATION OF INCREASINGLY DIFFERENTIATED CONCEPTS AND FORMING PROCESSES

Children are generally nearing the end of the scribble-drawing stage when they first enter school. This distinction, however, can not be rigidly applied because children grow at different rates of speed. We can only safely assume that all children have been or still are in the undifferentiated stages of scribbling, in which productive and thinking aspects are poorly related. In such stages, the precognitive store of experiences is small but motor skills, in most cases, are developed sufficiently to make it reasonable to plan a program for correlating the precognitive and productive processes. Such planning should be made with the understanding that both processes are at an early stage of development. Through planned enlargement of children's experiences, which will increase their precognitive store, and through increased skillfulness in the productive processes, the children's rate of differentiation may be accelerated.

The planned enlargement of children's experiences involves the development of a program for helping children perceive and recognize increasingly new and important things. When children are ready for certain kinds of knowledge, the teacher should plan field trips, slide or film showings, picture study sessions, or readings and storytelling. These experiences can easily be related to child participation in related activities, such as discussions, question and answer periods, and role playing or dramatizations. In this way, particular experiences may become increasingly vivid. The manipulative processes are important during this phase of development. Manipulative processes involve working with materials related to the subject, making pictures, writing poems, playing musical instruments, or acting parts that might be related to the subject. Through such activities, the children's understanding of a subject or an experience is broadened. Such acquaintance can provide avenues that lead to more detailed knowledge.

Differentiation evidences itself in children's art work as increasing detail. However, the mere accumulation of detail is not enough evidence of growth. A function of the art program is to help children understand, through kinaesthetic and visual processes, the way details can be related to form wholes. When all aspects of a completed work are well related, there is a possibility that the harmony of the relationships will result in an aesthetic experience.[2]

Children's abilities to establish relationships between the details of an experience must be understood in art activities in terms of the level of motor skill possessed by the children. Motor skill is an important consideration. Without motor skill, children will be handicapped in their efforts to represent the relationships between the visual-plastic parts and the structured metaphors they evolve from experiences. Apparently children's motor skills are fairly well developed by the time they enter kindergarten. For this reason, it seems safe to involve children in programs designed to aid in the achievement of correlations between the understanding, forming, and structuring of increasingly detailed experiences.

GESTURE DRAWING AS AN EXPRESSIVE MEANS

Gesture drawing is an advanced form of the undifferentiated scribble. Participation in gesture drawing indicates a readiness for participation in a planned program of productive thinking. Gesture drawing, in its earliest phases, is the uninhibited scribble drawing or painting. The scribble is the result of an arm and body movement. The gesture is the same movement controlled by an expressive purpose. The expressive purpose causes the gesture to come into being.

[2] See Chapter Eleven.

Individuals often supplement their conversations with expressive gestures, which consist of descriptive movements of the hands, arms, and sometimes even the entire body. Gesture drawing is a charting of the expressive gesture. A gesture transferred to a picture or sculptured form is the expression of a physical response to an idea or a concept. A gesture may be the expression of a deeply felt feeling or of a profound need to communicate. Gestures grow out of kinaesthetic responses to experience.

A unique function of the art education program is to provide the concepts, purposes, and feelings expressed in gestures with a purposeful structured physical form. From this point of view, it might be said that art activity is made stronger when its motivation evolves from experiences with other forms of kinaesthetic expression. If motivation causes children to explore music, drama, dance, and poetry, their understandings will be broadened. Each art form requires a particular emphasis on a particular sensory experience. Thus, participation in varied art activities promotes sensory interaction, which tends to increase the quantity and quality of children's detailed knowledge.

If children happen to be considering a visit to a shoe factory they may try to describe the smell of the leather with words. With musical instruments, perhaps a rhythm band, they may describe the rhythmical sounds of the working factory. With descriptive movements of their bodies they may describe the rhythm of workers and machines; with clay, paint, or paper they may describe the images of shoes being made, of machines, and of people at work. Their paintings, if they make paintings of the visit, will incorporate the sensations of movement the children described with their dance. The visual rhythms will grow out of or supplement the sounds of their musical expression of the experience. In this way, the painting is at least, in part, the product of a cultivated series of expressive body movements.

The high level of sensorimotor ability possessed by children at the beginning of the kindergarten year is evidenced by their combining of gestures with developing skill in the use of precognitive thinking. Sensorimotor ability involves the association of gesture drawings and manipulations with kinaesthesia. Such associations become increasingly qualitative when they are employed in productive processes.

EMERGENCE OF AESTHETIC VALUE

An increasing smoothness of the interaction between thinking and productive processes is marked by an increase in aesthetic quality. Aesthetic quality exists partly because of effective interaction of the precognitive and productive processes. This interaction contributes to the development of useful thinking and learning processes.

In order to achieve the objective of smooth correlations between precognitive and productive thinking during the first year of the primary-school period, it is necessary to engage in a curricular program that is designed to make use of the natural modes of child art activity. The achievement of smooth interrelations between precognitive and productive processes can not take place until a useful store of precognitive experience has been developed and some skill in productive work has been learned. Consequently, it is very important that skill and experience, as well as knowledge about the structuring of image-symbol forms, accompany and parallel each other. A separation of the factors is artificial. If any one of the factors is separated for learning purposes, the ultimate achievement of smooth interactions will be very difficult.

PRIORITIES IN DEVELOPMENT OF CHILD ART

The manipulation of tools and materials is the first process with which children gain familiarity. The next process to be clearly defined in the evolution of child art is the naming of the results of manipulative activity. At the beginning of this phase, the child is unable to correlate the results with the names he gives them. This inability can be demonstrated by suggestion. At this point, almost anything an adult suggests to a child may prove worthy of consideration. When the child resists this kind of suggestion, he is either very stubborn or he actually considers his manipulative result to represent some symbol or concept.

During the earliest phases of the manipulative processes, children will be satisfied with naming their manipulative results, in spite of the fact that there is no real relation between the names, the processes of manipulation, or the manipulative results.

The beginning of a useful correlation between precognitive and productive thinking takes place when the child names his work because of suggestions its accidental forms make to him. This stage represents the beginning of an interaction between material, manipulations, and thoughts. The naming of a manipulative result according to an object or concept it suggests may be the beginning of useful precognitive thinking; it may provide the basis for dynamic interaction between precognitive and productive thinking processes.

Some children, even during the earliest phases of the manipulative processes, may find suggestions for concepts that may lead to an interaction between suggestions from manipulative accidents and deliberate continuations of the original forming process. This kind of interaction is highly desirable because it is an interaction between materials, tools, manipulations, and the subconscious and conscious aspects of the precognitive processes.

Even at the earliest stages of the primary-grade period, some children may have image-symbol concepts so vivid that they interact with, and frequently dominate, the productive processes. In such cases, it may be necessary to help these children correlate their imagery with gestures, tools, materials, and manipulations.

ASPECTS OF LEARNING THROUGH MANIPULATION IN EARLY CHILD ART

According to some early research into the character of children's art, the representation of movement and action is one of the poorest and weakest aspects of early child art.[3] We have reason to believe this is true when children attempt to represent a concept or a symbol in purely visual terms. When this happens, the kind of multisensory interaction that may result in the expressive gesture is obviously ignored. Efforts by children to make pictures of only visual experience usually result in neutral representation. Neutral-

[3] See Helga Eng, *The Psychology of Children's Drawings* (London: Routledge & Kegan Paul, Ltd., 1954).

14-1. PORTRAIT
Runnemede, New Jersey, Public Schools.

14-2. DRAWING
Chalk. *Author's collection.*

ity in this case means that stiffness, stereotypes, or otherwise awkward relationships between parts dominate the art work. We have reason to believe that this will happen even when children are encouraged to employ expressive gestures and are helped to achieve a successful interaction between gestures and concepts. An excellent example of neutral representation is Figure 14-1. In painting this figure, the child paused in his manipulative process and lost the sense of rhythm. The fault here may result from the child's great dependence on visual experience alone. The child attempted to make a picture of what he saw without forming the corresponding symbols that result from other kinds of sensory experience, such as taste, smell, and hearing. By contrast, Figure 14-2 represents a sensitive forming of rhythmical movements correlated with symbols that constitute an expressive metaphor of a specific experience.

When emphasis is placed on purely visual perception, to the partial or complete exclusion of other forms of sensory activity, particularly kinaesthetic activity, expressions become stereotyped. The fact that such stereotyped expressions are not unusual in early child art indicates that the children's creative imagination is being blocked by too great an emphasis on visual perception. Children's sensitivity to this shortcoming in their art expressions may be indicated by their common practice of using gestures and verbal descriptions to add life to their stereotyped symbols. Purely visual emphasis results in poor correlation between naming and productive thinking.

In child art, the indication of a beginning interaction of other sensory responses, with main emphasis on the kinaesthetic response, will be represented as a connection between the parts of a motion. The representation itself will be static, but it will provide a symbol for the felt need for motion. Figure 19-4 is an example of this type of representation. The enlarged and elongated arms and hands provide a connection between the symbol for the child and the concept of the action he is trying to express.

Motion may be represented in symbol form. This kind of expression is frequently cultural or imitative in origin. An example is Figure 14-3, a chalk drawing of birds in flight. The drawing of the birds themselves is static, but the curved lines in front of the birds represents a sign of movement. This method has been copied from newspaper comic drawings.

The combination of gestures, feelings, thoughts, and manipulative processes aids knowledge. Through such a combination, expression becomes more effective because understanding of the subject increases as a result of muscular activity. According to Sanford, ". . . it is conceivable that the nervous system stores up experience through a recording of past muscular movements, and that now, in the face of a problem, it 'thinks' by reactivating muscular patterns of response." [4]

The interaction between thinking and doing, between precognitive thinking and the manipulative processes of productive thinking, is evidenced by changes in concepts. These changes take place during the period when the group is being motivated to form concepts in plastic materials. Apparently, no matter how effective and complete the processes of motivation may be, the form of thinking, its structure, and its depth and breadth change considerably during the productive thinking phase of art activity. The reason for this development is easily found in the processes of manipulating concepts, image-symbols, and materials.

We do know that an individual's thinking processes—his attitudes, concepts, selections from precognitive sources, and his general purposes preliminary to engagement in the productive processes—are all affected by and related to the patterns of neural activity in his cortex. Neural activity results from stimulation of the sensory receptors. By changing the order of the responses of the sensory receptors—in other words, by changing their patterns of stimulation—the pattern of neural activity will also be changed. In the same way, manipulative processes that cause unexpected movements result in changes in the expected pattern of muscular response. "Therefore, a change in muscle tension, by changing the pattern of neural activity in the cortex, may change the content of a person's experience." [5]

[4] Fillmore H. Sanford, *Psychology, a Scientific Study of Man* (Belmont, California: Wadsworth Publishing Company, Inc., 1961), p. 359.
[5] Krech and Crutchfield, *Elements of Psychology*, p. 491.

The form of the symbol and the character of the concepts children develop in their art activities change as a result of the effect of manipulative processes on the whole of the art experience. This is one of the reasons why a plastic material, interacting with a concept and its image-symbols, forms a completely new experience. In actual practice, the interactions that govern the evolution of the processes of productive thinking result in the evolution of new levels of experience. An effective productive thinking process never results in the formation of replicas of past experience.

The changes in concepts and thinking that evolve from manipulative experiences with art materials must be subjected to continuous examination by both the children and the teacher. The specific responsibility of the teacher is to help children see how the images they form with art materials are affected by the character of the materials used and by the requirements of the manipulative processes unique to the materials. Children should be helped to observe the interaction of materials with image-symbols. Such observation involves a process of becoming aware of the changes that take place in images, concepts, and thinking. This process of knowing and doing is the process of evaluation. Evaluation, in this sense, is group and individual participation in continuous study and analysis of the way art forms develop. This process can not be complete unless the relation of the children's thinking to their development of art forms is also considered. From this point of view, conscious evaluation of the products of productive thinking is an important part of the processes of knowing what has been accomplished and of formulating plans or directions for continued activity.

REPRESENTATION IN CHILDREN'S ART

Because healthful correlations of the physical, social, and psychological environment influence the evolution of useful experience and learning, mere representation of visual experience is detri-

14-3. BIRDS IN FLIGHT
Chalk. *Author's collection.*

mental to processes of learning through art. Replicas of purely visual experience may tend to be overloaded with data not needed for a particular expressional purpose.

Early forms of child art may sometimes be the results of efforts to make replicas of visual experience. This tendency is to be expected in a social environment where the visual form is, illogically, supposed to represent other visual forms. The art work of children, however, is seldom purely visual, in spite of its typical emphasis on visual duplication. As visual representations, such art works fall short of precise duplication because of the severe limitations of children's representational skills.

The child art form that is a polished replica of visual experience is rare. During the early primary stages, children will draw shapes that stand for the totality of a visual experience. Such forms are usually the products of a gesture designed to embrace an experience. Shapes that are made in this way are not cognitively formed symbols of what the child knows nor are they abstractions; they are usually shapes that are easily made from the materials used.

We have reason to assume that art activity is largely controlled by efforts to represent. These efforts increase in intensity as skill in manipulation increases. An important function of the program of early childhood art education is to provide children with experiences that can be formed into expressive metaphors.

An expressive metaphor is a combination of visual experience and of several manipulative and other sensory processes that are most suited to its definition. Not all art expressions require the same kinds of sensory activity. Some perceptions benefit most from hearing, some from smell, some from tactile sensations, and some from the purely rhythmical movements seen with the eyes. In every case, however, the kinaesthetic sense functions as a source of knowledge gained from muscular interaction with the productive processes.

EVOLUTION OF METAPHORS

Children's art activity, which begins with the gesture and its continuation in precognitive and productive thinking, must result in an economic selection of experiences. This economy is essential to the effectiveness of the constructed metaphor. The art education program should provide a means for helping children select the gestures, materials, and processes that will best enable them to express the experiences they select from the multitude of stimulations with which they are surrounded during a routine day. Such help in selection is gained through the development of programs designed to select experiences that are important to young children and to develop these experiences through role playing and dramatization.

SUMMARY

The natural development of child art forms indicates a basis for construction of the curricula for primary-grade art education programs.

The processes of art activity indicate that the child becomes acquainted with his world through manipulations.

Manipulative activity functions in combination with the sensory receptors to provide effective learning through art activity.

The visual experience is a learned experience; used by itself, it is insufficient to contain a complete learning process.

During the earliest developmental stages, children's perceptions and concepts are generally undifferentiated, regardless of whether their mode of expression is visual-plastic or verbal.

At the beginning of art activity, immediately prior to and during the early part of kindergarten, interaction of the sensory modes is awkward. Smooth interaction of the sensory modes occurs as children gather experience in art activity. The degree of the smoothness of sensory interaction may be proportional to the degree of aesthetic value achieved in results of productive thinking.

Because of their low level of skill during the earliest phases of art activity, children see and know more than they are able to incorporate in their productive work. For this reason, it is necessary that the art program be devised in a manner that will avoid overloading the sensory receptors. Overloading results in unsuccessful activity because the metaphoric structures, when they are formed, are confused and, therefore, lose much of their useful function.

We have reason to believe that the activities of drawing, painting, and manipulating pliable but solid materials are closely related to thinking. Thus, we believe that the application of muscular and manipulative activity such as in painting, drawing, and the shaping of three-dimensional materials contributes to the most productive thinking processes. On the basis of this belief, it is felt that the effectiveness of the forming or productive thinking processes determines the probable extent of useful learning processes.

The occurrence of stereotypes and increasing differentiation indicates the direction of the processes of education through art activity.

The stereotype comes into being as a catchall. It functions in much the same manner as the language stereotypes that are so typical in early childhood. Stereotypes are common in early childhood art because of the low level of development of the children's precognitive and productive processes.

Differentiation results from a maturing of the precognitive and productive thinking processes. If stereotypes persist during the growth processes, it is likely that the precognitive processes are not operating effectively. Proper development of the precognitive and productive processes should result in decreased rather than increased use of stereotypes.

Fifteen

GENERAL CHARACTERISTICS OF THE ART

OF OLDER ELEMENTARY-SCHOOL CHILDREN

The art of older children is the product of an increasingly complex interaction between the children and their environment. The teacher needs to know the specific characteristics of the children's growth before effective planning is possible for educationally valid art activities.

There are important differences in the art forms made by primary-grade children and by children in the intermediate and upper grades. A knowledge of these differences aids in the planning of educationally effective art programs for older children.

GENERAL ASPECTS

The earmarks of art made by older children can be known in a variety of ways. One useful way in which this knowledge can be achieved is by making comparisons between the physical, intellectual, and emotional growth patterns of the younger and older children. This kind of study will also involve a study of the effect of the cultural and physical environment on primary-grade and older children. Such a study should supply us with understandings that we can relate to comparisons of primary-grade art forms and art forms made by intermediate and upper-grade groups.

CHILD GROWTH AND FORM IN ART

Useful understandings of elementary-school art are possible when we are able to examine a complete pattern of growth over a period of many years. This pattern of growth can be constructed from the interaction of growth factors. Examination of the art work done by older children often reveals evidence that this pattern of growth affects patterns of forming with art materials. In the forms produced by primary-grade children, the location of the ground- and sky-line in landscape drawings and paintings is often the product of modes of thinking and feeling among young children. In much the same way, particular concepts of the natural and socio-cultural environment can qualify and direct the way older children use materials during the processes of art activity. Among the primary-grade children this environmental influence is evident in the spiral forms of the earliest expressions and in the geometricized forms of the later phases of primary-grade achievement. In the art forms produced by older children, there is evidence that the socio-cultural environment increasingly influences the structure of the metaphoric forms.

A purpose of planning art activities for older children is to provide some means for improving the children's understanding of their environment. Art activities should be planned to help children find forms that will satisfactorily express their growing knowledges. The interaction of experience with forming processes must maintain the kind of flexibility that is possible if the teacher can encourage attitudes conducive to exploration, research, and improvisation with materials and working processes.

If we are able to develop a program for older children that supplies their needs for healthy growth, we may then be able to observe patterns of growth in their art work. This kind of tangible evidence will offer a strong base for evaluation of their growth. Such evaluation can provide the teacher with the knowledge necessary to plan a successful art education program.

COMPARISONS BETWEEN ART OF OLDER AND YOUNGER CHILDREN

There are general characteristics that can be observed in the art work of children in elementary school and in the intermediate and upper grades. The older children are roughly from nine to thirteen years old. The general characteristics of the art of children from eight to nine years old are more easily defined than the general characteristics of the art of older children. As children grow older, they become increasingly complex persons; consequently, their art expressions become correspondingly complex.

The increasing complexity of the lives of older children does not always make it possible to predict the kinds of art work they will do. If such predictions are to be meaningful, they must be formed from detailed knowledge of the children's experiences, cultural backgrounds, personalities, needs, and interests. Before it is possible to know what type of educationally useful art work older children are capable of, it is necessary to know a great deal about the children. This requirement for information is based on the idea that the metaphoric forms children make to express their experiences, concepts, and aspirations are products of the children's total pattern of living.

ROLE OF RATIONALITY IN ART OF OLDER CHILDREN

Rationality plays an increasingly important role in the art of elementary-school children. The older children's increased use of rationality leads to an increase in the number of modifications and qualifications they feel a need to consider in their forming processes. Such considerations lead to efforts to express more subtle nuances of meaning, more detail, and greater accuracy. These new and increasing concerns often lead to a dryness of expression that is looked upon with disfavor by many art teachers. By comparison, the forms produced by primary-grade children are more direct, uncomplicated, and spontaneous. Such forms possess a freshness of expression that often results in pleasurable and sparkling metaphoric wit.

RATIONALITY AND SENSORIMOTOR SKILL

One of the most obvious changes that takes place as children grow older consists of an increase in sensorimotor skill. This increase should be accompanied by a corresponding growth in reasoning skill. If these two skills do not mature together, a serious imbalance in the child's development can result. The older child's ability to form complex image-symbols and concepts can become a dead end if the child's sensorimotor skill is not sufficiently developed to enable him to form suitable metaphoric expressions.

Younger children do not feel as great a need for skill in forming as do older children. This need is felt by the older children because their skill in critical thinking has reached a relatively higher level. Growth in critical thinking must exist before the need for sensorimotor skill is felt, although in actual practice it is difficult to establish an order of importance. The two factors should be developed almost simultaneously. Neither one of the factors should be permitted to get too far ahead of the other.

The difference in critical thinking and sensorimotor skill between primary-grade children and older children is easily observed in their methods of working and performing. The younger children display a simpler approach to working, a naïveté, and a freedom that is restricted mainly by the natural limitations experience must eventually impose. The older children realize that not all problems can have absolute answers. For younger children, all people have round faces with two eyes, a nose, and a mouth. For older children, all men and women have unique personalities. The more expressive a child's experiences become, the more aware he is of individuals and individual uniqueness. For this reason, older children find it difficult to express a face that stands for the faces of all people; the circle with two eyes, a nose, and a mouth is no longer a satisfactory generalization. The accumulation of experiences leads to increasing recognition and understanding of individual differences. In a general way, it is possible to say that increasing experience logically leads to the increasing differentiations in the art work of older children.

EMERGENCE OF CLICHÉS AND STEREOTYPES

There is a fair degree of uniformity in the art forms produced by primary-grade children. For this reason, we refer to some of the earliest works of the primary-grade period—the circular scribbles and the first evidences of correlations between concepts and formed images—as stereo-

types. An example of such stereotypes can be seen in the gesture drawings of young children. The first gesture drawings are often made from circular movements, which are kinaesthetic responses based on the gesture of the arm intended to describe a human face. In typical fashion, the uncritical child then places two spots in the circle to indicate eyes, a spot to indicate a nose, and a short line to stand for a mouth. The head made from a circle is a typical early symbol for a person because a child's thinking about people begins with the gesture for head and because the natural circular movement becomes a gesture that represents a form that can easily be made into a head. As the child matures, it becomes increasingly evident that such simple generalizing gestures can no longer communicate the child's more complex thoughts and experiences.

For a short time during the primary-grade period, the developing maturity of the children's art work appears to follow an approximately predictable pattern. This pattern is most easily recognized if the cultural backgrounds of the children and the program of their school experiences conform to the over-all curricular framework.

At some time during the later stages of the primary-grade period, children become more influenced by their socio-cultural environment. This influence results in an increasing differentiation in the kinds of image-symbols children use to form their metaphoric expressions.

When children's critical awareness first becomes an important influence on the art forms they make, the children become more and more dissatisfied with their ability to form what they consider to be suitable metaphors. At this time they realize that their art work fails to express as much as they have to say. Although verbal explanation of what they are expressing in their art work seems a satisfying technique for younger children, the relationship between "telling" and doing does not justify the incompleteness of an art form for more mature and critically aware children. If good guidance is not provided by the teacher when this kind of dissatisfaction arises, the children may resort to tried and proven art forms, which will be clichés or stereotypes. The most unfortunate thing about this development is its occurrence at a time when there is a need for more inventiveness and for an exploitation of what should be a developing precognitive store,

15-1. PAINTING
New York City Public Schools.

increased sensorimotor skill, and maturing creative imagination. If children have to resort to manufactured forms, ideas, metaphors, and techniques, they will have no opportunity to exercise their precognitive processes, their imagination, or their creative faculties.

It is difficult to know just when social forces begin to cause children's art work to become less typical and increasingly differentiated. It is possible that children in one community may show more rapid development and achievement of differentiated image-symbols than children in another community. The impact of cultural influence on the living, thinking, and expressional patterns of children may be more varied, and sometimes less predictable, than the differentiations that arise from the development of the physical, intellectual, and emotional characteristics of children.

Children in most American schools differ in many details of their cultural environment. These differences can be observed in the art work of older children and, to a lesser degree, in the work of primary-grade children. For example, children in suburban communities draw houses that have peaked roofs and are seldom more than one story in height. Children in urban communities tend to draw houses that are multiple dwelling units; apartment houses are common in the drawings of children from the urban communities. Figure 24-12 is a drawing of a multilevel, multiple-unit building that was made by a child in the latter part of the kindergarten year. The same child, during the early part of the kindergarten year, did not draw apartment buildings. This particular kind of cultural differentiation was the result of a planned observation.

Children will show evidence in their art work of increasing differentiation and influence from their cultural environment when they are encouraged to know their cultural environment.

Figure 15-1 is an example of a primary-grade painting that demonstrates an effort to describe physical differences among children of different races. This painting was made in a school in which racial groups were mixed. At this early stage of the child's school career, he has become conscious of differences and has been able to represent these differences in a sympathetic manner. Children who are not members of an intercultural community can be provided with experiences that can result in a similar, although perhaps less complete, understanding of different racial and cultural characteristics. Under such conditions, these understandings may not be satisfactorily developed until after the primary phase is completed, but it is helpful if they can be developed at the beginning of the intermediate phase. Generalizations regarding phases of development in art expression depend upon a complex of factors among which is the immediate social and cultural environment. For example, a rich intercultural environment will be more likely to influence children to develop more differentiated understandings of people and to express these understandings in their art work.

It is possible to generalize about the differences that are characteristic of the art work done by primary-grade and older children. These differences are correlated with the children's developing awareness of their socio-cultural environment, and this growing awareness is correlated with the children's perceptive and sensorimotor skill. An increasingly differentiated motor skill is necessary to express increasingly differentiated image-symbols and increasingly complex ideas and responses to experience.

As children grow older they become increasingly skillful. Upper-grade children display more physical dexterity than do primary-grade children, but there is apparently some point at which skill ceases to change. Apparently, skill develops rapidly during the earliest years, as does the physical body. The most striking evidence of change comes at the beginning of the intermediate period, which occurs around the end of the eighth and the beginning of the ninth year. At this time, understanding and conception appear to exceed manipulative skill. This situation may be partly the result of previous training in technical and manipulative art processes.

In terms of the forces acting upon children, the formation of stereotypes and clichés is unnatural. Almost every aspect of a child's growth indicates a need for the development of creative imagination. Physical growth, growth in critical awareness, and sensitivity to socio-cultural forces require continuous adjustment by the child. If the goals of art education are used to guide the planning of the art education program, the child's growing becomes a rich experience full of educational opportunities.

GENERAL CONCLUSIONS REGARDING GROWTH PATTERNS

It is difficult to establish definite distinctions between the art forms produced by children of different ages in the lower grades because traits or tendencies that are considered to be characteristic of one age group are often found to be equally characteristic of another age group. However, unique and obvious distinctions can be observed in the art forms produced by children in the seventh and eighth grades. This uniqueness may result from the children's rapidly changing physical characteristics. Many of the physical changes expected in the seventh and eighth grades are not strongly evident until the children have entered the first recognizable stages of the adolescent phase. In the upper grades, it becomes evident that these changes are more easily recognized among girls than among boys.

In the upper grades, some noticeable distinctions in the productive work of the sexes may appear. These distinctions can easily be observed in the children's art work. The more rapid maturation of girls tend to form a pattern of behavior and performance, which is conditioned by recognizable cultural patterns. Since the sexual factor comes into being before children reach seventh or eighth grade, evidences of such biologically caused differences are sometimes found in the art work produced by boys and girls in the intermediate grades.[1]

In a very general way, it is possible to describe the art work of children in the intermediate and upper grades. However, because transitions between some recognizable phases of development during these stages are extremely subtle, it is not wise to make distinct separations between any of the recognizable phases. For this reason, it is not wise to base the planning of an art program on supposedly clear differences between age groups above the primary grades. In each phase of development, varying situations may cause individual differences and exceptions. The impossibility of knowing all of the qualifications and exceptions for every situation is one of the factors that makes all teaching a very creative enterprise. Life in our society is too complex and changeable to allow for accurate forecasting.

Qualifying factors that make the work of older children less subject to categorizing than the work of the younger children are:

1. Increases in the scope of the children's experience.
2. Greater awareness of the physical environment.

[1] The culturally caused differences that are found in the art work of boys and girls are discussed and illustrated in Chapter Nine. Our present discussion is concerned with the differences that are caused by biological factors.

3. Increasing manipulative skill.

4. Increasing familiarity with techniques and processes.

5. Increasing self-consciousness.

6. More critical attitudes toward their own work, as well as toward the work of other children in the group

7. Greater susceptibility to cultural influences.

8. Growing desires to be acceptable to the group. Such desires result in tendencies toward conformity, which strongly affect attitudes toward personal standards of accomplishment and achievement.

9. Increasing desires to achieve adult standards, although skills and experiences are not yet sufficiently advanced to make this goal easily attainable.

10. Increased structuring of personality characteristics results in increased potential for individual uniqueness.

RECORDING GROWTH IN CHILDREN'S ART FORMS

The art activities of older children are easier for the teacher to understand because histories of past performance are more extensive for this group. Younger children have not had time to accumulate such detailed patterns of growth and development. For this reason, it is important that we have records of what older children have accomplished during their primary-grade experiences. This kind of history will exist if primary-grade teachers prepare written records of the children's backgrounds or folders containing examples of the work individual children have done. Such work is most useful if it presents a picture of growth patterns. If a representative example of work from each stage of a child's development is kept in a folder, it will be possible for the upper- or intermediate-grade teacher to know the kind and rate of progress a particular child has made.

On the basis of information about a particular child or group of children, objectives can be established for a program of art education. For example, if a child persists in forming stereotypes, we know that he needs work that will encourage him to seek new forms with which to express his experiences. To provide such encouragement, the planning of the art education program for this child would be based on his need for exploring materials and ideas, for experimenting, and for improvising.

PLANNING IN TERMS OF CHILDREN'S GROWTH

The planning we do for children, in terms of their needs, is based on a concept of growth, change, and continuous flux. We now know that children are not static entities; consequently, we have to think of planning as a means for giving direction and purpose to their growing and changing. This concept of planning is important in all levels of elementary school and also in the upper grades, where it takes on added meaning.

If the planning of an art education program does not make provision for children's growth, some phase of the art activity might lag behind the physical, emotional, and intellectual understandings the children acquire. When this happens, there is a possibility that the children will find some aspects of their art activities inadequate. This inadequacy may manifest itself as the children's inability to find suitable expressive means for the needs they recognize as important to them. This inability may cause the children to develop inhibitions, fears, and a sense of inadequacy regarding their art abilities. Fear asserts itself as the fear of not being able to form a concept into a suitable metaphor. Inhibitions may be displayed as an unwillingness to experiment, to improvise, and to try new directions, methods, and techniques. In practice, we call this tendency "conservatism." In actuality, it is a product of the children's finding refuge in forms with which they have had earlier successes. This attitude often leads to dependence on stereotypes, which lose expressive force because they can't meet the needs of every new and unexpected experience.

CLASSIFICATION AND IDENTIFICATION OF OLDER CHILDREN'S ART

The first thing a teacher needs to know in order to accomplish planning that will discourage fear, stereotypes, and inhibitions is that children themselves are never stereotypes. There is really no "typical child," nor is there any rigid and typical expressional mode by which an age group can be identified. It is possible, however, to generalize about groups of children in particular social, economic, and physical environments as we demonstrated in our discussions regarding the work of primary-grade children. We know that certain kinds of forms made by very young children are often products of the children's physiological and neurological make-up. Because these factors continue to exert an influence on the children, as they mature, we can make use of them to form some very broad generalizations about older children. Such generalizations make it possible for us to describe, in a very general way, the work of the older age groups. However, it is important to remember that the older the group we are describing, the greater the need for qualification and specification of unique characteristics and conditions.

Before we can begin to plan effective art activities for post-primary-grade children, we must realize that older children are less subject to strict classification as "types" than are younger children. Comparisons made between the various art forms produced by older children are most valid if the comparisons are made in terms of patterns of flux and change. We can not acquire a reliable picture of the art of older children if we assume that their work can be described as typical expressional forms of their age group. The "typical" expressional modes are convenient myths and generalizations that must be qualified by cultural, emotional, physical, sociological, psychological, geographical, and any other factors that may influence children's behavior.

SELF-CONSCIOUSNESS IN OLDER CHILDREN'S ART WORK

Teachers in elementary school often note that the work of upper-grade children tends to be very self-conscious in comparison with the work of primary-grade children. This self-consciousness is often manifested as great concern with the techniques of representation. It is often felt that older children, with their increasing awareness, their developing self-consciousness, and their natural tendency to raise their own standards of accomplishment, become unsure of their ability to reach the goals they feel compelled to set for themselves. This unsureness contrasts sharply with the general observations we can make of the certainty, sureness, and lack of self-consciousness that is characteristic of the art work of younger children. It is interesting to note that younger children also show less self-consciousness in social situations than do pre- or early-adolescent children. In art activities, the increasing self-consciousness of older children is evidenced in their tight or cramped drawings, in their tendency to use monochromatic colors, and in their uncertainty about the best way to express an idea.

Some of the first evidences of tight and cramped art work may be found in the later phases of the primary-grade period. The art work of nine- and ten-year-old children frequently represents the children's efforts to make forms that are beyond their abilities. It is believed that older children often produce inexpressive art work because their conceptual skill may develop more rapidly than their manipulative skill and technical knowledge. The older children's realization of this shortcoming leads them to fear that they will not succeed in giving form to their conceptions.

One of the problems of art education planning for the intermediate and upper grades of elementary school is the need for a plan that will make it possible for children to continue in their ability to conceptualize, to find suitable image-symbols for their experiences, and to make effectively formed and structured metaphors that express their understandings, needs, and purposes.

The individual intermediate- and upper-grade child must feel that his productive work is expressive of his purposes. Because such expressive achievement requires skill, an effective art education program should provide the means for helping the older child select useful concepts for art expression. The older child needs to be able to find a means for establishing what he believes are valid relations between materials, forming processes, and the resulting art forms.

INTERACTION BETWEEN BEHAVIOR, PERSONALITY, AND ART ACTIVITY

In order to plan effectively for an art education program that will help older children engage in educationally useful art activities, it is necessary to know something about the relationship between older children and the processes of art activity. We have already noted that there is a pattern of growth that helps us recognize transitions from the art forms made by very young children to the art forms made by various groups of older children.

There is probably no specific characteristic that can be said to represent a distinctive change from the art of primary-grade children to the art of older children. We have noted that the most easily observed distinctions are those created as a result of the natural changes that are part of the children's growing processes. The most useful distinctions appear to exist in general modes of behavior among children. For example, we can begin with the observation that the modes of effective forming during art activity are more critically considered by older children than by younger children. We have seen that art activity for the very youngest children can be almost pure pleasure in the manipulative processes. We have also seen that increased interest in rationalization enters into the processes as younger children mature. The result of some of this application of the rational processes to art activity results in the establishment of relationships between experiences and art forms.

ART TECHNIQUES OF OLDER CHILDREN

Childhood techniques evidently end with childhood. The six-year-old child's techniques and modes of working are not useful modes for the seven- and eight-year-old child. In spite of our understanding that the modes of the youngest children have a freshness and naturalness too often lost in the work of older children, we must also be aware that little can be gained if we attempt to perpetuate these modes.

As children grow older, their increasing perceptiveness makes them more aware of how their efforts compare with the efforts of other people. It is this awareness that often causes older children to establish goals that are beyond their abilities. It is the responsibility of the teacher to help children know what standards they are ready to attempt to achieve. The teacher should help each group of children establish objectives and standards that are reasonable for them.

ASPECTS OF EMOTION IN OLDER CHILDREN'S ART ACTIVITY

Changes in emotional sensitivity influence the character of the art work of older children. Dur-

ing the growing processes, there may be many times when rational thinking processes and emotional motivations are not properly balanced. This problem is illustrated in the two kinds of work older children produce. Some of their art work can be too deliberative and analytical. Such art forms will be dull and lifeless; they will lack the power to convey depth of meaning and to inspire understanding as a product of the purpose of effective communication. On the other hand, many art forms made by older children may be too emotional, too spontaneous, or too uncontrolled by reason. In either case, an extreme of too much or too little reason or emotion results in unsatisfactory art activity. One of the teacher's main responsibilities is to help children explore both the emotional and rational qualities of life and to achieve a balance between the two qualities.

The teacher should help children develop qualitative emotional responses, which are profound, sensitive, and selective responses to experience. We have noted in discussions about the work and behavior of primary-grade children that a lack of self-consciousness makes it possible for them to maintain forcefulness, clarity, and a sparkling verve in their art expressions. This is a characteristic that should be developed as children grow older. For this reason, young children should be encouraged to develop their emotional life in a useful manner; they should not be forced to suppress their emotional responses. When children reach the intermediate-grade levels, they should be growing increasingly sensitive to the values and uses of qualitative emotional responses. ". . . if the child, adolescent or adult is to have a full and rich emotional life, if he is to continue to grow in conceptual, problem solving, and creative-thinking abilities, he needs to retain certain capacities for being fearful or angry, or inquisitive—not to mention certain capacities for joy and affection. The problem in emotional life is not one of elimination but of development. As the child matures the expression of emotion becomes more controlled and symbolic. That is, emotions take on a pattern through dynamic relationships with the thinking process. Like percepts and concepts, emotions become structural modes of response, organized through experience. As such they pervade the child's thinking—his play, his fears and dreams, his interpersonal relationships, his ethical views, his humorous and aesthetic concepts." [2]

A GENERAL SUMMARY

In our discussions of the work of primary-grade children, we described the way their physical development relates to expressive art activity, which is thought of as being at least partly the product of cultural characteristics, thinking, and feeling. Most important, our discussion emphasized the fact that the total pattern of both the younger and older children's lives and behavior must be understood in order to make possible useful understandings of the educational values of art activities.

The characteristics of children's art are changing characteristics. Because it is difficult to find rigid standards for all aspects of children's art activity, we describe the work of the youngest children according to the phases that generally represent the characteristics of their growth and change.

The major problem in our definition of the art of primary-grade groups is the problem of

[2] David H. Russell, *Children's Thinking* (Boston: Ginn & Company, 1956), p. 178.

establishing a specific time for each phase of the children's development—for example, a time for the early scribble phase, the late scribble phase, the gesture phase, the forming phase, and the phases in which effective metaphors are beginning to be made. These phases in the development of childern's art activity can be recognized, but they can not be categorized in terms of specific age groups or time periods.

The problem of knowing when art work done in elementary school is typical of intermediate- and upper-grade children is confused by the increasing complexity of the older children's thoughts and emotions. For this reason, the art of intermediate- and upper-grade children is not as easy to describe as the art of primary-grade children. Description is possible; however, as children grow older, increasing numbers of qualifying factors that may vary within schools, communities, and cultures come into being. During the course of our discussion, we shall find that the art forms made by older children are different from those made by younger primary-grade children. Because the older children's art forms are less easily placed in categories, it is not likely that we will be able to establish as simple a developmental pattern for their art as we did for the younger children's art.

Sixteen

EMOTION AND FEELING IN CHILDREN'S ART

Emotion in children's art develops in the same way that their art evolves: from the unstructured, uncertain, and amorphous to the formed or the qualitatively and purposefully structured metaphor.

A purpose of the art education program should be to develop emotional responses that are the products of multisensory activity. The art education program should be planned to provide opportunities for children to learn to form useful emotional patterns from the many different kinds of sensory experience.

EMOTIONAL AND RATIONAL QUALITIES

Emotions are an important part of the expression in children's art work. If we attempt to separate and define the emotional and nonemotional aspects of children's art work, we will surely experience difficulties. What may appear to be emotional to the adult may be something the child made by accident. It may very well happen that for the child there is no real distinction between the emotional and rational aspects of his work.

The teacher will often feel a need to make distinctions between the emotional and rational qualities in children's art work. If some guide could be developed, some standards for determining when a child's work of art is overly emotional or rational, it might be possible for the teacher to help the child gain a better balance between the two elements.

A child may make a picture of a circus. The teacher should ask the child to tell the class what the circus is like. It might be best to wait until the picture has been started, for after the art activity is underway, the teacher can take note of the kinds of things that are in the painting. Among some older children, the work will perhaps be tight and cramped. Figures will be drawn with hesitation. Much time will be given to outlining objects, hesitatingly, with pencil lines. This hesitation in picture making is some indication that the effort of making the picture is taking precedence over the emotional exhilaration experienced at the circus. To help the child express his feelings about the circus, the teacher should ask questions. "Was there a lot of noise at the circus?" "What did the trapeze performers do?" "What did you see when one of the acrobats let go, when he seemed to fly through the air and was caught by another acrobat on another swinging trapeze?" "Show me the direction and the speed of the trapeze performer as he flew from one bar to another." "What colors did you see while the acrobats were performing?" "What were the clowns like?" "What were the colors of their costumes?" "Do you remember their noses?" "What did the clowns wear on their heads?"

The solution to the problem of making a picture about an experience involves rational understandings. The rational qualities in a child's art work might be defined as the technical means used to make the pictorial form. These rational qualities include methods for making objective statements and for recording data. The emotional qualities might be defined as the manner in which technical processes are used to give form to a concept, to make possible the existence of a poetic metaphor. From this point of view, the emotional qualities escape definition. We expect the emotional aspect to be a poetic metaphor, the unique expression of one child's response to his own experience. It is impossible for us to define the form of such an expression before it is made because a unique form must be unexpected; it must be a form that never existed before in exactly the same way. From this point of view, the emotional aspect is the product of imaginative thinking; and the role of imaginative thinking is to give meaning to emotional responses to ideas, experiences, or concepts.

The more proficient art work produced by older children may be the result of their familiarity with materials, tools, and processes. Familiarity makes it easier for children to find techniques that make the expression of emotion increasingly effective. This kind of effective emotional expression may not be as possible in the work of younger children because they have not yet acquired enough knowledge of objective techniques, which is a knowledge of tools, materials, and processes. As children mature they learn that different methods can be used to achieve certain kinds of expressional requirements. Growth in expressional skill implies increasing ability to find suitable technical means to express emotional and intellectual responses to experience. The purely technical painting, the art work that is a product of a developed skill, is not our objective.

In the early work of primary-grade children, less skill may be evident than in the work of older children. Among the younger children, the teacher should be concerned with their ability to know, to appreciate, and to give meaning and purpose to experience. Technical means for the expression of experience and concepts will be developed as a result of the children's need to give form to experience and concepts. Children's pictures are not made for their own sakes; they are made as a result of the children's need to complete their experiences by providing them with direction, form, and increased understanding.

Emotion, feeling, and rational understandings interact with the rational means required for painting a picture or shaping a sculpture. At its highest level, in the work of the artist, emotion can be expressed through a sophisticated interaction between emotion and reason. This kind of interaction was described in our discussion of Picasso's "Guernica." [1]

How can the teacher guide children in their use of emotion and reason? The first thing the teacher must do is respect the individual child's subjective judgments. If a child "feels" that his

[1] See Chapter Nine.

method of working is right, he should be permitted to develop his work according to his judgments. However, it is the teacher's responsibility to ask questions in order to make the child think about what he is doing. Guidance of this kind can take place when the teacher believes the child has reached a stage when he can be helped to understand what he has done, when he can begin to think about other directions for forming his purposes, or when his purposes can be redefined. For example, if a child uses a certain combination of colors, he might be asked to notice the colors of objects in his own surroundings and to think about whether or not the color combination he used really contributes to the purposes he established for his painting. Or the teacher might show the child a painting by a great artist, pointing out the artist's use of color and asking the child to tell how this use of color helped the artist achieve his purpose in the painting.

It is not unusual for primary-grade children to make some objects too much larger than other objects. Children may make figures of people or animals many times larger than trees or houses because of the importance they attach to the figures. For example, fathers are often drawn as very big men because of their perceived stature from a child's point of view. Sometimes this sense of importance as shown in size is culturally inspired. Or it might just happen that the largest object in a picture is the first object the child draws. If this is the case, the other objects the child adds to the picture have to be smaller because the first object takes up most of the room. The child expresses emotion in his picture in this way because the first object drawn is usually the object the child considers most important. If the child changes his opinion of the relative importance of the objects after his picture is completed, the picture will no longer be a true expression of his emotions. Nevertheless, such a picture will still be useful to the extent that the experience of creating it acted upon the child's emotions.

Children may maintain rational or irrational concepts with a great degree of emotional conviction. Because such convictions are notable for the short duration of their emotional intensity, the teacher need not be overly distressed by children's convictions regarding the rightness of their seeming irrationalities. It is the teacher's

responsibility to help children understand their irrational concepts and to provide suggestions and guidance that will lead the children to new and meaningful approaches to expression. The teacher should realize that children's emotional convictions, which often seem like downright stubbornness, can be very useful if they are directed to form a basis for improved understandings. We have already seen that in art activity, and in most useful thinking and learning processes, emotional conviction gives force to the art education processes and it gives life and meaning to art expression.

In light of our understanding of the teacher's role in using the logic and irrationalities of children for educative purposes, we shall now consider how the teacher can direct the development of logical and illogical thinking. It is important that the teacher realize that children's illogical or irrational thinking should be explored rather than discarded because:

1. What might at first appear to be irrational to the teacher could actually be a child's approach to understanding. For this reason, it is wise to explore the meaning of the child's concepts. It might happen that the child is simply approaching understanding in terms of his own level of development.

2. The seeming irrationality of a child's thinking and expression could actually be a satisfactory mode for the expression of a valid emotional response to experience. In this sense, the value of the response might be based on the child's level of growth. What is valid for a child, and a child's thinking, may not be valid for an adult. This understanding can easily be justified by the educational cliché, which is also an educational truism, that we must take children from where they are.

The expression of irrationalities in children's art creates confusion among adults but seldom among children. In the art work of primary-grade children, we can recognize stereotyped patterns, which are rarely acceptable to adults as representations of visual experience. It may very well be that a child will realize that his own purposes are not always acceptable to adults. For this reason, the teacher should take time to consider whether a child is satisfying his own needs or merely trying to do what he knows adults want him to do.

An excellent example of an irrationality that

is useful to children is the typical sky-line and ground-line concept in children's art. Children often paint the sky as a line of color at the top of the paper and the ground as a line of color at the very bottom of the paper. All objects that are normally earthbound are placed on the ground-line. Between the ground-line and the sky-line is the world of childhood, where each part of the world assumes a relation to space that the child believes is correct according to logical adult standards. The sun or moon is located in the open space below and close to the sky-line. The sun is relatively far above the earth or the ground-line. All objects of the earth, such as people, animals, flowers, trees, and houses are securely located on the ground-line, from which they extend upward into the space above the earth. The earth does not extend behind the objects belonging on the earth.

Although the ground-line and sky-line mode of representation appears correct according to the child's sensations of knowing and feeling, we know that it is not correct according to the facts of visual experience. It would be difficult, however, for us to try to explain why the child is wrong. We might have to buttress our argument with technical explanations of the facts of linear perspective. Such an explanation would be difficult because it is based on the modes for pictorially describing optical illusions. The child can counter with the argument that, when standing, we are perpendicular to the earth. The sky is above us; it never really touches the rim of the earth. In fact, the sky never exists behind us or behind a tree or a house. The sky is above all of the earthly objects that are such common paraphernalia in the drawings and paintings of primary-grade children.

Some writers on the subject of children's drawings believe it is ridiculous to assume that children draw only what they know. Children's range of knowledge is too limited for them to construct abstractions, such as the ground- and sky-line, for the things they "know" to be "true." Teachers sometimes assume that children draw a ground- and sky-line because they are beginning to learn how to write between two guide lines.

It is important to realize that children frequently begin to use ground- and sky-lines while they are still in kindergarten before they begin to learn to write between guide lines or on ruled or lined paper. It is also important to note that children locate their objects in a rational manner between the sky- and ground-line. The heads of their figures do not touch the sky-line in the same manner that the tops of the letters they learn to write must touch the top of the guide lines on a ruled page. In the same manner, objects not earthbound, such as the sun, touch neither the top nor bottom line, but are located at a reasonable distance from both lines. There is a logic in these space relationships that has nothing in common with the problems of writing between lines. The most important thing about this logic is that it is a logic of relationships. The influence of the writing experience is of small importance.

It is possible to find multitudes of reasons why children superimpose a rational relationship upon the irrational sky- and ground-line mode of representation. Some understandings of this phenomenon may be useful for the development of valid art education programs. We have reason to believe that the ground-line and sky-line modes of representation contain a useful logic for children. If the children don't have a conscious understanding of this logic, much may be gained by pointing it out to them. By taking this kind of positive approach, rather than demonstrating the faults of what adults conceive to be an irrationality, a teacher might gain a useful means for aiding the children's emotional and intellectual growth.

Our first approach to children's typical irrationalities should be to help them see the usefulness of their peculiar brand of logic. The value of their logic is derived from our understanding of the essential rightness of their space relationships and their concept of ground- and sky-line pictorialism. The children's feeling of rightness could be destroyed if we were to impose upon them understandings about optical perspective. With this feeling lost, all that would remain would be an intellectual understanding, a technique.

SOURCES OF EMOTIONAL BEHAVIOR

Children's emotions develop in much the same way as their drawings develop, that is, from the amorphous and uncontrolled to the structured. Structured emotion is defined as emotion ordered by rationality.

Unlike other aspects of children's growth that

are important to art activity, emotion is only partly acquired through experience. Many emotional responses are involuntary. Much emotional behavior is cultural in origin. The quality of some emotional responses may be acquired as the result of heredity. Inherited emotional characteristics are significant because they may contribute to the intensity and quality of emotional responses that are otherwise nurtured, formed, and developed.

USES OF EMOTION IN THE ART PROGRAM

Emotions may interfere with the critical aspects of the productive thinking processes. Such interference results from the lack of a properly directed and guided program for individual and group evaluation. In a carefully guided productive thinking process, the effect of emotion on thinking may be highly desirable. An important function of the art program is to provide an effective means for correlating rational thinking processes with emotion. We can carry this understanding even further by saying that irrationality may sometimes generate a useful emotionality, which in turn may be structured in a satisfactory manner by rational processes. Figure 16-1, a chalk drawing of an airplane, is an excellent example of this kind of structuring. To the child, the airplane is a thing of the upper spaces; it floats above the earth. Even when it is not in motion,

the child believes it must be located in the space above us. This concept itself is an irrationality that results from the child's lack of experience with airplanes. The child's irrationality, nevertheless, finds a rational solution to the problem of entering the airplane. This solution consists of the ladder that hangs from the bottom of the airplane.

The child's feeling for spatial relationships causes him to locate the airplane in space to make it hover above earth and mountain, alongside the sun, and beneath the blue sky. In this simple manner, the child uses the ground-line and sky-line symbolically to represent a spatial concept, which contains a felt symbolism. The child's sense of space and of the airplane's location in space is continuously qualified by his rational understandings. For example, because the child has heard that airplanes must roll along the ground on a runway before they take off into upper space, he has provided the airplane with adequate wheels.

EMOTIONAL BASIS OF CONCEPT FORMATION

The child's feeling about the airplane as a thing that hovers in space, his representation of techniques for entering such a vehicle, and the symbolism he uses to describe these concepts evolves from an emotional base. In this sense, feeling and emotion interact to form the concept.

16-1. AIRPLANE
Chalk. *Author's collection.*

16-2. FIREMEN FIGHTING A FIRE
Chalk. *Author's collection.*

Emotion guides feeling, which generates a sensitivity to relationships and symbols that are suitable for expressing the child's sensation of what "feels right" in combination with his conceptions of the facts of gravity and space.

KINAESTHESIA AND EMOTIONS

Emotions tend to guide sensitivities, which are expressed with kinaesthetic means. This kind of emotional motivation to forming is well illustrated in Figure 16-2, where the sense of the third dimension is emotionally rather than logically perceived. The firemen fight the fire by bending every effort toward directing the water into the fire. It is as if the force and pressure of the movements themselves will snuff out the flames that oppose the fire fighters. The fire directs the lines

of its consuming flames toward the hoses, the ladders, and the firemen. Note that the firemen, the ladders, the hoses, and the fire trucks are represented as solid masses of color and line. The burning house, on the other hand, is drawn with a light line and lacks solid masses of color; it is insubstantial. In this way, the strong and the consumed are unconsciously described, emotionally felt, and kinaesthetically symbolized.

PROPORTIONS AND SIZE AS INDICATORS OF EMOTION AND FEELING

We have already noted that the proportions children use in their drawings are often indicative of their feelings. Feelings and emotions guide children in giving emphasis to parts of their metaphoric structures. This emphasis can be achieved by variations in sizes, by making important objects large and less important objects smaller. During the earliest phases of child development in art, when qualitative emotional factors are in a very raw state, size relations may be determined as much by undeveloped motor skills as they are by emotional attitudes that are not subject to much critical thinking.

Children's natural inclinations to express feelings through size variations can be educationally useful. The teacher's problem is to find a means for helping children add a useful degree of rationality to their natural means for expressing their feelings. One simple means for making children aware of the facts of size relations is to have them observe and report. Such activity might be done in group sessions. This kind of observing and reporting can provide children with a basis for evaluating their art work. Another effective way to teach a group of children about the facts of visual size relations is to encourage conceptions of size relations in terms of the children's communication needs and purposes in art expression. This procedure must take into account the important requirement that more than one sensory mode be involved in all art activity. Children usually want to know how a thing feels, smells, sounds, etc. The teacher should help children recognize and use the sensory modes that are most useful for the expression of a particular experience.

Generalizations about children's methods for establishing size relationsips need continuous qualification. Size relationships in children's art do not always result from emotional attitudes. During the earliest phases of the primary-grade period, it is possible that visually inaccurate size relationships may result from children's natural inability to grasp the totality of a concept. According to Helga Eng, children have a ". . . feeble capacity for synthesis; they cannot, when occupied with drawing the details, retain a grasp of the whole. The parts are drawn piece by piece without taking the total effect into account." [2] It must be realized that children's inability to conceive of wholes and their lack of awareness of the need to establish effective relationships be-

tween parts provides them with freedom to be guided by emotion. On the other hand, children are not always unable to estimate relative sizes and proportions correctly. During the stage of rational thinking when they are able to make use of geometric structuring, children can correctly appraise relative proportions and sizes when they are asked to do so; however, their habit of allowing their emotions to guide their understandings persists and many children continue to produce illogical size relationships. The teacher should encourage the children to balance their emotions with rational thought to produce logical proportions and size relationships in their art work.

EMOTIONS AND MULTISENSORY EXPERIENCE

Size concepts are most useful when they combine emotion plus multisensory perceptions. The senses of smell, sight, touch, and hearing can direct emotional attitudes that, in turn, interact with processes of thinking about the formation and structuring of complete metaphors.

The significance of this understanding regarding the relation of size perception to emotional perception is strengthened when we understand that concepts of size are not, during the more advanced phases of the primary-grade period, formed during a moment of visual perception. Size concepts may be cultural, economic, or social. Concepts of size, as well as of space, depth, and distance, are the products of many sided experiences. Size variations may be the products of emphasis that is emotionally inspired. The expression of emotion through size variations may have sources in cultural, psychological, physiological, or environmental factors.

LINES AND EMOTIONS

The way children use lines in the early phases of their art work may be indicative of the existence of useful emotional forces. Expressive lines may begin as graphs of a gesture. Lines form graphs of gestures when the gestures are charted by being made intrinsic parts of a drawing or painting motion. A gesture is the kinaesthetic part of a multisensory response. It is an effective means for communicating responses or emotional reactions to experience.

[2] Helga Eng, *The Psychology of Children's Drawings*, p. 163.

The variety of sensory responses expressed by a gesture, or by combinations of gestures, may be indicative of the emotional depth of a child's experience. A gesture, and its painted or drawn equivalent, is vital in proportion to its ability to communicate a rich texture of emotional overtones.

Lines become a means for describing the rhythm of a gesture. Especially in paintings by children, lines often comprise the direction of a mass. This rhythmic movement of mass is actually motivated by the same expressive gesturing that gives a rhythmical line its energy. The width of the brush used very often causes masses to become extensions of lines in children's art work. This curious characteristic is evident in a typical painting such as Figure 18-2. In this case, the masses bear the marks of the linear intent. For example, the mass in the upper left shows the linear brush strokes from which the mass is made. The drawing of the face itself is made from wide lines rather than masses. The linear mass begins as eyes and a nose at the center of a linear spiral and then becomes many masses in the outer shape of the face. From here, the child gradually evolves masses from the natural character of his wide brush. If a pencil or pen had been used instead of a brush, this figure would have been a line drawing rather than a painting made up of colored masses. The emotional impact of the painting is derived from the rhythmical and linear flow of the brushed masses rather than from the fact that the painting itself is composed of masses. In other words, the structure of the painting is linear, its framework is a skeleton of linear movements, which find origins in the expressive and descriptive gestures made by the child. In terms of the emotional force of this painting, we know that the gestures are the products of a motivation that caused the child to re-enact, with paint and brush, the action of sweeping and cleaning.[3]

The art work of the kindergarten period is less likely to exhibit a variety of sensory responses and emotional depth than the more mature work of primary-grade children. For example, Figure 18-2 is mainly a painting of movement sensa-tions, which are associated with the motivation that led to the painting, the discussion and class-room dramatization of the school cleanup campaign. Sensory responses other than those related to the actions of cleaning are not noticeable in this painting. It seems logical to assume that the sensations of movement the children learned during the school cleanup campaign are the only sensations that are expressed in this painting. On the other hand, Figure 18-5 clearly communicates an image of a little girl with very long, wavy, and well-combed hair. Combined with this image-symbol is a total metaphor that emerges from a young girl's fascination with long, wavy hair and her excitement with caring for her hair. The texture of the hair is clearly indicated and the total metaphor emerges as a rendering of feelings about the child and the cosmetic quality of her hair rather than as a purely visual image of a child with long hair. A similar emotional depth is easily found in such works as the painting of the circus, Figure 5-2. In this painting, the qualities of colorfulness, acrobatic action, and the magic of the circus as seen through the eyes of children find expression in the images of flowers, exaggerated movements in the figures, exaggerated sizes, the rhythmical flow of line and mass, texture, and vivid color.

In children's art, lines appear to be used most frequently as expressions of the kinaesthetic response. However, mass is also often used in much the same way to express the kinaesthetic response. When used in this way, mass is the product of a linear effort. We have seen how this translation of line into mass takes place in paintings such as Figure 18-2. At a more elementary level, this phenomenon is exhibited in the emerging geometricity of the scribble painting as in Figure 18-1.

On the basis of our examples, it seems reasonable to conclude that line is the ancestor of the expressive mass in early child art. As the product of a gesture, lines or related masses may express feeling, emphasis, direction, size, shape, force, energy, character, or structure. The vitality of each of these qualities is determined by their emotional content.

The significance of the multisensory and emotional aspects of lines in early child art becomes a possible guide for the development of

---

[3] Similar characteristics, in a sophisticated form, are found in the work of Franz Kline.

goals in curriculum planning. For example, we find that drawing is most useful if it is an expression of qualitative emotional responses to experience. We know that drawing may begin with lines, which may serve as the basis for forming masses. However, the vitality of lines or masses will be determined by precognitive experience, by rationality serving as a brake on irrational or uncritically spontaneous responses to experiences.

Our understanding of the function of lines as the products of expressive gestures in early child art must also lead us to the realization that drawing as pure representation of visual experience may become a mere outline of visually perceived masses. Such outline drawing is lacking in emotional depth. The omission of multisensory experience causes the lines to lack emotional power. To avoid such outlined forms, proper motivation must be provided in the classroom. For example, the teacher can encourage the children to dramatize their experiences, perhaps through role playing, in order to help them develop a greater awareness of the many modes of knowing that are available to them.

An important objective in early child art education is to reinforce the children's sense of line as a gesture of expressive forming and communication. From this point of view, line is conceived as expressive rhythm. Expressive rhythms communicate meanings as an integral part of image-symbol structuring, that is, as an essential part of the formed metaphor.

COLOR AND EMOTION

The fact that color appears to have little intellectual significance in the art of the early kindergarten period contrasts with the large emphasis adults place on the function of color as a means for communicating emotion. During the later parts of the primary-grade period, color may be used to communicate feelings in terms of culturally inspired symbols. For example, in our culture blue-violet may symbolize profound melancholy, red danger, white purity, yellow cowardice, and green envy.

SUMMARY

Emotion and the sensitivities that generate emotions may be expressed in the art work of children in the following ways:

1. Through gestures reflected in the rhythms of kinaesthesia.
2. Through suitable symbols, which are not necessarily representational but which suit the symbolic purpose (such as Figures 18-2 and 18-5).
3. Through size differentiation.
4. Through modes for establishing relations between parts.

A lack of feeling and emotion can be noted in work in which precognitive thought has been partially or completely destroyed by an overabundance of conscious thought. When this happens, the rhythmical movements of effective kinaesthesia are lost. The result is a tight, cramped, and stilted drawing.

A function of the program of art education during the primary-grade period is to provide the emotional responses of children with quality. This purpose will be achieved if children can develop means for using their emotional responses in constructive ways. Emotional behavior must not be destroyed; it must be used as a means for providing children with understanding and recognition of the need for constructive expression and achievement. In art activity, emotional drives accomplish the following:

1. They motivate the forming of symbols that are expressive of feelings, concepts, and thoughts.
2. They direct the effective structuring of forms, that is, they give vitality to structured forms.
3. They provide the energy necessary for the completion of a concept and for its formation in physical materials.
4. They increase sensitivity to make sure that the most useful selections are made from experience.

Seventeen

INTERRELATION OF THE SENSORY RECEPTORS

The mutually supportive interaction of many senses is necessary for the development of an educationally valid art activity. Our understandings of the educational values of art activity are helped when we become aware of the manner in which all of the senses interact and strengthen each other during processes of precognitive and productive thinking.

We have previously noted that the visual experience alone can not provide an individual with sufficient information and knowledge to make possible the creation of educationally useful art forms. In actual practice visual experience becomes most useful when it is supplemented by the activity of other sensory receptors.

The unified action of the senses during processes of perceptual experience is the result of a physiological phenomenon. Understandings of the physiological basis of sensory activity will prove valuable in providing us with the knowledge necessary to construct guides for the organization of an educationally valid art program.

PHYSIOLOGY OF SENSORY ACTIVITY

The unified action of the sensory receptors takes place in a network of neurons in the lower mid-brain. This network is made up of interconnections, which form a structure known as the reticular formation.

The reticular formation is divided into two parts; one part is devoted to sensations ascending to the cortex and the other part is devoted to sensations descending from the cortex. These two parts are referred to as the ascending and descending reticular formations. Impulses received from the various sensory receptors, such as the eyes, ears, nose, skin, etc., ascend to the cortex by way of the ascending reticular formation and are then distributed to the various parts of the brain. The cortex is activated by neural impulses from the ascending neural formation.

The interrelatedness of the neural responses to sensory perception is largely the result of the ability of simple sensory responses to alert all parts of the brain. The old concept of the brain as a central switchboard alerted by separated and insulated nerve fibers, much in the manner of a system of telephone wires, simply does not exist in the human organism. In actuality, when a neural impulse is received from one receptor, it is spread over more than one section of the brain. In many areas in the human body, particularly along the paths of conduction to the brain, in the sensory organs, and in the brain itself, what happens in one area causes a modifying and supplemental action to occur in another area.

IMPLICATIONS FOR ART EDUCATION

A useful program of art education should properly evaluate the significance to art education processes of the functions of the ascending reticular formation. This evaluation must be conducted in terms of the content of precognitive and productive thinking. The experiences that make up these processes are essentially visual. Our knowledge of the functions of the ascending reticular formation indicates that a set of purely visual sensations can not be sustained unless the neural impulses from the ". . . ascending reticular formation are diffusely discharged into [the] cortex at the same time." [1]

The physical structure of the human being emphasizes the need for planners of art educa-

[1] Krech and Crutchfield, *Elements of Psychology,* p. 491.

tion programs to be fully aware of the interaction of many senses, of how the total human is formed and conditioned by the diverse aspects of his environment: the physical, the socio-cultural, and the economic. The interaction of the senses in art activity carries implications for the development of art education curricula. Possible illustrations of the way in which these implications are reflected in program planning may be found in the curriculum for the Bauhaus.

The art program of the Bauhaus was designed, in part, to encourage sensory interaction and to make this interaction qualitative. Sensory activity was directed toward the manipulation of tools and materials. The correctness of this method seems to be verified by the information available to us today regarding the physiology of sensory activity.

NATURE OF VISUAL PERCEPTION

We know that during the processes of visual perception an impulse is received from the retina. When this impulse is sent into the reticular formation, the entire cortex is alerted. The descending reticular formation plays a surprising role during this process of sensory activity. This formation first receives signals from the cortex; then, it transmits these signals to the fibers from the receptors. The result is that signals ascending and descending the reticular formation meet each other. A sensory impulse originating with the eyes may block an impulse originating with the ears. As a result, the action of one sensory receptor may prevent another sensory impulse from reaching the cortex. For example, if an individual is completely absorbed in a visual experience, it may not be possible for him to hear someone talking to him. In other words the individual's entire sensory apparatus may be absorbed in one activity.

Because of the functional structure of the human reticular formation, our perceptions are inclined to be strengthened by sensory interaction. On the basis of this knowledge of the human sensory apparatus it is possible for us to conclude that our perceptions are rich in memories, past experiences, and emotional qualities, and that the usefulness of this organization is largely a result of the interrelatedness of the senses.

SENSORY ACTIVITY AND PRODUCTIVE WORK

The interaction of the senses is noteworthy in terms of its influence on productive thinking. Since the richness of our store of precognitions depends on experiences gained through sensory perception, the interaction of the senses enriches our productive thinking processes.

EVIDENCE OF SENSORY INTERACTION IN GROUP PAINTING

The earliest work of children, especially the work of children in the preschool stage, is notable for the awkwardness with which sensory activity is correlated with productive work and thought. It is possible that sensory activity is so completely related that children are unable to distinguish between types of sensory perception. It is not uncommon for a young child to investigate new things, objects, and experiences, by touching, looking, smelling, tasting, and manipulating.

Most preschool and primary-grade art work displays evidence of the children's general inability to represent the interrelatedness of sensory experience in their art products. The paintings of a bus trip, Figures 17-3 and 17-4, are excellent examples of this problem. Figures 17-1, 17-2, 17-3, and 17-4 all indicate that the children's sense of touch, their response to tactile sensations, was given little consideration. Available evidence leads us to believe that children do not translate the tactile sensation into paint unless they are guided to do so. Children's concern with tactile sensations becomes most evident when they are given different kinds of materials, and are asked to cut or tear them into planned shapes to be used to organize a picture.

The paintings illustrated here are typical be-

17-1. PAINTING BY NANCY
Author's collection.

17-2. PAINTING BY JOHN
Author's collection.

17-3. PAINTING OF BUS TRIP
Author's collection.

causc thcy demonstrate that the children's only concern with tactility is with the tactility of the art materials themselves. Apparently the children do not feel that it is possible or necessary to convey sensations of touch with paint. This general lack of concern with the expression of tactility might result from the children's frustrated attempts to represent the sensation. In the painting by Nancy (Figure 17-1) and in the painting by John (Figure 17-2) there is some indication of an attempt to paint an irregular surface. In discussions, Nancy first said that the irregular marks were "spots." One of the other children in the class said he thought they were the children in the bus. The teacher asked why some of the spots were yellow, some orange, and some blue. Nancy then said that the spots represented children's hair, to which another child responded that nobody in the group had orange or blue hair.

The child who painted Figure 17-3 was asked what the little curved lines covering the surface of his painting were supposed to represent. He said they represented all of the children. It must be noted that the child said this after he had listened to the discussion regarding the spots painted by Nancy.

When John was asked why he did not paint any of the children in his picture of the bus, he said that all of the children were in the bus and, consequently, could not be seen.

None of these paintings display any conscious effort to represent tactility. In each case, the child's explanation for the irregular surfaces was given in terms of a description of the picture as a replica of experience.

Observation of the children's processes of painting Figures 17-1, 17-2, 17-3, and 17-4 seems to indicate that their points of emphasis, in terms of sensory activity and expression, were as follows:

1. There was a concern with the manipulation of the paint.
2. In each case, a concentrated effort was made to represent the bus and the children in it.
3. The concern with representation was repeatedly forgotten and the art processes, during periods of nonrepresentational concern, became dominated by the rhythmical movements of a brush on paper.

The first factor, the manipulation of the paint, was largely a matter of attempting to control the paint as it dripped on the floor and of keeping it from dripping on the paper and spreading out of control. The difficulty in paint manipulation caused the children to scrub the paint drips on the paper with a brush. This scrubbing usually assumed a side-to-side motion or a semicircular motion closely related to the scribbling processes observed to take place in the art of very young children. During the process of scrubbing, the children's attention often wandered; they would

17-4. PAINTING OF BUS TRIP
Author's collection.

forget their original purpose and their attention would become centered upon scribbles or semi-circular manipulations of the brush. This side-tracking of the original purpose (to paint the bus experience) is evident in all of the paintings made by this group. For example, the painting by the boy who did Figure 17-4 is dominated by three large semicircular masses, one at the bottom left, another just above it and toward the pictorial center, and another just below and toward the bottom right. In each case, the semicircular masses are overlaid with several coats of paint. The mass on the top right is dominated by a number of short strokes whose rhythm is lost to the picture because they are different in color from the strokes under them. This rhythmical pattern serves a number of interesting purposes. During part of the painting process, the strokes making up the pattern were attempts to erase drippings of paint; at another point they became an expression of the child's concern with pure rhythm. This process, which continued because it became pleasurably kinaesthetic, caused the short curved strokes that cover the surface of the painting. In a very interesting fashion, this kinaesthetic manipulative process provided the child with a means for leading into his representational purpose. The pleasurable movement sensations combined with the child's effort to form a sense of depth and space related to his understanding of the volume and structure of the bus, as well as to his recollections of the bus trip experience.

We have some evidence that the tendency of children to concentrate on one aspect of a problem causes all other aspects to be blocked out. Such evidence is particularly notable in the painting by John. John said that the inside of the bus was very big. He began his painting by making a large orange curve for the top of the bus, which he followed by two orange sides. The shorter green curve on top of the orange roof seems to have been a concern of all of the children. In Figure 17-1, this section is the area in which the symbols for the children are placed. This placement is typically illogical. During the course of the painting process, the child appeared to lose feeling for the relationships between the parts of the bus experience. The same curious phenomenon occurs in the painting by John (Fig-ure 17-2). In John's painting, the depth of the bus, which to a child is very great, is represented through John's inept use of an extension of the mass of paint used to paint the interior void. This extension becomes a diagonal mass extending out from the right side of the bus. In Figure 17-4, the main section of the bus is the rectangle in the lower right of the painting. However, this area has been covered by the child's process of painting a curving mass to cover the paint drippings and related short curved strokes of his kinaesthetic experience. This process left room in the upper area of the painting for the children in the bus. The child who painted Figure 17-4 recognized this area as the necessary void associated with the interior of the bus.

In Figure 17-4, the kinaesthetic sensations of painting curved masses in an attempt to cover drips of paint is later translated (on the left side of the painting) into an effort to represent the bus as three-dimensional. This attempt to represent three-dimensionality is more detailed than that made by John because it includes the location of the bus driver in relation to the children in the bus. The child who painted this picture knew that the bus driver was located at the front of the bus. In accordance with the driver's importance, he is painted to appear very large. The child painted the driver's head with a rhythmical transfer of kinaesthetic brush strokes. The rest of the driver's figure was not painted because of the child's loss of interest, which may have been caused by his recognition of the difficulty of the representational problem. Below the bus driver's head are a number of strokes that were a beginning effort to represent his hands on a steering wheel. Below these brush strokes is a square mass, which was intended to represent the bus' radiator. In a curious manner, the driver is represented as sitting at the front of the bus on the left side of the painting and the children are mislocated beside him as symbols for the interior volume of the bus. Most significant is the evidence of a rhythmical attempt to represent the receding dimension of the bus area behind the driver. In both Figures 17-2 and 17-4, a searching effort to combine rhythmical movement sensations with a concept of three-dimensional space is evident.

The interrelation of sensory activity is largely derived from role playing and group discussion.

During the course of the painting of Figures 17-1, 17-2, 17-3, and 17-4, there was much discussion by the children about what they were trying to do. As they painted, the children became frustrated in their efforts to relate the several sensory experiences associated with their subject. In order to make up for this deficiency they dramatized their desire and need for correlated sensory experience by talking, acting, and naming the unexpected and unplanned results of their unconscious and uncontrolled kinaesthetic rhythms.

The function of kinaesthesia and its tendency to overpower the original purpose of representation is illustrated in a more extreme manner by the painting made by Nancy, Figure 17-1. Nancy began her painting with the large form in the center, which was intended to represent the bulk of the bus. She then attempted to represent the windows with the open oval form painted in almost the exact center of her paper. By the time she reached this point, her kinaesthetic sense began to dominate and her representational purpose diminished rapidly. The overpowering influence of kinaesthesia is indicated in this painting in a most interesting manner by the rhythmical repetition of the oval window form, like a smaller teardrop, on the upper right side of the picture. In the first oval form, Nancy had been thinking about the bus window and she painted a face looking out of the window. She later returned to this face and, not recognizing it as a part of her original purpose, she blocked it out. At this point, the painting became completely dominated by movement sensations and Nancy began to think in terms of colored forms. The discussion around her about the bus, however, caused her to recall her purpose and she made a brief and destructive effort to paint the floor of the bus on the upper left side of her painting. This effort completely destroyed the rhythmical flow of line and color that was just beginning to dominate her painting.

OBSERVATIONS

Our observation of the children painting their bus trip experience revealed several interesting and typical things about sensory interaction in the art activity of young primary-grade children.

1. In the art of kindergarten and first-grade children, manipulation of materials and concepts is very important.

2. During the early primary-grade period, children have a fairly well developed sense of three-dimensional space and they make an effort to express this understanding. It is expressed most frequently as a feeling for movement through space. This expression assumes the form of a gesture that is related to gestures from the earlier stages of circular scribbling.

3. A lack of skill in the representation of space and the location of objects in space does not lead to frustrations too frequently at this stage of child development. It is interesting to note that the children's efforts to represent space are made in terms of sensations of movement through space rather than in terms of a recession in space expressed by typical perspective techniques or color changes. The children's search for a suitable means for representing space leads to the exploitation of kinaesthesia rather than to the discovery of purely intellectual means, such as linear or aerial perspective. Note should also be made of the similarity between the children's method of kinaesthetic movement through space and the method used by Jacques Villon in his painting, "Abstraction," Figure 13-14.

4. There is a noticeable interaction between movement sensations and the materials used. This interaction is not smooth; each factor tends to influence the other. Nevertheless, the characteristics of the movement are colored by the manipulative limits of the materials used during the productive processes.

5. The children's lack of representational skill frequently causes them to attempt to substitute motor movement for other modes of expression. The resulting interaction of kinaesthetic sensation with the representational purpose causes a continuous shift from one mode to the other during the processes of productive thinking. This shift leads to changes in the direction of thinking, and it sometimes appears as a lack of continuity that expresses itself as awkward changes and pauses in the rhythmical structures of the paintings. This shift will sometimes cause one mode to overlap the other, thus causing an interaction of the two modes. Such interaction usually results in the strengthening of both modes. Interaction

between two separate purposes calls forth a corresponding interaction of different sensory modes; the result is a primitive but useful interaction of diverse senses.

6. The interaction of several sensory modes frequently results from attempts to correlate verbal description with visual, auditory, and tactile experience. Our observations indicated that auditory and tactile sensations can be recalled if children are reminded of these experiences. We also noted that experiences centered around the senses of hearing and smelling do not lend themselves to children's natural inclinations to use gestures and their manifestations in rhythmically painted movements.

7. Our observation of the interaction of materials with sensations during the productive processes lead us to conclude that experience would aid the children in their appreciation of possible interactions between sensations and their representation with art materials. In practice, the productive processes become experience. They are partly an extension of the experience the children set out to describe but, in essence, they are new experiences rather than a duplication of previous experiences. This fact is worthy of special note because it indicates a means for making the art activity a developmental process.

8. It is generally observed that the art of young primary-grade children is full of confusions. The children's sensory interaction is fragmentary, and they quickly find substitutes for their lack of skill. An example of such a substitute is the children's naming of parts of their pictures with little reference to what really appears to exist.

9. Our observation of the children's selection of sensory modes for representing their bus trip experience revealed the importance of the decisive role the teacher must play in aiding the children in strengthening their perceptions. Because some senses are more useful than others, all senses are not always needed for all art activities. The senses that contribute to the development of learning in art activities should be determined and activated by the skilled teacher.

IMPLICATIONS FOR PROGRAM PLANNING

The sensory receptors play a very important part in the art education program. A purpose of the art education program is to increase the sensitivity of the senses and to find the means for making their action both economical and effective for learning purposes.

Earlier references to the art curriculum of the old Bauhaus are pertinent here.[2] The Bauhaus emphasized the need for training the senses in order to increase the individual's sensitivity to experience and the expression of experience through sensitive forming of materials. At the elementary-school level, we try to train the senses in a number of ways to make the children increasingly perceptive and observant.

Sensitivity to experience must be guided in order to help the children select and use their experiences in an intelligent effective manner. The objectives of increasing children's perceptiveness, their sensitivity to experiences, and their ability to make good selections may be achieved through well organized and directed motivational experiences. Effective motivations are most easily arranged when the experiences are firsthand. Vicarious experience is more difficult to know. Experiences, both firsthand and vicarious, may be provided with increased understanding through field trips, picture showing, dramatizations, role playing, and group discussions. The most useful motivational experiences will be those that are designed to involve the children immediately in related manipulative processes.

[2] See Chapter Two.

Eighteen

STRUCTURE-FORMING PROCESSES

The planning of primary-grade art activities ought to be based on children's natural modes for relating thinking and feeling to body movements. Such natural expressional modes provide a core around which an educative process can be formed through art activity.

THE SPIRAL AND THE GESTURE

Some of the earliest drawings made by kindergarten children may be nothing more than lines moving rapidly in a large spiral. If children are watched during the early stages of kindergarten art activity, it becomes obvious that the symbols they create are products of the large spiral movements they make with their arms. These spirals are large or small depending upon the speed or fearlessness of the movements made by the arm pivoting from the shoulder. The earliest drawings made by children often reveal a transition from uncontrolled scribbled movements to a controlled circular rhythm, which may become related to the gesture. Children, like adults, will describe the size or shape of something with a movement of their arm or hand. In art activity, this simple kind of gesture can change a painted line into a symbol for something the child wants to communicate.

179

FUNCTIONS OF GESTURES

We have already discussed the way a gesture may become a means for expressing feeling and thinking. As the child matures, his gesture drawing or painting may become the product of increasing amounts of reasoned thought.

Gestures are motivated by kinaesthetic responses to experience. The function of a gesture is closely related to the quality of the emotions and rationalizations connected with an experience. If gestures can lend meaning to expression, it becomes possible to structure forms that are expressive of children's participation in experience. From this point of view, gestures are part of a most important aspect of the learning processes. Qualitative gestures grow out of the processes of manipulating aspects of experience. The controlled manipulation of experience and of the materials related to experience is a very important part of any learning process.

We all know that we can know a thing best if we can work with it, if we can hold it in our hands. We know how to drive an automobile by operating the controls, by taking the automobile into traffic and by getting the "feel" of the engine and the steering. In a similar fashion, we buy clothing by feeling the texture of the fabric and by trying on the clothing. All of these processes involve manipulation. In art activity, manipulative operations, which provide us with knowledge through physical participation, become qualitative and gain increased depth and breadth if they make use of the feelings that are related to experience. Feelings may be given form by the body movements they generate. When these body movements are employed by us to communicate, they take form as gestures. Sometimes gestures are translated as dance movements. Responses to rhythmical music are often expressed as a pattern of organized and expressive body movements. Such body movements are actually muscular responses to the rhythm and quality of sound. Through our participation in such muscular and physical movement, we feel part of the musical experience. In much the same way, we respond to experience with painting, drawing, or sculpturing.

The close relationship of the gesture to the sense of participation and to the desire to com-

municate feeling makes the gesture a suitable means for developing understanding. Mere movement or physical involvement in experience may be insufficient to make the experience educationally useful. If gestures are incorporated into the movement, they can provide the opportunity to enhance an experience with qualitative factors if they bring the following to the experience:

1. A desire for communication.
2. The interaction of many modes of thinking and doing.
3. Clarification of the experience through the development of expressive physical activity.

Gestures are muscular responses to sensory experiences. The senses of smell, sight, hearing, and touch interact and tend to stimulate muscular activity. The activity of these senses also stimulates desires for participation in an activity. Muscular or kinaesthetic participation and the stimulating of interest help to initiate thinking and feeling. When children's thoughts and feelings about an experience are stimulated, the children are more likely to be encouraged to seek recollections from past experiences that will enrich their present experiences. In this way the factor we have referred to as precognitive thinking comes into play.

The relationship between gestures and the processes of precognitive thinking should be understood. Gestures become qualitative and are more useful when they aid in the association of other experiences with a new experience. Experiences drawn from other art activities are just as useful as experiences drawn from events in the past that contribute meaning and clarification. This process of association requires much direction and aid from the teacher.

RELATIONSHIP OF GESTURES
TO CHILDREN'S EARLY ART

According to our earlier discussions about children's scribble paintings, we have some reason to believe that there is a relationship between the scribble and the sensations of movement experienced by the child while he is painting.

If a gesture is truly an effort to communicate through physical movement, it must be characterized by a desire to be understood. In the work of the youngest children, this desire may be only partly felt, if it is felt at all. The teacher must help the children develop an awareness of their need to be understood. With the development of such an awareness, the children will show evidence of growth through their increased efforts to make their gestures meaningful and understandable. This process involves an increasing effort on the children's part to think about the movements they are translating into pictorial or sculptured form. Such a process requires that thinking be applied to feeling and selecting, and that the products of unconscious behavior be rationally examined.

In order to understand how children evolve a qualitative relationship between gestures, forming, and thinking, it is important that we know what happens when gestures are given form in art materials. This understanding is part of the total understanding we must have of the early stages of productive thinking processes.

Observation of children performing in painting, for example, reveals much that we need to know. Examination of their paintings and discussions with the children help increase our understanding. We learn from such observation that children have difficulty if they are given too much direction. If the children are told to make pictures of things beyond their range of understanding or of their motor skill, they become confused and frustrated. We need to work with children in terms of their own level of achievement and ability to know and perform.

We know that children, from the beginning of the kindergarten period, are usually advanced beyond the stage of making unstructured and purely meaningless scribbles. They are either naming their scribbles or they have begun to form and structure in terms of the manipulative skills they have achieved.

An obvious characteristic of the structured scribble painting is its implication of a rapid outward movement from the center. The center is dynamic because, like the center of a coiled spring, it represents a source of energy. The outer edges of the spiral rhythm of the total rhythmical pattern express a diminishing energy. Evidence of the expended movement is found in the increasing differentiation of the forms toward the outer edges of the painting. Increasing differentiation may be accompanied by an increasing deliberateness, an increasing conscious effort to form. We have noted in earlier discussions regarding the role of subconscious thinking in the precognitive processes that too much intrusion of conscious thinking on the productive processes may hinder the smooth and necessarily rapid development of productive thinking during its earliest stages. When such interruptions occur, there is danger that the continuity of the original rhythm will be disturbed.

We know that the flow of unconscious thinking must eventually be subjected to examination by conscious thought processes. However, the relationship of conscious or critical processes to unconscious processes is not clearly established in young children's art. This aspect of art activity needs to be planned. Children have to learn how to be critical of their art work.

IMPLICATIONS FOR CURRICULUM PLANNING

An important purpose of curriculum planning for the early stages of art activity should include plans for developing correlations between differentiated structuring processes and the dynamic rhythms of initial gestures. If this kind of correlation is not sought, achieved, and maintained, the development of image-symbol structures and the evolution of effective metaphors will be seriously hampered by the gradual domination of conscious over unconscious forming processes. As indicated in our discussion about precognitive thinking, conscious thinking is most effective as a device for scrutinizing or evaluating the products of unconscious activity. If conscious thinking dominates, art activity becomes hindered by the slowness of the conscious modes and the resulting metaphoric forms tend to lose rhythmical interaction between their parts. The result is a loss of harmony and of effective interaction between related aspects of the total metaphor. When conscious thinking dominates a child's art activity, the child shows hesitancy in his productive processes, which causes unnecessary fragmentation of his art work.

An objective of early childhood art education is to maintain the interaction of gestures with feeling, thinking, and communicating and to in-

18-1. SCRIBBLE
Painting. *Author's collection.*

18-2. PAINTING
East Orange, New Jersey, Public Schools.

clude all of these aspects as part of the manipulative processes of productive thinking. After this interaction has been accomplished, the teacher should form a curricular plan that will help increase the scope and content of the children's precognitive experience. The educationally useful result should be the effective interaction of the physical body with precognitive and productive thinking. In actual practice, this achievement will be recognized when the children are able to select useful experiences from their store of prior experience to contribute to the productive parts of their art activity. The action of kinaesthetic and manipulative processes will become one with the processes of transforming the selected experiences into structured art forms.

The teacher's observation of children who participate in art activities will provide the most useful basis for planning the art education program. Observation, however, will be most useful if the teacher knows what to look for. The basic thing to observe is the quality of the interaction between thinking, materials, and motor activities that are related to the forming processes.

It should be noted that there is a relationship between natural modes of engagement in art activities, motivations to art activities, and the ways in which thought and behavior evolve out of the art processes. If we can observe this relationship and if we can demonstrate that its results contribute to the effectiveness of our learning goals, we might have established an educationally valid art process. The following examples provide evidence of the existence of this relationship.

Figure 18-1 is an example of a painted scribble. This painting is not based on image-symbols. Its forms grow from rhythms made as the result of the whole arm gesturing from the shoulder. The smaller areas, which surround the large main form of the painting, are considered to be more differentiated than the central area because they are smaller and because they evolved out of the familiarity with brush and paint that was gained from making the large central form. The increase in differentiation is shown in the painting of the letter "H" in the lower left-hand corner. This picture is a gesture painting, from which an image-symbol structure barely begins to emerge. The structuring of the image-symbol is discovered in the evolution of the gesture as curving painted forms. Experimentation with structuring symbols of shapes, which are made from brush strokes combined with gestures, results in some rudimentary structuring. The letter "H" represents an effort to give form to an image-symbol drawn from a precognitive experience.

METAMORPHOSIS OF THE IMAGE

Figure 18-2 has the same general forming characteristics as the scribble painting, Figure 18-1. The difference between the two paintings lies in the interaction of the images with the painting processes. The child who painted Figure 18-2 was a member of a kindergarten group that participated in a school-wide clean-up campaign. The image used in the painting grew out of discussions about the campaign, its purposes, and the ways in which the purposes could be met. The concept that supplied the basis for the image-symbol formation was the product of an experience that involved discussions and participation in forms of constructive social behavior. Related to the discussions and activities was a clearly defined social goal, in this case, to help in cleaning and ordering the school and the home. This group of children talked about places that needed cleaning and ordering and, by mutual consent, decided that home basements and floors were in most need of cleaning. Figures 7-2, 18-2, 18-3, and 18-4 are pictorial expressions of what these children did as part of their cleaning activity.

The major difference between Figures 18-1 and 18-2 is found in the nature of the motivation that preceded the forming of the paintings. Figure 18-1 is concerned with almost purely permissive painting; Figure 18-2 is grounded in a planned, many faceted experience.

IMAGES AND PROJECTION OF SELF

Like Figure 18-1, Figure 18-2 grows out of a dynamic center. But in Figure 18-2 the dynamic center is the child himself. The forming of a face at the center of the paper becomes an extension of self. It becomes the child's most immediate, direct, and fully felt projection of experience. The projection is at the point of greatest sensitivity. The gesture required to project this self-image is a spiral but it is also the gesture of throwing, which describes the act of energetically removing trash from the basement of the child's own house. The gesture is a sensation of participation, and the encompassing descriptive movement is intrinsic with the child's thinking about purposes and his accomplishment through doing.

The masses of color surrounding the symbol for self are continuations of the spiral activity in combination with lines and masses representing felt or sensed continuations of self. Here we have an interaction between image-symbol structuring through movement sensations and pure gesture interacting with pleasure in kinaesthesia, the projection of self, and the diminishing intensity of the original motivation to productive thinking. This diminishing intensity causes the painting to revert to the kinds of differentiation in the expended outer part of the spiral movement that are evident in Figure 18-1. In Figure 18-2, this differentiation is partly controlled by an effort to paint the torso and limbs of the projected self.

It would be interesting to know if the projection of self in child art is an attempt to represent the visual image of self and if children's earliest efforts to structure experience in plastic materials represents an effort to express movement sensations correlated with a social purpose. There is, however, no conclusive way in which we can answer these questions.

In order to develop an educationally valid process of art activity, the productive thinking processes should be correlated with a varied assortment of sensory experiences. For this reason, regardless of whether or not an art activity is part of an effort to represent a visual experience, it is desirable that children be helped to structure combinations of sensory experiences.

CONFLICT BETWEEN VISUAL AND KINAESTHETIC EXPERIENCE

Figure 18-3 demonstrates the emerging conflict between visual and kinaesthetic experience. Uncertainty regarding methods for describing the cleaning process results in a fragmented and disorganized arrangement of dissimilar masses. This painting begins with a projection of self, which is no more competent than the symbol of self in Figure 18-2. In Figure 18-3, the child

conceived of self in relation to the object being cleaned. This object, according to the child, was a rug. The child attempted to shape the rug, but his developing awareness of the cleaning action controlled his shaping of the intended form structure. It may be that the child was unsure of how to shape the rug and his developing movement sensations evolved toward the more accurate rhythms of the large sweeping gesture that encloses the figure and the rug masses. It should be noted that in this painting the processes of manipulating the paint created a problem because the brush kept running out of paint after only a section of the total gesture had been painted; the child had to pause repeatedly to dip his brush in fresh paint. It is to the child's credit that he did not forget his original purpose and that he continued to paint the gesture until it was completed. The short strokes on the right side of the painting indicate the child's final effort to describe the cleaning action. This final effort indicates that the child's motivating purpose was never lost; and that the child felt aware of the completeness of his metaphoric structure.

Figure 7-2 (see Chapter Seven) shows evidence of a successful correlation between the productive thinking processes and the correlated sensations that emerge from the precognitive phases. Like Figure 18-3, this is a projection of self involved in the cleaning activity; however, the movement sensations are sustained throughout. The figure is symbolic rather than representational; the black lines are used to define the movements rather than to outline the symbol, and the dust rising from the action of cleaning is pictured as a series of rhythmical spots on the outer edges of the dynamic spiral action.

Figure 18-4 indicates an interesting variation in method from the previous examples. The initiation of the productive process is the same as in the other paintings and the progression from a dynamic center evolves in much the same way, but instead of a direct rhythm from the projection of self at the core of the spiral, there is a deliberative structuring of the body. Differentiated curvilinear masses radiate from the head, and the arms are painted out of all proportion to the size of the projected self. The arms are no longer projections of self; they are extensions from the self to the structured symbol of the

18-3. PAINTING
East Orange, New Jersey, Public Schools.

18-4. PAINTING
East Orange, New Jersey, Pub-lic Schools.

activity in which the self is involved. The large size of the arms and hands is intended to indicate the basic tools and methods involved in the processes of cleaning. The size is dictated by sensation rather than by a predetermined plan to produce a visual description of arms and hands. The hands are capable of holding objects, which become part of the circular forms that comprise the outer parts of the spiral. In this painting, visual experience is merely a part of other correlated sensations.

The weakness in Figure 18-4 is the painting's lack of smoothness between the various parts of its visual-plastic expression. The transition from the sensation symbols formed by the hands and the attempt to describe the torso objectively does not relate rhythmically to the total spiral movement.

DIFFERENTIATION: EVOLUTION FROM SUBJECTIVE TO OBJECTIVE FORMS

A more highly differentiated forming of an image-symbol structure into an effective economical metaphor is the self-portrait by a little girl in Figure 18-5. This is an economical metaphor because the child has selected her hair as the object of expression. The movement sensations in the painting have been concentrated on the visual and tactile characteristics of the child's hair; its waviness and what it feels like when it is combed or when it is looked at in a mirror. The correlation of the metaphor with sensations, visual and felt, results in a structure that is more highly differentiated than those of the more rudimentary spiral form. The difference between this self-portrait and the paintings based on the spiral is a matter of increased discrimination between aspects of diverse experience. This is a type of differentiation that takes place simultaneously in all other aspects of expressional experience. For example, animals are not all classified as "bow-wows" and people are no longer just men and women. It is obvious, however, that complete differentiation does not exist in this painting. The eyes still appear as circles, the nose as an elongated spot, and the mouth as a horizontal upward curve.

Figure 18-5 also represents an increase in structural discrimination. Unlike the earlier examples, the head in this painting is poised on a neck and a neck is firmly located on a torso. There is also indication of an emerging representational effort, which is made evident by the child's slight effort to indicate that the portrayed object exists in space. When the child painted a sky at the top of the picture surface, she began to represent some of the things she knows, such as her observation

18-5. PORTRAIT WITH LONG HAIR
Painting. *East Orange, New Jersey, Public Schools.*

that the sky is above us and that the space in which we exist is the void encompassed by the sky above and the earth on which we stand. Considerations of the child's modes for defining space are not as important as the fact that the child conceives of her symbols as existing in space. At this stage in a child's development, it becomes possible for the teacher to place major emphasis on the art processes as a means for expressing sensations of many kinds rather than mere descriptions of purely visual experience.

FORCES AND TENSIONS

The most important understanding we can draw from an investigation into the ways children express and communicate ideas in visual-plastic form is that children are concerned with forces and tensions, with sensations and some degree of conscious comment on the totality of an experience.

Tensions are conveyed through the use of the spiral form as a rudimentary mode of plastic communication. The spiral results from a combination of elementary descriptive gestures and an attempt to define experience with an all inclusive wave of the arm. The evolution toward a greater differentiation is made through increasingly detailed and descriptive motor activity. This motor activity results from a form of kinaesthesia that combines observation with muscular responses to sensations.

An important function of the art education processes is to aid in the differentiation of kinaesthetic response and to increase differentiation between various kinds of sensory response. Correlated with this increase in the interaction of sensory modes must be a program that is designed to develop the store of experience that feeds the precognitive processes.

When we speak of forces and tensions, we are referring to motivations to activities. If we can find a means for making children want to partici-pate in art activities, we will have created tensions and forces that impel them to become involved in art activity. This kind of motivation, the development of useful tensions, requires involvement in all kinds of human activity. We have noted that the physical, mental, and emotional being should be involved in the development of art forms. In order to thus involve the total being, the forces and tensions we create must elicit a total or complete pattern of responses during the individual's processes of art activity.

In classroom practice, the involvement of the individual in the processes of art activity requires a purposeful guidance program rather than a schedule of preplanned activities. Too much preplanning of separate art activities may neglect to take into account unexpected events and the individual's possible need for a change in direction. Changes in direction may be made necessary by needs that can not be known during the early phases of an art activity.

It may be discovered that the best kinds of art activities are those that evolve from the interests and needs of the children in a particular group. The teacher should accept the responsibility of helping the children examine the art activities they select.

During the processes of art activity, the teacher should continue to guide the children's thinking about their activity. This guidance should take the form of an individual and a group evaluation process. As the result of guidance or critical evaluation aids from the teacher, the individual child will be helped to explore the implications of his efforts. Some of the most effective guidance and useful motivation to new and increasingly satisfactory achievement can be accomplished in group evaluation sessions. Such sessions are extensions of motivations that lead to the initiation of art activity. If group evaluations are conceived in these terms, all of the children's art activities can be helped to maintain a meaningful continuity.

Nineteen

GEOMETRICITY

Geometricity first appears when forming results from the application of rational criticism to otherwise irrational processes. Geometricity is a natural mode, which may be used to help children make strong, expressive metaphoric structures.

Geometricity in early child art refers to the presence of organized patterns of lines and shapes, such as spirals, ovals, partial circles, rectangles, and lines placed at any angle. Children's art that involves geometricity shows evidence of the children's attempts to structure concepts in terms of lines and shapes that are predominantly geometric rather than representational.

REPRESENTATION AND GEOMETRICITY

Geometricity may exist in a form that combines representational and geometric shapes. In such cases, it is preferable that the interaction of the geometric and representational factors be so complete that representational concerns do not destroy the final structure. Geometrical forming in art places a large emphasis on the construction of the form rather than on mere definition of symbols. Geometrical concepts provide a structural basis that supply art forms with a cohesiveness and

188

clarity of purpose that sets them apart from the purely descriptive symbolism of strictly representational art.

KINAESTHESIA AND GEOMETRICITY

The first evidences of controlled kinaesthesia comprise the earliest kind of genuine geometricity, which is dominated by circular, semicircular, and spiral movements. Our example of a kindergarten child's painting about cleaning out the basement, Figure 18-2, is a good example of such geometricity. This entire painting represents a diagram of the rhythmical action of cleaning—the sweeping, circular movements of the arm pivoting from the shoulder.

LOCATION OF GEOMETRICITY IN DEVELOPMENTAL PROCESSES

Geometricity is a developmental characteristic of child art. Its first appearance is a sign of the emergence of control by the child over the amorphous forms of undifferentiated scribbling. Geometricity may represent an attempt to bring order out of the confusing diversity of experience. In its earliest forms, it may be an unconscious charting of controlled kinaesthesia. At more highly developed levels, kinaesthesia itself represents a process of attempting to isolate a selected concept from the general mass of experience to enclose it in some kind of ordered rhythm. This ordered rhythm is drawn from the child's own sense of body movement. The process of isolating and ordering a concept, of structuring, and of constructing a framework that will provide meaning as well as clarity results in the use of geometric lines and shapes.

Geometricity may achieve a high level of usefulness as a forming process during the first year of the primary-grade period. Teachers should provide the kind of guidance necessary for the emergence of a useful geometricity during this period. In its most useful form, geometricity is a means for making children self-conscious and critical of their productive thinking during art activity. However, geometricity becomes a useless mode of forming if self-conscious and critical views lead to stereotypes. Geometric stereotypes exclude the need for establishing relationships between concepts, image-symbols, and visual-plastic materials.

COMMUNICATION THROUGH GEOMETRICITY

From its earliest appearance as structured scribbling, geometricity should be the result of an effort to seek a means for communicating the uniqueness of experience.

The painting by a kindergarten child, Figure 19-1, is an example of an attempt to think productively, to express precognitive thinking

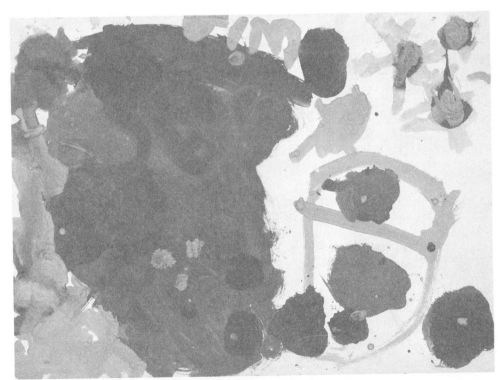

19-1. SCRIBBLE PAINTING
Landscape? *Author's collection.*

through the forming of a physical material, in this case, poster paints. The painting is essentially a scribble brought under limited control as the result of an effort, apparently centered around a desire to paint a landscape. The painting began on the left side of the paper. Both the dripping paint and the uncertainty regarding the appearance and location of the symbols causes the child to correct his earlier efforts repeatedly. This process of correcting indicates an effort to structure, but the child's inability to eliminate his earlier efforts effectively results in the obliteration of everything on the left side of the paper. The child profits from this experience, however, by gaining familiarity with the materials. The child uses a clean brush dipped into a contrasting color to superimpose small circular spots on the overpainted area. The child continues to paint the spots and, with this increase in number, there is an apparent increase in the child's confidence. Correspondingly, the spots increase in size and boldness as they move with rhythmic stateliness toward the right. A naming process accompanies the painting of the spots and this helps the child discover forms that suggest trees and plants. As a result, a geometric form is painted to enclose two circular forms in the clear space to the right of center. Throughout the painting of all of the shapes, the rhythm of the painting is dominantly circular.

FORMING GEOMETRIC STRUCTURES FROM VISUAL IMAGES

The circular character of Figure 19-1 is typical early evidence of geometricity. The teacher may recognize such a painting as evidence that the child is making an effort to give meaning and form to experience on his own terms, according to his own experience and level of intellectual, social, physical, mental, and emotional development.

Geometricity in its earliest form often indicates much more than a child's frustrated effort to represent a visual impression. Although the child himself is often not aware that the visual sensation is merely a part of the total experience, he may unconsciously attempt to express a multitude of sensations.

Because of the multisensory nature of early experience and because of children's efforts to express experience in geometricized forms, it is important for the teacher to be aware of the following factors:

1. Children will not be able to grow in expressional skill through art if they are taught to represent images that are entirely the products of visual experience. Such a procedure tends to destroy the totality of experience and to diminish the vitality of sensations.

2. Proper and effective teaching requires that emphasis be placed on the total concept of the images or image-symbols of an experience rather than on visual impressions alone.

We know that concepts are the basis for effective metaphoric constructions and that children develop concepts from many different kinds of sensations. To attempt to fragment these sensations and to isolate the purely visual from all other possible kinds of sensation results in the weakening or destruction of the value of an entire experience. The purpose of the precognitive and productive processes is to make possible the structuring of a total experience into coherent effectively expressive forms.

Because knowledge must be verified by more than one sensory mode, the development of experiences as combinations of concepts and structures based on multisensory perception provides the only effective basis for the development of an art education process. In our discussion of the physiology of learning, we shall discover that all possible sensory perceptors and all possible parts of the cortex must interact in order to provide the most useful and productive learning processes.

The process of an evolving geometricity is illustrated in Figure 19-2, a more advanced painting by a child who signs his picture Larry. This painting illustrates a developed geometricity; the structured use of rectangles, triangles, circles, lines, and solid masses is a part of the painting. Geometricity is not artificially superimposed on a representation or a symbol.

Figure 19-3 provides an interesting contrast to Figure 19-2. Figure 19-3 is a logical next step along the road to representation. This painting began as an expressed desire to paint a landscape.

19-2. PORTRAIT BY LARRY
Painting. *Runnemede, New Jersey, Public Schools.*

Larry Winters.

19-3. LANDSCAPE
Painting. *Author's collection.*

The large mass at the bottom of the painting was made first and was intended to be the earth. This mass is significant because it is differentiated. Instead of simply painting a ground line, the child tried to give a contour to the earth. The irregular mass directly above the apex of this ground area is a continuation of the initial rhythms; it vaguely suggests an effort to establish a structure on the pinnacle of the ground mass. Naming took place both before and after this irregular mass was painted. Before he began to paint the mass, the child said it would be a tree; after it was painted, he named it a house. The child washed the blue paint from his brush in a jar of clear water and dipped it in red paint. Then he continued the original undulating rhythm beginning on the bottom left and curving upward toward the center and down to the bottom right. The result was a repetition of the triangular form of the ground mass; however, the curvilinear rhythm of the pre-symbol stages caused this movement to continue near the apex of the triangular mass as a series of smaller diagonal ovals. At this point, the child added several other colors to fill in the area created by the lines of the half-scribble, half-symbol mass. These colors were used to enforce the child's expressed conviction that he had painted a mountain. Next the child's representational purpose was extended to a reconsideration of his original effort to paint a house, or tree; he dipped his brush in blue paint and overpainted the area until his representational purpose merged almost completely with his controlled scribble. Then he painted circular masses in the sky, beginning with a sun and ending with other masses, which he named clouds.

The significant thing about this painting is the geometricity that arises from the interaction of naming, scribbling of an advanced sort, and a beginning effort to represent through the use of symbols. Representation is not an expressed effort to duplicate the visual experience. The symbols are formed as indicators of what the form is like.

Figure 19-2 is an example of geometricity developed beyond the controlled scribble stage. This formation of geometricized lines and masses is deliberative in a way that the controlled scribble is not. The lines and masses are rhythmically related as pictorial units as well as expressions of a unified kinaesthesia. For example, the head of the figure is made with a clean single stroke of the brush. From this large movement, the child was able to change his rhythm to the smaller controlled movements needed for placing the eyes, eyebrows, nose, mouth, and spots of color on the cheeks. There is a sensitive relation between the character of the brush stroke and the character of the feature being painted. The general circular line defining the head is simple, large, and is made with a wide stroke. The stroke used for the mouth is undulating in thickness; and the strokes used for the eyes, the nose, and the eyebrows are given an emphasis suitable to the tactile sensations associated with the expressive character of each part. The circular shape of the head is used as a source from which the triangular structure of the body begins, descending to a base which forms the bottom of the dress. Semicircular lines curving outward from the apex of the triangle form the shoulders and hands.

Figure 19-2 is an example of controlled rhythms structured to express the character of a particular

individual, perhaps another child in the class. This characterization is continued in geometrical form through the arrangement of squares made from vertical and horizontal lines that define the texture of fabric and the print design in the child's blouse. Solid masses of color provide this sense of textural change in the skirt and in the lower part of the blouse.

Larry's portrait is a differentiated structural form. This kind of forming is to be expected from children during the middle of the primary-grade period. All children do not arrive at this level of detailed and structured forming at the same time; however, this level provides a general standard of achievement during this phase of the children's development.

LIMITATIONS

Geometricity can become a useless stereotype if it is used as an easy means to make "designs." Figure 19-1, an arrangement of curvilinear shapes, could become a useful arrangement of forms; but unless the child is aware of an expressional purpose, the arrangement becomes meaningless. Before such processes can be useful, it is necessary for children to have much experience in finding exciting shapes and textures in invented shapes made from many different kinds of materials.

Figures 19-4 and 19-5, chalk paintings of a truck and a rhythmical arrangement of rectangles, suggest a means for developing children's natural inclination to use geometricity as a means for

19-4. TRUCK
Chalk. *Author's collection.*

19-5. ABSTRACTION
Chalk. *Author's collection.*

structuring experience in an organized fashion. It is notable in the drawing of the truck that the spiral effect of gradually increasing size among angular units begins in the cab of the truck, continues through the motor area, and gradually becomes lost in the rear of the truck body. The isolation of the entire object in empty space is indicative of a motivating representational purpose that dominates the rhythms of the rectangles. If it had been possible for the teacher to guide the child in investigating the structure of the truck as a series of rhythms extended into surrounding space and related objects, such as buildings or other vehicles, the child might have established a satisfactory relationship between symbol and expression. This kind of over-all rhythmical unity is achieved in Figure 19-5, but its value is lost because it has no purpose beyond the making of rectangles. It should be noted that the child was aware of this limitation, and made an effort to give his picture some additional sym-

bolic meaning through the vinelike forms on the left and right side of his picture.

THREE-DIMENSIONAL STRUCTURAL METAPHORS

Geometricity is a natural means for securing purpose and coherence in three-dimensional form structures. When children use very plastic three-dimensional materials, such as clay, geometricity provides a basis for forming the materials. When this understanding does not exist the forms created are amorphous or, if symbols are attempted, they are structurally weak and quickly fall apart.

An example of typical forms made by children will clarify the function of geometricity in three-dimensional work. If the material used is heavy and nontransportable, such as beach sand or snow, children manipulate it and form and structure it on its own terms.

When a material can be shaped while it is held in the hands, it loses it contact with the earth. When it is shaped, it must continue to hover in space because it has no base on which it can rest. When children work with such materials, they almost instinctively conceive of them as having their own gravitational center. Under such circumstances, they structure the form around an imaginary nucleus. Rolls, slabs, coils, and sticks are stuck onto the center. The material may be shaped, pushed or pinched, but it always grows outward or radiates from its artificial independent gravitational center, its nucleus.

This outward progression of three-dimensional structures is similar, in many respects, to the metamorphosis of forms from the early structured drawings of the rudimentary spiral form. However, the typical small scale of plastic clay structures, and the resulting emphasis on building with the fingers, does not encourage kinaesthesia. As a result, such forms are more divorced from the rhythmical experience and from the forming of a keenly felt metaphor than are the paintings or drawings.

The shortcomings of three-dimensional art work, however, are not as serious as they may seem. If structuring is done with heavy materials, the need for geometric forming is obvious. Concepts of space and mass are tempered by engineering requirements. As a result of the demanding nature of such forming processes, children are encouraged to combine critical processes with their precognitive and productive thinking.

SUMMARY

Geometricity in early child art may be the beginning of form. It may be the child's means for forming concepts into structured metaphors. During its earliest phases, geometricity is predominantly circular and spiral-like. Although differentiation in the evolution of the rudimentary spiral is associated with differentiation in kinaesthetic movement, in geometric forms it is expressed as triangles, squares, rectangles, vertical and horizontal lines, and partial and complete circular forms and spirals.

The development of a useful geometricity requires:

1. Experimentation with various types of movement sensations.
2. Exploration of the structural characteristics of various materials.
3. Exploration of image-symbols and their potential for structuring in order to achieve metaphoric effectiveness.

True geometricity in child art is not an imposition of geometric forms on symbols according to the belief that suitable metaphors will result. Such procedures result only in the imposition of one mode upon the other in such a way that rhythmical continuity and coherence of thinking is destroyed.

PART FOUR

SKILLS IN ART EDUCATION

Twenty

SKILLS IN EARLY CHILD ART ACTIVITIES

Our discussion of the art work of primary-grade children suggests that skill is an integral part of art activity.

The youngest children are less concerned with manipulative skill than are older children because of the immaturity of their critical faculty. Skill in drawing, in manipulating materials, in representing visual symbols, and in forming them into coherent structures becomes of increasing concern to children as they mature. Children's concern with skillfulness in art work is a by-product of their developing awareness of the need for better means of solving problems in art. This concern often begins to manifest itself during the first half of the primary-grade program.

THE COMPOSITION OF ART SKILLS

Our knowledge of how children think and learn indicates that the interaction of the senses plays a basic role in the development of art skills. The healthy maturation of children involves an increasingly complex body of experiences, which forms the basis of the precognitive processes; these processes are the bases of art activity. In our earlier discussions, it was noted that precognitive thinking is most useful when knowledge and experiences are organized in a purposeful fashion. These organized, related experiences are the raw materials of skills.

The degree of organization of stored experiences determines the quality of a skill. The artist is able to perform technical manipulations with ease and expertness because of his vast, purposefully organized experience. The ability to interrelate experiences purposefully becomes a skill when the experiences can be drawn upon with ease and discrimination. An experienced artist can easily develop techniques and use them effectively to express a concept because of his skill with respect to experiences with art processes. A lack of skill is manifested by hesitation, lack of discrimination in choosing techniques and materials, and awkwardness. Skill makes it possible for an artistic response to exist as the result of spontaneous action rather than as the result of a series of consciously manipulated processes. The proficient artist can use color relations, manipulations of paint, drawing processes, and various expressional techniques in such a way that each interacts harmoniously with the others and becomes a useful and efficient tool of the art activity.

A successful work of art is one in which the artist's skill has enabled him to develop his image-symbols and concepts into meaningfully structured forms. In an unsuccessful work, the artist has not been able to do this.

ADAPTIVE SKILLS

Adaptive skills, those most conducive to productive thinking in art, must be developed in children as the result of flexible patterns of thinking, conditioning, and memorization. Skills developed in specific, rigidly controlled art experiences are nonadaptive, and lead to stereotypes of thinking.

Nonadaptive skills arise in children as the result of inflexible precepts, for example, those requiring that blue always be harmonized with blue-green, that color opposites such as blue and yellow never be used, that representation of an object always be in proper perspective, that standardized modes of light and dark shading always be used, that a human figure always be six, seven, or eight heads tall, that human eyes be properly located on the head by means of a line drawn midway between the chin and the top of the head, and so on.

SKILL AND CREATIVE IMAGINATION

The development of adaptive skills requires the habitual use of creative imagination. This correlation between adaptive skill development and creative imagination is learned.

Young children show a tendency to look for stereotyped art techniques and to repeat them. This tendency, if developed, may interfere with creativity. Children's development of form structures at the beginning of the primary-grade period is noted for an undifferentiated symbolism, which is as much the result of their formulated construction of simple symbols as it is the result of their sparse precognitive processes. Their earliest efforts in art, therefore, are marked by a lack of knowledge of experiential patterns and the dominance of newly developed formulas that quickly become stereotyped techniques for form construction.

IMPLICATIONS FOR CURRICULUM CONSTRUCTION

One of the first considerations of a teacher in making a curricular program for the early primary period is to provide a means for the learning of skills that are applicable to a variety of situations. This can be accomplished by a program that emphasizes the flexible, rather than inflexible, ordering of the parts of a skill. Attaining flexibility is more important at this time than trying to achieve the kind of smoothness that characterizes the highly developed skill of the adult artist.

The way to achieve adaptive, flexible skills is mainly through the development in the child of habits of exploration, experimentation, and improvisation. Adaptive skill, then, will involve learning the habit of investigating ways to adapt aspects of the art experience, as well as conditioned responses to it, to new, unpredictable happenings.

The development of flexible skills must be achieved through guided experience with productive processes in the art activity. Achieving adaptive skills involves exploring the physical characteristics and sensory qualities of materials. Qualities such as texture, softness or hardness, pliability, color, and structural characteristics are discussed in terms of their suitability to the expression of particular ideas. Such understandings may be referred to when a quality of a particular material suggests a means for making a concept meaningful. For example, yarn makes excellent whiskers for lions and domestic cats and flash-bulbs could, when painted red, make excellent noses for puppet clowns.

It would be a simple matter to list purposes and situations that might arise in a kindergarten or first-grade art group, along with the materials and techniques that would be most suitable for these purposes and situations. But when we do this, we may be hampering children who need to find materials and techniques that are most suitable for the things, the images, that are part of their unique experiences. To provide shortcuts in this seeking and finding process by giving answers might easily destroy its advantages so far as learning is concerned.

Twenty-one

SKILL IN EXPRESSION

Adaptive skill in expression can be developed in children as the result of their participation in art activity. Expressive skill involves skill in experimentation, in making discoveries, and in developing metaphoric structures to suit experiences.

SOME REQUIREMENTS FOR EXPRESSION

The relation of materials to expression is a never-ending problem of art activity. Each expressive purpose poses new problems, for each requires techniques and materials best suited to its uniqueness.

As children grow older, they become increasingly sensitive to the ways techniques and materials can be manipulated to communicate most effectively their responses to experience. One of the aims of art education for older children, therefore, will be to develop in them the habit of seeking means suitable for their expressive purposes.

The ways children will approach problems of expression will depend to some extent on their cultural backgrounds. We have seen how the cultural environment affects our views of surroundings, modes of thinking, attitudes, concepts, and even the kinds of metaphor we use to embody expressive purposes. Within this cultural context, the previous experience of a child will determine how he thinks and does things. The things he does will, in large measure, be products of his total personality, in turn the product of his physical, social, and mental characteristics. The quality of these products, these solutions to expressional problems, will depend in good part on his creative skill, his imaginative power, and his aesthetic sensitivity, the elements with which art education works. For this reason we must be concerned with the ability of children to express concepts in image-symbols and metaphoric structures, as well as their ability to draw, to paint, to carve—to manipulate tools and materials in order to embody their concepts and achieve their expressional purposes.

READINESS AND EXPRESSION

The child's readiness to seek out relationships between materials and concepts is an important consideration in planning art activities.

In art activity, the child has motivations and purposes that are not too different from those of the professional artist; the chief difference between the two is experience. In order to plan art activities most effectively, it is evident that we need to know what the child is ready to accomplish at any phase of his growth. At all times, however, what the child does in his art work has profound importance so far as his experience and stage of growth are concerned, for the expressive value of art work is not determined by quantity of experience; it exists if the expressive form can communicate the level of growth of the child, not that of the adult or professional artist.

EXPRESSION AND VISUAL EXPERIENCE

The older child's images of experiences are constantly changing. In the work of the youngest child, there is little relation between expressive purposes and the forms made with art materials. Early evidence of the developing relation between concept and form can be seen when the kindergarten child makes a ground-line–sky-line picture. His maturity is indicated by his ability to conceive and express an image of himself as related to the earth. The ground- and sky-lines are visual images that express a child's concept of the physical universe.

The older child's increased rationality and more critical thinking result in his inclination to place greater emphasis on the evidence of visual experience. His art is more objective and less concerned with the expression, in art forms, of inner feelings than with forming replicas of visual experiences. When the older child sees the ground as a plane which meets the plane of the sky at an imagined horizon, he is acquiring knowledge of environment with only one sense, that of sight. The younger child forms a ground- and sky-line concept on the basis of feeling as well as sight. The ground-plane–sky-plane image of the older child is an attempt to duplicate the visual experience.

The ground-plane–horizon mode of expression is not caused entirely by the same kinds of influences that cause younger children to form a ground-line–sky-line concept of their environment. When this mode of expression is used, the child is probably ready for a program of guidance which will help him to correlate his increased visual perceptiveness with increased expressive skill.

LINE AND PLANE AS EXPRESSIVE MEANS

Some of the most expressive art forms of primary-grade children are the linear patterns which have their origins in an expressive gesture. In discussing the planning of primary-grade art activities, it was emphasized that there is an early need to provide for forming gestures into communicable metaphors. The natural means of providing for this is geometricity; because some of the most expressive and coherent art forms produced by primary children tend to be geometrical structures of line patterns.

The professional artist is inclined to insist that there is no such thing as a line in nature and, in fact, he is right. Many of the finest modern works, such as the calligraphic expressions of Franz Kline (Figure 21-1), convey the strong and dissonant rhythms of contemporary living through flowing planes that grow out of line movements. The expressive line becomes a massive plane and then returns again to the line. This alternation between line and plane is part of the technique for encompassing sophisticated understandings, for structuring profound metaphoric conceptualiza-

21-1. MAHONING
By Franz Kline. *Collection of the Whitney Museum of American Art, New York City. Gift of the Friends of the Whitney Museum of American Art.*

tions of nonvisual experience. These paintings are gigantic gestures in stark space. They are mature because they embrace concepts of emotion and human experience which transcend accepted notions of top and bottom, up and down; the artist is little concerned that for most of us "down" is a force directed toward a center of gravity. He is drawing from the experience of modern man, which has told him that the center of the earth is not the center of the universe, and that therefore, direction need not always be measured in terms of it, or in terms of a north and south pole. The astronaut loses these points of reference, and the entire human orientation may someday have to be changed. This transcending of old values and notions could easily destroy orientation to life itself if human beings can not quickly adjust to new concepts of living.

On a less abstract, less rich experiential level is the line of the expressive gesture of a child, drawn in terms of his level of understanding. There is certainly a vast difference between the expressive gestures of a Franz Kline and the groping gestures of a young child, although the child is doing exactly what the mature, adult artist is doing, using a linear rhythm in terms of his own experience.

The planning of art activities for older children, then, requires some knowledge of the expressive functions of gestures and of how rhythmical lines express concepts. We must provide for nonvisual experiences and understandings communicated through the gestured movement of line and plane.

The teacher could help children relate concepts to movements by having them participate in workshops emphasizing expressive plane and line rhythms with respect to specific subjects. A subject could be the American eagle. The children could be asked to describe its flight with colors and with arm and body movements. Perhaps a relationship might be established with the soaring rhythm of Brancusi's sculpture, "Bird in Flight."

It is fortunate that the child uses line as a natural expressive means, for it then may be possible to broaden his understanding by helping him evolve mass and plane from line. The evolution of mass and plane as expressive continuations of line is evident in the Kline painting, as it is in the successful efforts of older children. The teacher must devise means to help children evolve mass and plane from line and correlate them with texture and pattern to embody their critical conceptualizations. If this help is not provided, the expressive powers of children may not grow as the children grow.

Figure 21-2, a painting by a sixth-grade child, shows how the older child may be encouraged to use line movement expressive of a subject being painted. The movements associated with a particular kind of bird have been used as a basis for design. The drawing of the bird grew out of the rhythms, which are illustrated as a charting of a kinaesthesia. Expressive linear rhythms rather than pictorial representation are used to form the image of the bird. When conformations can be observed that suggest the bird itself, they are given emphasis with line, color, or texture. Thus emphasis on a movement, a line, or a shape makes it possible for others to see these conformations.

Like Kline's, this painting is intended to communicate much more than a purely visual experience, although the conceptualization of the child is immature in comparsion with the profundity of Kline's images, feelings, and thoughts. The child's purpose, clearly related to that of the artist, has been to explore the forms he can make with his coloring materials in terms of his expressive gestures, to give form to his intellectual and emotional responses to sensation, his response in this case to experience. The artist's response is that of an adult to his experience in the twentieth century, while the child, less concerned with the relation of man to his world, responds directly to his immediate experience. This is not to say

that the mature artist would not concern himself with something so simple as animal life; but if he were to do so, he would evolve forms commensurate with his maturity, as does the child.

The emergence of the forms of the bird from the linear rhythms of the painting indicates the origins of planes, which are themselves dynamic movements. The line patterns are transformed into textures, which also convey the elemental rhythm of the expression. This evolution of line into plane is essentially the same as that which takes place in the painting by Franz Kline. In the Kline painting, in the transformation of dynamic lines into powerful planes, the forces of the line rhythms are spread into broad and expressive planes that create the impression that the lines are growing like living forces. This vital power is also a characteristic of the calligraphic techniques used in Chinese writing, where lines spread into planes and then return to lines, strengthening the communication of the writer.

From the beginning of his intermediate grade experience the child is ready to evaluate critically the line-forming gesture as an expressional device. To ignore this natural inclination to evaluate could easily lead to the destruction of expressiveness in art activity. Children of the post-primary

21-2. BIRD
Collection of Theodore Lynch.

period are becoming increasingly aware of how they can form and express their conceptualizations. Their problem is to combine this thinking with their natural abilities.

Our understanding of children's need to combine expressive gestures with a growing critical consciousness is increased when we can recognize this need. Art education would fail if we could not find a means for invigorating thought with feeling, such as with gestures. As teachers, we need to increase the fine sensitivity of children to this means, and to wed the means to the rational, critical, probing mind. We know children are ready to combine thinking and feeling when they are no longer satisfied with purely manipulative processes.

Figure 21-3 shows how the rhythmic movements characteristic of an experience suggest a method for making a drawing of the experience. Here, line is used to define the shapes of the dancing figures. In Figure 21-2, lines were used to indicate the rhythmical movements of the bird, and only partly to suggest its shape. In drawing these figures, the child began with the rhythms of the dance. This need not be the first drawing the child made in this fashion; it could be the result of a series of experiments with the rhythms of this particular kind of dance.

Figure 21-4 is a painting by a primary-grade child. It is indicative of the kind of training a child should have before he enters the intermediate grades. Here, not line but rhythmical masses of color have been used to form the figures. The colors as well as the rhythmical masses have been evolved from kinaesthetic responses to movements.

Figure 21-5, drawn by an intermediate-grade child who has much skill in making representational forms, illustrates line movement consciously formed in a specific kind of rhythm. The likenesses of the horses are not only formed with a great degree of manipulative control, but they are also correlated with the expressive rhythms of the horses, increasing the value of the representation.

REPRESENTATION AND EXPRESSION

Many of the expressional forms children use require skill in representing parts of the natural environment. Children learn this skill when they need it, usually in the early intermediate and upper grades, when it becomes necessary to duplicate visual experience in order to insure effective expression.

It does not follow, however, that strict representation of the visual experience is the best mode of expression. Duplication of the visual

21-3. DANCING FIGURES
East Orange, New Jersey, Public Schools.

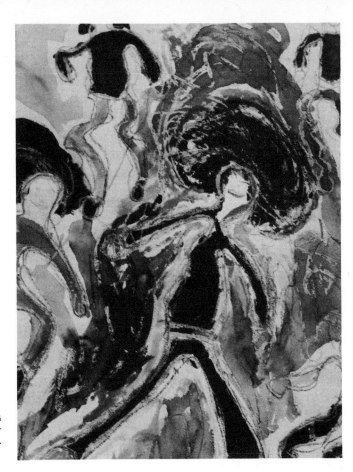

21-4. PAINTING
East Orange, New Jersey, Public Schools.

21-5. HORSES
Drawing. *East Orange, New Jersey, Public Schools.*

experience in two or three dimensions is only part of the purpose of art activity, and should be employed only if strict representation is the best means available for the expression of a concept. As was mentioned before, older children are more apt to assume that it is only reasonable that things they see during an experience be represented according to visual evidence. They do not realize that the visual sense is not the only one we use to know experience. They must be encouraged to use as many senses as they need for the complete perception and the expression of experience.

The teacher will have to help them explore experience with as many senses as possible. To do this, it may be necessary to resort to technical aid; visits to artists, advertising design studios, and museums may provide the necessary aid. Library research, motion pictures, or talks by invited artists may also be useful.

The classroom teacher may require technical help from special art teachers during the later phases of the elementary-school experience, because as children mature and their critical awareness increases, they need increasing amounts of technical information in order to develop more sophisticated representational skills. But even without technical help the classroom teacher can develop the art education program as long as the need for expression exists.

SENSORY SOURCES OF EXPRESSION

If the art work of children is to be educationally useful, it must draw on senses other than the purely visual. Thus the planning of the art education program at all grade levels, especially in the upper grades, requires that provision be made for multisensory experiences. At the primary level, it is enough for the teacher to be able to help children maintain their many-sided responses to experiences, as well as their natural ability to use different senses for different expressional purposes. In the upper grades, it is important that the teacher be able to maintain and develop expressive abilities achieved in the lower grades and to help children continue to grow in their expressional and visual-plastic communcation skills.

Children's many-sided sensory responses become increasingly useful when they are encouraged to find means to express their responses. This encouragement involves helping children select those sensory aspects of an experience that

21-6. WINDY DAY
Painting. *New York City Public Schools.*

21-7. ABSTRACTION
Painting. *New York City Public Schools.*

21-8. WINTER IN THE CITY
Painting. *New York City Public Schools.*

would make the expression of it more meaningful.

The development of skills to express multi-sensory experience begins in the primary-grade art experience, when simple means are used to express more than purely representational ideas. A few examples will suggest how this development begins.

In Figure 21-6, a primary-grade painting, symbols have been used to create a total metaphor for wind, rain, wetness, and chill. Cool blue colors, low in tone, emphasize these sensations. Wind has been suggested by the figure's leaning forward, the backward tilt of the umbrella, and the diagonal lines suggesting wind-driven rain. The darkness of the day is indicated by the bright house windows and the traffic light at the extreme left of the painting.

Figure 21-7 shows how the forming of visual symbols into metaphoric structures is developed in the intermediate and upper grades. This painting greatly emphasizes expressive rhythms, sound, and tactility. Rhythm is suggested by the staccato pattern of short, abrupt, sharp movements. Sound comes from the staccato rhythm and its contrast with the long, smooth, lyrical qualities of the flowing lines and masses. Tactility is suggested by the patterns of texture, the emphasis on surface quality. This painting places more emphasis on sensation than on visual representation.

The painting thus has a unique charm and a quality that can be infused into paintings describing the sensory experiences of children. For example, Figure 21-8 shows how a child was able

21-9. WIRE AND PLASTER SCULPTURE
New York City Public Schools.

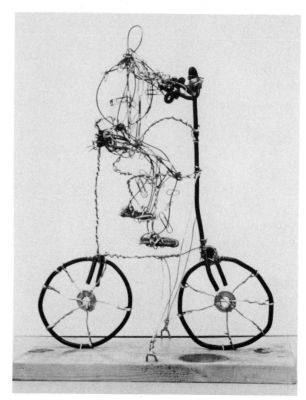

21-10. WIRE CONSTRUCTION
Author's collection.

to use tactile, kinaesthetic, and sound symbolization in a painting of a winter day in the city. An achievement such as this could be made after a teacher has discussed the application of the symbols used in a painting such as Figure 21-7 to pictures of the things children see around them.

Skills in using symbols for sensation in combination with rhythm need not be restricted to two-dimensional art. The meaning and purpose of these skills, as well as the ease with which they are used, will be enhanced if they are developed in a variety of two- and three-dimensional media.

The three-dimensional line construction in Figure 21-9 shows how physical form can be given to a gestured line rhythm moving through real space. The problem here was to find a means for making a line form a gesture that described the emotional and physical characteristics of a figure. The means in this case is ordinary string, dipped in a rapidly hardening plaster. It could just as easily have been wire, perhaps coated with melted crayon to give color and to enhance the effect.

The wire construction in Figure 21-10 employs the same kind of approach as that used in the line

sculpture of Figure 21-9. But it poses a different kind of problem, for heavy coat-hanger wire could be too difficult for primary-grade children to manipulate, although older children could cut, bend, and twist it with pliers and wire snippers. Soldering tools would make possible other techniques.

The clay sculpture in Figure 21-11 is akin to the three-dimensional structures in Figures 21-9 and 21-10. Of course, the nature of the clay changes the character of the expression completely. Its pliability, lack of tensile strength, and tendency to require compacting results in a form that is dense in comparison with the openness of the other two three-dimensional forms. Here too, the medium interacts with the gesture-like quality of the expression. The representational element is not dominant, rather, it tells us what the pattern of line and mass is about. The effectiveness of this representation is, in large part, a product of a child's manipulative skill with the particular kind of material used.

The materials used in each of these three-dimensional forms contribute a quality of tactility, touch sensation, important to the total expression. This tactility is most evident in the clay sculpture, where contact between fingers and material is direct and rapid because of the pliability of clay. It is also evident in the string and wire sculptures, where the tactile sense is associated with the looseness and flexibility of string and wire. Here, sensation contributes to the sense of the flowing movement of the expressive gesture. The teacher must help children develop this kind of touch sensitivity.

We have reason to believe that the discovery of techniques of forming is related to expressive purpose, and that the development of these techniques is begun without preconceived ideas about the relationships between materials, processes, and concepts with respect to expression. The child attempts to create relationships between these elements as he goes along. This is a good thing, because not every expressional purpose is served by relating materials and processes to previous experience; purposes are also discovered and served during manipulative-experimental processes.

Much of the art of the youngest kindergarten children is done for its own sake. A painting can be pure scribbling, pure manipulation, and the naming of it that comes afterward can be on the basis of what it looks like to the child, in terms of his previous experience. In the work of more mature kindergarten children, growth is considered to have taken place when manipulation and experience are related in an art form.

It is possible to help older children structure forms from materials that become metaphors expressive of the art processes themselves.

21-11. CLAY SCULPTURE
New York City Public Schools.

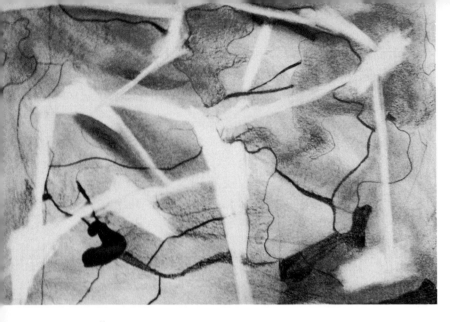

21-12. PENCIL DRAWING
East Orange, New Jersey, Public Schools.

21-13. PENCIL DRAWING
East Orange, New Jersey, Public Schools.

Figures 21-12 and 21-13 are made with soft pencil on white drawing paper, the purpose being to find out what kinds of designs can be made by manipulating a soft pencil in a variety of ways. In Figure 21-12, tones have been produced with the side of the lead and then rubbed to make soft modulations. The point has been used to produce dark lines. A soft eraser has been employed to remove black and gray areas so that the white of the paper comes through to produce an additional tone and pattern. The child has discovered ways to make the surface seem to modulate, as well as means to make contrasting tones from patterns that echo other toned patterns. In Figure 21-13, an entirely different kind of surface and textural pattern has evolved because the point of the pencil has been used.

Each pencil drawing has resulted in an abstract pattern of shape, tone, texture, and rhythm, the product of the natural qualities of the materials alone. Each is based on the sensory experience of working with the materials, rather than on visual kinds of sensory experience.

Older children can be given similar opportunities to exercise their critical awareness in experiences dominated by the spirit of "let's see what will happen."

Figure 21-14 shows how expressional purpose, material, tactility, rhythm, and gesture interact in a complete expression. This Halloween ghost, made by a seventh-grade child is evanescent, pale, and ghostly as a result of the use of cheesecloth for the body and a white ball for the head. Cheesecloth makes a thin, wispy, airlike shroud which emphasizes its unreality. The over-all effect of a flowing garment hanging in space also adds to the sense of ghostliness and unreality. The tactility of the materials has increased the effectiveness of the expression. Here, as in the string, wire, and the clay sculptures, purpose and material successfully interact.

A material should not restrict expression, since expression should come first. The purpose of experimentation, discovery, and invention is to find materials that will most effectively embody an expressive purpose. If the purpose is to express the feelings of a boy and girl doing a fast dance, it might be worthwhile to experiment with many different kinds of materials. In Figure 21-15, colored electrical wire conveys the sense of whirling movement involved in popular, teen-age dances. The wire creates a sense of excitement by combining pirmary colors with spiraling movement; the twistings of the wire describe the dynamic rhythm of the two figures. Neither the color of the wire nor the movement inherent in the forms is intended to reproduce a visual image, a specific dance, or a pattern of sound. These qualities are communicated in the total pattern of rhythm, color, and composition. Representation is a product of total purpose, and it is impossible to say where it begins and ends.

21-14. HALLOWEEN GHOST
Toms River, New Jersey, Public Schools.

21-15. WIRE SCULPTURE
Toms River, New Jersey, Public Schools.

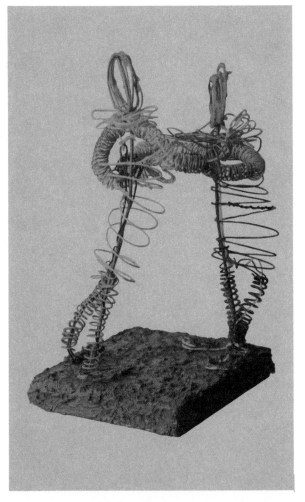

21-16. MOSAIC
Toms River, New Jersey, Public Schools.

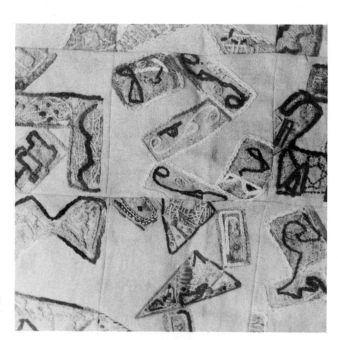

21-17. STITCHERY DESIGN
Collection of Theodore Lynch.

Figure 21-16, a mosaic made by an upper-grade child, is the product of the experimental arrangement of tiles on a board. The rigid, angular shapes of the tiles themselves have suggested the form that eventually comes to dominate the total design.

EXPRESSION IN GROUP ART ACTIVITIES

The mosaic pattern of shapes and colors serves as an interesting contrast to the stitchery design made by a group of intermediate-grade children.

Here, each burlap rectangle was threaded with a pattern of colored yarns by a different child, and all the squares were sewn together to produce the total pattern. The varying quality of this pattern is the result of the different kinds of detailed individual yarn patterns, whereas the mosaic is dominated by a single concept, itself dictated by the essentially similar, angular tiles.

Like the stitchery design, the puppets in Figures 21-18 and 21-19 are products of group cooperation by children in the intermediate grades.

21-18. HAND PUPPETS
New York City Public Schools.

21-19. PAPER SCULPTURE
Campus School, Glassboro State College.

Puppets can be made in a variety of ways. Heads can be made from wads of paper, paper pulp, soft woods like balsa, or from papier mâché. The costumes can be made from fabric scraps, stockings, or other materials.

The clowns in Figure 21-19 were made by a class from construction paper and were stapled to a bulletin board as part of a three-dimensional circus. Each child either selected a part of the circus to work on with two or three other children or was assigned a part by a chairman. Some children were assigned the job of over-all organization, as well as responsibility for background and other designs necessary to make the circus complete. All the children helped organize the circus on the bulletin board.

In each of these group efforts, the major job was organizational. The children had to determine how to give meaning to an area of study. In the case of the puppets in Figure 21-18, the area of study was a dramatic production. Such a production, of course, could have been handled in a number of ways. For example, the children themselves could have participated as actors, costume designers, and set designers. Because of interest, previous experience, or suggestions from the teacher, however, they decided on a puppet play.

A teacher should never force a particular decision on a class if she is unable to convince the group of children of its desirability. A good teacher will permit the group to engage in some other enterprise if the children insist on it or if they demonstrate that it would be more desirable.

After the initial planning, the children became involved with the problem of how to make the puppets and the puppet stage. Some of them may have had previous experience with puppets or marionettes, and could make suggestions as to how to solve this problem. It was still the responsibility of the teacher to determine the group's ability to make certain kinds of puppets. The teacher might have decided that research or a movie on puppet- or marionette-making would be useful. Perhaps the teacher arranged a field trip to a puppet or marionette maker, or invited a professional puppeteer to talk to the children. Maybe a special art teacher was brought in.

The entire process, then, involved group analysis and solution of the problem, and the children's assumption of responsibility for the various parts of the job. The only problem that then remained was to make expressive puppets for the dramatization of a particular story. This involved experimentation with materials, improvisation, invention, and finally the making of the puppets themselves.

SUMMARY

To achieve skill in expression, children must think of the art activity as a problem-solving process in which there are no absolutes, specific answers, or formulated methods for arriving at solutions. Expressional skill involves the ability to seek and discover, improvisation and experimentation, effective means for expression.

Skill in visual representation should not be confused with skill in expression. The mere representation of an object as we see it is not an objective of the art education process. Representation is only a part of expression, and its use may or may not be justified, depending on the expressive purpose. Expression, the forming of meaningful metaphors with plastic materials, is dependent on all possible sources of sensory experience.

A teacher must be sufficiently sensitive, creative, and imaginative to be able to help children benefit from experimentation and improvisation, and to make them aware of the discoveries they achieve.

Twenty-two

SKILL AND INVENTION

Invention is the product of discovery. The process leading to invention is a learning process for which some careful planning must be done. Successful invention is the product of a process of creative action based upon developing imagination and a growing repertory of experience. The evolution of critical awareness is a necessary ingredient in the achievement of educational value in this aspect of art education processes among the older children of the elementary school.

Complex skills are required to form the conceptualizations of children in the intermediate and upper grades into suitable metaphors. Such skills make possible a process of invention. Inventiveness evolves out of the ability of the creative-imagination to take advantage of discoveries made during children's experimentations and improvisations with art materials and image-symbols.

DEFINITION

Inventive skills are adaptable skills. The older children in elementary school can develop adaptable skills if the following resources can be increased both quantitatively and qualitatively:

1. *Image-symbols.* The store of image-symbols can be increased if

217

planning for art activity includes provisions for widening the children's experience and for helping them form visual concepts of their experiences. This goal can be achieved by discussions about experiences to be used for art activity and by continuous group and individual evaluations of the progress of an art activity. This kind of evaluation procedure motivates the children to consider means for forming images that can be evolved into suitable metaphors.

2. *Techniques for forming materials.* The older children will have increased ability to use tools, to explore a variety of hand and power tools, and to work with an increasingly larger number of different materials.

3. *Techniques for exploring and experimenting with ideas and materials.* Knowledge about the techniques of experimentation with materials and ideas is adaptable and flexible. Skill in using such techniques requires habits of analysis of materials, experiments with forming in terms of the structural and plastic qualities of materials, and the ability to recognize qualities that might be useful for forming purposes. There is no formula that can be used to guide thinking about this procedure. The technique is mainly one of being alert to suggestions, evaluating results, and imaginatively projecting techniques.

Skills in invention are not developed according to patterns and sequences. Skills developed as stereotypes hinder, rather than encourage, the development of useful forms among older children. For example, if children are told how to draw a face according to some standards or formulated procedures, they will most likely be able to draw a satisfying and recognizable representation of a human face. This kind of achievement, however, requires a nonadaptable skill because the end result will not be the product of an unexpected interest, an unforseen need, or an unexpected requirement. The face the children will have learned to draw will not be a face that is intended to exhibit the characteristics of a particular person; it will be an unidentifiable face that the children learned to draw by rote. Such nonadaptive skill may be interesting and may win some plaudits, but it is a very limited skill and makes extremely limited contributions to the totality of the children's education.

INVENTION AND CHILD GROWTH

Among the older children, the process of invention may be thwarted by the children's natural tendency to conform to group norms. Such group norms are often the products of previously established standards or of standards that are most acceptable to the group. The natural tendency of older children to want to be part of the group, to conform, to win the approval of the group, often encourages the children to learn nonadaptive skills because they are most acceptable. Thus, the nonadaptive skill becomes an easy way out of the more difficult problems of invention.

The natural manipulative processes of children will serve as a means for beginning effective experimental processes that, through growth, may lead to aesthetically satisfying and expressionally valid purposes. For example, the processes of

22-1. CLAY FIGURES
Author's collection.

building three-dimensional forms from clay can evolve into techniques for discovering useful expressional means.

The sculptude in Figure 22-1 was made by a primary-grade child. This sculpture follows the dynamic forming tendency discussed earlier as the pressing of elements on a central core (see Chapter Nineteen). The result is an evolving form that springs from a central nucleus. The cause of the form is in the nature of the materials used. Clay is a material that is so pliable it naturally lends itself to a building-up process. Young children first form round shapes because the plastic material conforms to their hands. Soon after the children learn that they can make rolls and slabs with a gentle pressure, and they build forms by applying odd slabs, coils, and bits of clay to the round ball, which becomes a central core. In effect, this is three-dimensional scribbling. As the children's skill increases they observe relationships between their three-dimensional scribbling and forms. This observation is the beginning of invention.

For older children, the beginning of forming with a material as plastic as clay is the beginning of experimentation. The resulting experiments are critically studied for suggestions of forms that express some purpose.

The sculpture in Figure 22-2 is not merely a clearly defined nucleus from which dynamic shapes radiate; however, elements of earlier scribbling tendencies are still observable. These might be listed as:

1. *Building.* The mane of the lion and the collar and hat of the figure are added slabs and balls of clay.

2. *Pinching.* The snout of the lion and the collar and hat of the figure are pulled and pinched.

From this simple and natural beginning, the older child, who made the sculpture, was able to develop a more complex technique, which is largely the product of experimentation. The added sections of clay that form the mane of the lion, for example, might have been made by pressing the clay through a sieve. The spaghetti-like clay that emerges from the sieve could form the textured material that becomes a metaphor for hair.

The sculpture in Figure 22-2 illustrates the manner in which one child's growing critical

22-2. CLAY FIGURE
New York City Public Schools.

awareness serves to structure a concept of man and lion in terms of the natural qualities of the art material used, in this case, clay. These qualities are:

1. The clay is plastic and easily formed.

2. The natural manipulative processes involve a form of structuring that is additive and subtractive and results from hand pressures on the clay. The additive process is the process that encouraged the child, from his first experience with the material, to add rolls, slabs, and bits of clay to a central core or nucleus. Pinching is a natural process that aids in giving shape to the clay. The subtractive process is a process of removing clay by pulling or cutting. The subtractive process is less important to primary-grade children than it is to older children. Subtraction becomes a means for making changes easily when applied to processes of pushing, pulling, and pinching.

3. The plasticity and softness of the clay makes it possible for a clay object to sag and fall apart

if the structure is too heavy in any one part. For this reason, the art of the young primary-grade child, shown in Figure 22-1, revolves around a central core. In the work of the older child, the form of structuring is more complex and purposeful. The head and body of the lion lie on the ground, the man's figure is as vertical as possible. With this mode of structuring, the natural compressive strength of the material is exploited and used for the essential character of the design. The design of this sculpture is as much dependent on the nature of the materials, their plasticity and structural characteristics, as it is on the expressive purpose of the metaphor.

From our understanding of the relation between materials and concepts, the structuring process and the potential metaphor, it should be evident that invention is a result of discovery. The things younger children discover are not necessarily new. From available evidence, it is obvious that primary-grade children discover very simple structures. They do not become involved in the same kind of detailed critical probing as do older children. In working with younger children, great emphasis must be placed on the things that can be made with materials. The young children's natural inclinations will usually be good guides to their art activity. It is during the art activity of the older children that the children's natural modes should be used as a starting ground, as a base of operations.

22-3. PLASTER AND EARTH BAS-RELIEF
East Orange, New Jersey, Public Schools.

MATERIALS AND INVENTION

A purpose in the program of experimentation and invention for older children is to help the children develop skill in dealing with new and unforeseen potentials of materials. This kind of skill involves the ability to look for the materials that will be most suitable for particular expressional purposes. Related to this skill must be the ability to use one's imagination to infer, from the character of a material, its potential for expression. Many of these understandings are often arrived at by accident. For example, children who have opportunity to experiment with paint sometimes find that wet colors blend with each other in unique ways that suggest methods for handling and controlling colors in order to secure useful effects. The ability to recognize and use the characteristics of materials is a skill that many contemporary sculptors, architects, and painters have developed. Sculptors, such as the American Flannagan, have been able to make exciting sculptures from natural stone formations. Many contemporary architects have used the qualities of construction materials and the engineering techniques such materials require in order to give their buildings a design quality related to the purpose of the building and the materials from which it has been formed. Skyscrapers of the best kind are usually good examples of this architecture. The long vertical lines made by structural materials are contrasted against the transparent horizontals of glass in such buildings as Lever House in New York City or the Carson, Pirie and Scott Department Store in Chicago. Henry Moore's sculptures, as in his "Reclining Figure" (Figure 7-3), suggest the fluid movements of mass and void suitable for cast metal.

Experimentation provides children with the opportunity to learn how to recognize qualities and configurations that are useful for expressional purposes.

Figure 22-3 shows how an eighth-grade child was able to improvise from natural materials to form a rhythmical combination of natural materials.

Figure 22-4 represents a rhythmical three-dimensional arrangement incorporating the perfectly natural qualities of clothespins.

Figure 22-5 is a construction made from ordinary toothpicks.

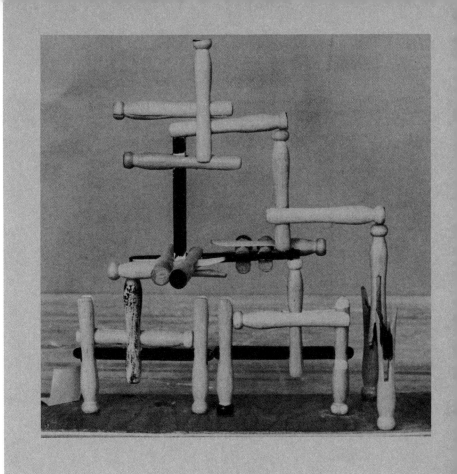

22-4. CLOTHESPIN CONSTRUCTION
Author's collection.

22-5. TOOTHPICK CONSTRUCTION
Author's collection.

Both Figures 22-4 and 22-5 are engineering feats as well as triumphs of a probing imagination. Neither construction is made according to a formula or according to any previously formed plan defining the character of the final form. In each case the child has had to study the qualities of the materials and he has experimented with them in a spirit of "let's see what will happen." Each of the structures, like the arrangement of natural materials in Figure 24-6, grew from the logic of the materials themselves. Through experimentation, children discover and learn to exploit the structural characteristics of materials. Out of this developing knowledge of materials, the creative-imagination helps fashion a form characteristic of the qualities of the materials themselves.

DISCOVERING TECHNIQUES FOR FORMING

The works represented in Figures 22-3, 22-4, and 22-5 indicate the importance of engineering skills. The need for this type of skill can not always be known in advance. The unique configurations suggested by the structural, tactile, and color qualities of a material may offer unexpected possibilities for invention. For example, methods for joining toothpicks to each other may not be known by the students when the teacher suggests that toothpicks be used for three-dimensional construction. In such a situation, the first problem posed for almost any group of children would be: How can the toothpicks be joined together? A similar problem must have existed in the wire and bottle top construction (Figure 22-6), in the combination of natural materials (Figure 22-3) and in the clothespin construction (Figure 22-4).

In program planning for the development of nonadaptive skills, the teacher should evolve a useful plan for helping children consider the relationships of the materials used in the preceding illustrations; the teacher would have to present the project as a problem in establishing relationships between the materials, the forming of possible structures, and the techniques for forming the structures.

The clothespins present a comparatively simple problem. Their structure suggests a method for joining them to each other. For this reason they could be considered much more elementary than materials such as toothpicks, clothes hangers, bottle tops, or other materials that do not, by their structure and original purpose, suggest a method for joining one to another.

The toothpicks presented an interesting problem for a seventh-grade class. The project was presented to the group as a problem in joining common materials. The teacher selected toothpicks and posed the following questions:

1. Can toothpicks be used for anything besides picking teeth?
2. Can toothpicks be used in much the same way large pieces of wood are used?
3. Does the size and shape of toothpicks suggest that they are adaptable to some unique mode of construction? If this is the case, is it possible to discover the mode or modes through some series of planned experiments?

The purpose of this group of questions is purely exploratory. It may happen that the children will have no answers. The teacher, in that case, must lead the discussion to possible answers. The purpose of this initial phase need not be precisely defined or planned by the teacher. It might be best to wait and see what possible directions for planning are suggested by the discussion with the children. The children might suggest directions for planning that the teacher had not thought about.

A purpose of the planning session is to propose techniques for investigating the potentials of the material for forming art objects. Since this purpose is formulated by the teacher, it is reasonable to expect some opposition from the children. Experimentation may be a process they can not associate with art activity. If this situation develops, the teacher must demonstrate the need for experimentation or must at least lead the planning toward experimental work with materials. For this reason, the purpose of the assignment for the children is to explore the materials and to attempt to learn what they can do to make the materials useful for the expression of ideas.

The techniques of experimentation have to be developed for children. This process requires the development of understandings about ways of working. For this kind of art activity, it is im-

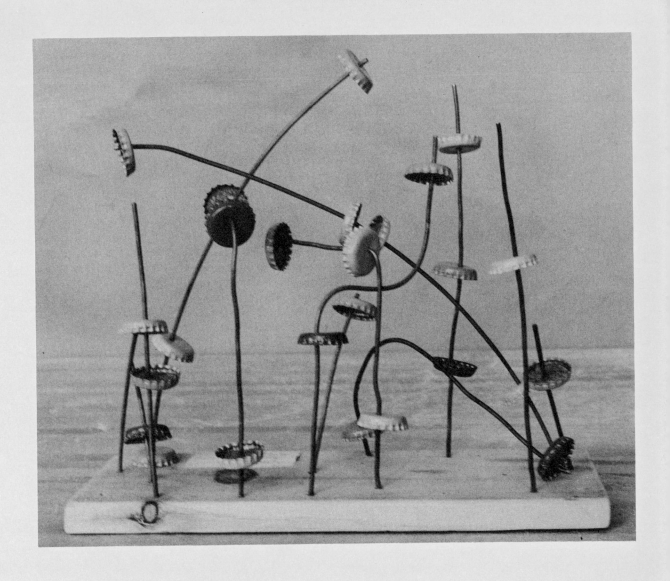

22-6. WIRE AND BOTTLE TOP CONSTRUCTION
Author's collection.

portant that methods of working with materials be examined, discussed, and agreed upon by the group of children. A suggested plan for experimentation might evolve in the following general manner:

The planning of the motivating sessions with the children should be concerned with finding means for answering questions. The kinds of questions posed should be drawn from the problems suggested in the questions previously posed as examples of questions that are fundamental to this kind of open-ended exploratory approach to art activity. The questions posed should actually indicate a technique for the experimental ap-

proach. For example, the following problems might serve as a basis for planning:

1. What are the structural characteristics of toothpicks? Can toothpicks be bent, curved, or formed into angles?
2. Can toothpicks carry weight? Do toothpicks have compressive strength? Do they have tensile strength?
3. How can toothpicks be joined?
4. Are there any examples available of constructions made from toothpicks by other people?

During the course of discussion, it should be pointed out to the children that the strength of materials changes according to the formations they are given. In the case of toothpicks, it is important to test the strength of the material when subjected to downward pressures, which may be described as compression. Some materials are ideally suited to carry this kind of pressure. A concrete foundation of a building, for example, can carry great weight; it has great compressive strength. Steel wire cables cannot support the same kind of downward pressures; however, they can hold much suspended weight. If one pulls on a rope of wire or a steel cable, the wire or cable will sustain and maintain the pressure. If equal pulling tension is exerted on a bar of concrete of equal size the concrete will probably break. Consequently, we say that steel wire cable has great tensile strength but little compressive strength. If we try a similar experiment with toothpicks, we may find that toothpicks have more tensile strength than compressive strength. We may also find that many toothpicks in combination have more compressive and tensile strength than one toothpick. Our findings may suggest that the kinds of structures for which steel cables, steel bars, or lengths of wood are useful may also be the kinds of structures for which toothpicks, in a proportionately smaller scale, are suitable.

A number of other things may be discovered about toothpicks depending on the extent to which the maturity of the children permits them to probe into the qualities of this material. For example, toothpicks are easily bent and broken, but often not all of the wood fibers break. Usually the fibers of the wood separate on the outside of the break but not on the inside angle and the toothpick thus remains whole. Now, if glue is added at the point of the break, the joint is made secure and strong. The resemblance between the tensile qualities of toothpicks and of steel suggests that modes of construction suitable for such things as suspension bridges may also be suitable for toothpick constructions.

The method of joining toothpicks suggests an interesting line of investigation. The glues ordinarily used for joining pieces of wood dry slowly. Although two toothpicks can be joined, they must be held in some manner until the glue has dried. This slowness of drying makes construction a very difficult problem, and certainly not one suitable for young children. However, if *extra fast drying* airplane glues are used, the joint

can be secured the moment two toothpicks touch each other.

PURPOSES

What happens in any one group after these problems have been posed depends upon many factors. The outcomes are rarely predictable in detail. In general, the purpose is to stimulate imagination, to encourage habits of creative action, and to provide opportunities for the children to acquire habits of invention, experimentation, and improvisation.

TIMING: WHEN DOES PLANNING FOR SKILL IN DISCOVERY BEGIN?

The next logical consideration must concern an understanding of when this kind of program for investigating materials should begin. In an effective program, this process begins in the beginning of the kindergarten year. The changes that take place from year to year are changes dictated by the children's readiness to work with particular materials. It is necessary to determine whether or not children may work with knives, sharp scissors, hand saws, wood planes, awls, and gouges. In many school districts there are specific rules that control children's use of various kinds of hand and power tools, scissors, carving knives, and chisels.

ROLE OF THE TEACHER

Is it always possible for children, under a teacher's guidance, to arrive by themselves at useful solutions to problems? Can a group of intermediate-grade children arrive at workable conclusions regarding toothpicks without being told some of the techniques that will make it possible for them to build expressive and aesthetically satisfying forms with toothpicks? Our answer must be that children develop such ability at times, depending upon the effectiveness of their teacher. If a teacher is familiar with modes for developing habits of creative action, imaginative thinking, exploration, and improvisation, the teacher will probably be able to help the children increase their ability to find answers to problems. This ability involves the ability to ask questions and to be persistently curious and willing to try many different approaches. Children need to learn that a failure is simply a sign that something else ought to be tried.

Children, especially younger children, need help in discovering solutions to problems. Information should be provided by the teacher as the children's need arises. In this way, the children's understanding of their ability to use new techniques will most likely be successful. The teacher should furnish children with the opportunity to try solving problems themselves before supplying them with explanations of the more standard techniques.

Since many art materials have been the subject of much study, we have a great deal of information available about applicable craft techniques. The teacher should investigate available literature on craft techniques, and should use with discretion the information gained. The teacher's purpose is to give the children opportunities to solve problems. The purpose of an art activity is derived from the structure of art education. The most useful kind of art activity emphasizes habits of creative action, imagination, and the seeking of relationships between the parts of a structure, concepts, ideas, and image-symbols. Much of the value of art education will be lost if children are given only answers. Prepared answers limit thinking and learning and the art forms that result may be stereotypes rather than unique expressions of unique individuals.

PART FIVE

BUILDING THE ART CURRICULUM

Twenty-three

READINESS

Planning the art program requires understanding of the readiness and individual differences of children. By the time children enter kindergarten, they are ready for involvement in activities that will encourage physical, mental, emotional, and social growth.

PHYSIOLOGICAL BASIS OF READINESS

The development of the brain and the nervous system reaches a high level of maturity when children are between five and eight years of age. The maturation reached during this period is sufficiently high to make it possible for us to begin a useful educational process for children in this age group.

The early maturation of the neural functions is accompanied by a similar growth in the sensorimotor skill of children. The almost simultaneous maturation of sensorimotor skill and the neural functions has specific advantages for the art education program. This combination of physical and mental functions makes early conditioning possible. Children can learn to perform in art activities. The children's physical and mental skill makes it possible for them to make paintings, drawings, sculptures, and constructions that can become valid expressive metaphors.

SKILLS AND APTITUDES

The relationship between the sensorimotor and the neural functions includes a relationship between the children's physical, emotional, and intellectual abilities. Because of this relationship children's behavior is related to their physical growth. The integral relationship of emotional, intellectual, physical, and sensory aspects results in a curious and important relationship between physical growth and maturation through experience, with its accompanying accumulation of varied skills and knowledges.

A child's readiness for art activity is shown by his physical and mental growth. According to this understanding, we know that children are ready for art activities from the moment they enter kindergarten. Experience in teaching has indicated that because of the maturation rates of the sensorimotor and neural functions, art activities do not need to be graded from simple to difficult during the primary years. All children, during this school period appear to have a potential for developing a high level of motor skill, sensory skill, and ability to evaluate their work.

INDIVIDUAL DIFFERENCES

Maturation rates do not progress at the same speed for all children. For this reason, the level of achievement for each child should be expected to vary from a theoretical norm. Nevertheless, it is necessary to establish a standard of achieve-

ment in art. The process of involving children in an art activity tends to increase their ability to progress in art skills and to communicate concepts with plastic materials.

In classroom practice, the skilled teacher will have to determine when a child is ready to do a job. It is difficult to know exactly when a child is ready to perform a particular kind of manipulation or to express a specific concept or understanding. Examples of how the teacher directs the growth of children's thinking, how she takes advantage of every evidence of readiness, is indicated in Figures 23-1 and 23-2, drawings of a turtle and a policeman by two different kindergarten children. Figure 23-1, the drawing of a policeman, began as a pure motor action. The child, stimulated by earlier discussions about the need for children to take proper precautions when crossing the street, started to scribble and said he was making a picture of a policeman. The teacher told him to make another drawing of a policeman because he had time for one more. The child turned his paper to the clean side and began to scribble again, but this time the teacher noted that he was making the gestures a policeman makes when he holds up his arm and cape to stop traffic. The teacher then suggested that policemen wear blue uniforms and white capes. From this point, the drawing begins to show the characteristic metamorphosis from scribble to geometricized form. The left arm of the figure is large and encompasses the broad gesture of the policeman's signal. The right arm appears to be

23-1. POLICEMAN
Crayon. *Author's collection.*

23-2. TURTLE
Crayon on cut out paper. *Author's collection.*

an afterthought. The right arm is not related to the action being expressed by the child; it is not related to the rhythmical and circular movement of the main gesture. The inclusion of the right arm is indicative of the child's purpose to form an image drawn from a concept of a policeman performing an important function. This concept is developed in rapid fashion as is indicated by the change in the circular scribbling to a stippling of the background with the point of the crayon. This is a significant change in movement. The manipulative process shows evidence of differentiation. The stippling process is an attempt to represent a change in texture from the figure to the background.

Figure 23-2, the drawing of a turtle, is also an indication of the child's readiness to communicate meaning through a forming process. The turtle began as a circular scribble, as is evidenced by the development of the turtle's form from the circular movements that are related to the texture of the turtle's shell. This form of development provides evidence of a clear relationship between the expressive gesture and the conscious forming

of an image. The incentive to form this image originated in discussion about a pet turtle, which was kept in the classroom and fed regularly by the children. This child, like the child who made the drawing of the policeman, is now ready to construct forms related to his own important experiences. The next step in the process is to provide the children with materials and techniques that will enable them to make pictures and models about the things they see and do as part of their daily learning experience.

GENERAL PRINCIPLES

On the basis of what we now know about children's growth, it is possible to establish the following general principles:

1. During the earliest phases of the kindergarten period, the children will exhibit some clumsiness in their manipulative processes. This clumsiness will be largely the result of the consistency of some materials, their resistance to shaping processes, and the amount of muscular strength required for handling certain tools.

2. The physical size of the children will limit their use of some materials and tools.

3. The ability to make judgments will govern the children's readiness for some activities. The children's ability to discriminate will affect their ability to recognize subtleties in materials and subtle differences regarding the uses to which various kinds of tools may be put.

4. Children's intellectual development progresses at different rates. Not all children will be ready at the same time for geometric structuring, or for the same kind of critical evaluation of their manipulative processes.

5. Not all children will have the same level of ability to communicate effectively through visual symbols.

6. Not all children are equal in their ability to respond to experience in visual-plastic terms.

7. Children vary in the intensity of their visual imagery.

8. Children vary in imaginative thinking ability.

9. Children vary in their ability to establish meaningful and unusual relationships between diverse materials and diverse ideas or concepts.

10. Children vary in creative skill. This understanding grows out of the understandings expressed in the preceding principles.

Twenty-four

DIRECTIONS FOR PRIMARY-GRADE PLANNING

The pace for thinking and performing in art education should be established at the beginning of the primary-grade period. Children form patterns early in their school career: attitudes toward art and art education, for instance, are formed during the primary period. During this time the general goals and methods for involving children in art activities need to be planned and related to other areas of the classroom program. If the initiation of the art program is not satisfactory, it may be difficult to make corrections in the intermediate or the upper grades. For these reasons, among others, the first years of the art program may be decisive.

Since effective art education is based on both the needs of children and their natural modes of expression, art education planning must make use of both the child's firsthand experience and his natural capacity for fantasy. In order to make the most of these natural inclinations, planning must be as much the responsibility of the children as of the teacher. Indeed, planning the art program begins with children.

BASIC CONSIDERATIONS

A basis for planning the art education program in terms of the characteristics of the children involved in it might be developed from

233

general guidelines derived from the children's needs and from the objectives of both general education and art education. The following proposals offer guidelines that could provide a foundation for program planning.

1. *The art experiences of children are most useful for educational purposes when they are based on the life experiences of the children.* A real life experience is one with which young children have a close contact. The five- to six-year-old group, for instance, has close contact with father, mother, brother, sister, pets, friends, school, teacher, and home. These experiences form the useful subject materials of art because they represent important and emotionally felt relationships. Art activities can clarify these relationships through the precognitive and productive thinking phases of the art processes. The art form becomes an objectification of experience, a meaningful relating of the parts of experience.

2. *As soon as possible, the natural manipulative processes should be related to the experiences that are important to children.* We have already noted that the drawing, painting, and modeling done by very young preschool children and children in the early part of the kindergarten year is often pure motor activity. This motor activity is pleasurable, and children sometimes accidentally discover a relationship between their scribbles and various of their own experiences. The planned art program from the beginning of the kindergarten year should *help* children discover such relationships. It should involve the children as early as possible with the techniques and processes of productive thinking.

Experiences important to children have emotional overtones that give a needed fullness, depth, and breadth to their thinking. Learning in art education depends on the development of meaning and a structured relationship between thinking, feeling, manipulative processes, and physical materials.

CHILDREN'S NEEDS AND ART PROGRAM PLANNING

The interests of children and the impact of firsthand experience are integrally related to the things children need to do, know, and discover about themselves and their social and physical environment. Plans for utilizing needs in the art program are based on the usefulness of art processes for helping children know and satisfy their needs, fulfill their interests, expand the range of their interests, and provide depth to their understanding of experience. The following needs are suggested as basic for the development of an art education program.

1. *Children need to know the physical world in which they live.* Young people need to become curious about their environment. They can be helped to discover and understand it if they are given opportunities to manipulate the physical materials in their surroundings. An art program designed to meet this need makes provision for children to work with many natural materials, to manipulate them, and to shape them in a manner suitable to their structure, color, plasticity, and their tactile, visual, and other sense qualities. Sand, for example, is used by children in a manner suitable to its qualities of cohesion when wet, its smoothness, and its plasticity. Children learn much about their environment when they are able to find natural clay and use it for modeling purposes. Stones, seashells, leaves, pebbles, gravel, and even vegetables can be used to form objects. The art program need not be designed to use only standard manufactured art materials. Paint, crayons, papers and commercially prepared clays play an important role at all levels of the art program. But a program designed to meet the children's need to know their environment, their world, provides opportunities to work with all kinds of materials.

Children should also have opportunity to explore the possibilities for art work offered by scrap materials, including ones they have found. Industrial scrap, if available, often teases the imagination. Children develop habits of thinking inventively when they utilize boxes, wire, scrap papers, woods, fabrics, buttons, burnt out electric bulbs, and many other materials.

2. *Children need to know themselves, their families, friends, and pets.* Children need opportunities to make pictures, clay sculptures, and imaginative constructions of people and animals important to them and places and things they see and are curious about. These imaginative constructions will be formed from materials with which the children are acquainted or from new

materials they have selected as most suitable to their expressive purpose of forming metaphors or interpretive symbols.

3. *Children need to learn techniques for expressing their experiences, their thinking, and their feelings.* The need to know oneself and one's friends is related to the need for expression, which begins with the individual child's need to find his voice, to communicate his feelings and his thinking. We all need to give form to our aspirations, our concepts, and our daydreams. Through working with plastic materials it becomes possible to give intangible thoughts an objective and physical form.

4. *Children need opportunity to establish their own directions for work and goals for achievement.* This is an individual goal strengthened by goals for group achievement. The relation between group and individual goals is one of mutual support. The unique individual draws strength from his membership in the group and the acceptance of his uniqueness by the group.

From the earliest phases of the primary period, children need opportunities to work alone as well as in groups. They need to be helped to discover their own modes for forming image-symbols into expressive metaphors. The responsibility of the teacher is to respect the child's natural uniqueness. Children do use predictable forms; the forms of child art tend to follow a characteristic pattern. But the youngest children are able to evolve modes and forms suitable to their own purposes, because they are not yet consciously confined to preconceived patterns of art expression. The teacher needs to be alert for evidence of uniqueness that is useful for a particular child's purpose. These examples need to be pointed out to the child as a means of obtaining a purpose important to him. We do know that children imitate each other; this is one of the ways in which they learn. But children also have to know what kinds of forms are most useful for their own special conceptions, their special kinds of experience. We also know that children during the earliest phases of the primary period can invent surprisingly fresh and expressive metaphors. The teacher must be able to recognize this kind of invention and should call the attention of the individual and the group to the effectiveness of the surprising metaphor, the expressive strength of freshness

and spontaneity, and the desirability of developing the germ of an idea in terms of individual thinking. Above all, the teacher must help the individual and the group appreciate the value of an individual point of view.

5. *Children need both activity and rest.* The rhythms of art activity involve doing and resting, action and recovery. Art processes themselves involve manipulation, evaluation, rest, recovery, and a return to activity. An effective art program makes use of these rhythms. It seeks to achieve a balance: between activity and periods of rest, between one type of activity and another type. The vitality of the activities and the ever-developing forms of achievement grow out of this balance. Because of it recovery is possible after activity, and new activity grows out of previous activity, evaluation, and rest. The balance is achieved through variations in types of materials manipulated, variations in manipulative processes, and a concern with discovering increasingly better means for expressing experiences. Art activities involving chalk may be followed by constructions made from paper or scrap materials; form-making with clay may be followed by collage; painting processes may be followed by three-dimensional constructions. And each separate activity is preceded and followed by contemplation, evaluation, discussion, and the formulation of new processes and plans for new experiments or investigations. The experiments with processes and the seeking out of suitable materials and techniques grow out of the directions indicated for new work during the periods when evaluations are made of completed jobs.

6. *Children need to develop a feeling for and an understanding of security.* Security can be achieved, at least in part, through the child's realization that he possesses the power to make useful expressions. Children need to know how to communicate the things they think about, feel strongly about, and experience. When they give a form to their experience, children become involved in a process that acquaints them with many of its facets. This process of manipulating materials can give meaning to experience; this is an aesthetic act because it involves the establishment of significant and useful relationships. This aesthetic is colored by the uniqueness of the child's own individuality. Children need oppor-

tunity to discover new meaning in experience through the process of art activity. Without the art activity, in fact, these new understandings will not occur. Given this opportunity, children make expressive forms that are unique expressions of their own personalities. This accomplishment can contribute to their own sense of worthiness; it can provide them with the security of knowing that they have a special contribution to make to the people among whom they live.

PROCESSES OF RELATING EXPERIENCES TO ART FORMS

It is natural for children to establish relationships between their manipulative processes and the experiences that are important to them. Typical examples are the stereotypes used by early primary-grade children in their art work. The moon is seldom represented in drawings of outdoor scenes. On the other hand, the sun is almost always symbolized by a circle with radiating lines. That some children's drawings have no symbol for sun frequently means that the child lost interest in the painting or that some other disturbance prevented the inclusion of the symbol. In a few cases, the child claims to have had no intention of painting the sun symbol; in others, when he is asked why he has not painted the sun, he immediately responds that such a symbol would be desirable, and he quickly makes the usual symbol. This is a most peculiar stereotype. It appears to have much in common with children's habit of beginning drawings of people by first making a circle for the head and then adding the rest of the body parts almost as if they were secondary characteristics. Somewhat related is the habit children have of including their name in a picture as if it were a major part of the work. All these stereotypes appear to be related to the natural ego-centered behavior of the very young child. For the youngest children, concepts are closely related to the self as the accepted center of the universe.

If we accept the idea that children relate their art activities to experiences that are important to them, it may then be possible to make some defensible assumptions. The ever-present sun symbol may represent the element in the sky with which children are most familiar. The sun is important to children because it represents their waking day, their time of activity. Young primary-grade children are expected to go to bed early in the evening, and they are expected to sleep until after the sun has risen. The experience these children have with the moon is very limited. The sun symbol is common; symbols for moon are rare. Night symbols occur at a later date in their experience.

The importance of the firsthand experience can be understood when we realize that the familiar is more emotionally colored than the unfamiliar. We feel emotionally attached to things close to us—to our parents, to ourselves. The things we merely hear about can not mean as much to us. For this reason children draw pictures of themselves and make symbols of people they know before they are willing or even able to draw pictures about purely fantastic ideas, faraway people, and purely imagined experiences and daydreams. These latter things are much more important to the pre-adolescent and the adolescent child than they are to the primary-grade child. This may be part of the reason why very young children symbolically place themselves in the center of each picture; they "draw" their names in prominent sizes and places on their papers.

That the young child draws pictures of people by first making the shapes that stand for the head, may be because many human creatures drawn by the child are identifiable as the child himself. The primary-grade child has difficulty projecting himself into the feelings of other people. He tends to confuse himself with many of the image-symbols he forms into metaphors of people. We have seen how this trait manifests itself even to the extent of appearing in many metaphors for pets and animals. An example is the face of the lion in Figure 6-2.

TRANSFORMATION OF EXPERIENCE BY ART PROCESS

Both the manipulative processes and the qualities of art materials affect the transformation of experience into an expressive metaphor through image-symbols. The qualities involved are the visual and the tactile: structure, texture, pliability, and color. That the use of different materials results in different works of art, even though the subject is the same, is obvious. A sculpture of a

particular cat is different from a painting of that same cat. The qualities of clay are not those of paint, and the differences are reflected in the form of art works utilizing those materials. But there are subtler considerations. In two-dimensional work, the picture space may strongly influence the form of the metaphor. In the crayon drawings of a railroad engine by two kindergarten children, this interaction of concept with pictorial space is demonstrated. The railroad engine drawn in the vertical picture space (Figure 24-1) seems to stretch vertically in order to accommodate itself to the space. Because of the vertical space, too, the engine is short and stumpy. The engine located in the horizontal space (Figure 24-2) is elongated. Again the child makes his metaphor fit the space in which it is placed. Both of these drawings demonstrate the effect of pictorial space and materials on the expressive purpose and its achievement in a metaphor. Both drawings resulted from the same classroom motivation, in which nothing was said about the picture space. There is, therefore, no reason to believe that the vertical or horizontal position of the paper was chosen for any particular reason. However, after the drawings were made, the child who drew Figure 24-1 said he wanted to show how high the locomotive was. The child who made Figure 24-2 said he wanted to show how fast the locomotive was. In each case, the child formed an expression of his purposes for the metaphor on the basis of the materials and processes of drawing.

The reasons children give for their method of handling a picture space may be afterthoughts—manufactured explanations, which are not necessarily the actual purposes that served as guides in the children's productive thinking. The discussion of the completed work or the evaluation often causes children to find or to invent reasons for having worked as they did. These explanations are often produced without prodding from the teacher. It is, however, important, that the teacher lead the children to consider relationships between their purposes and their methods of working and to be deliberative in relating their expressional purposes to the materials and processes of the art activity. In this way precognitive and productive thinking become part of the productive processes.

As a result of the guidance children receive from evaluation and discussion they are, hopefully, led to develop habits of relating the expression of experience to particular materials and processes. They are helped to learn to make suitable choices. Some kinds of experiences may be most suitable for expression in clay, some in words, some in dance, some in music. Our special concern is with those experiences most suitable for expression in pliable, plastic materials. In order to know how expression is related to purpose, it is first necessary to know the character of an experience and the most suitable means for making it meaningful, communicable, and understandable.

METHOD FOR RELATING CONCEPTS TO MATERIALS

Part of the process of relating experience to art must be discussion of the kinds of materials most suitable for the art activity. The art materials for a particular expression and the art processes to be used should be considered during preliminary discussions. In making their choices, children should understand why they chose certain processes and materials.

Often the form selected by children for objectification of experience is a combination of more than one kind of art form. An example is Figure 24-3, a story illustrated with a line drawing.

Figure 24-4 is a primary-grade child's picture of a bird cage. The feeling of reality is enhanced by cutting out the drawing. Cutting is often a means for overcoming the limited ability of very young children to construct three-dimensional structures. The same kind of purpose is illustrated in the cutout drawing of a turtle. Figure 23-2.

The problem of achieving reality within the limitations imposed by primary-grade skills is illustrated in the objects shown in Figures 24-5 to 24-8.

The person in Figure 24-5 is made from pieces of wood and buttons combined with paint on a wooden board. Use by the child of materials that can be held in the hand provides him with a direct sensory experience, an effect of heightened reality, and a technique for giving him added control over the manipulative processes. It also offers opportunities to experiment, because the child is able to move the parts of his object about before deciding where they should be located.

Figure 24-6 shows evidence of growth from the person shown in Figure 24-5. This representation of two people shows a discriminating use of contrasting materials that called for a detailed imaginative and creative process as well as a process of relating ideas or experience to diverse materials. The variety of differently textured materials contributes to the greater sensory detail of this work.

Figures 24-7 and 24-8 differ from Figures 24-5 and 24-6 in having been designed as elements in a dramatic presentation—they serve a social purpose. Like Figure 24-6, Figure 24-7 is an imaginative arrangement of materials. Figure 24-8 is an expressive arrangement of paper bags tied together and decorated with poster paints.

24-3. STORY AND ILLUSTRATION
East Orange, New Jersey, Public Schools.

Memorial Day

Memorial Day comes on May 30th. It is the Day when we remember the men that have served our country in time of war. There have been many wars. We decorate the graves of the men who were killed. We have parades and services.

Mann Turelli

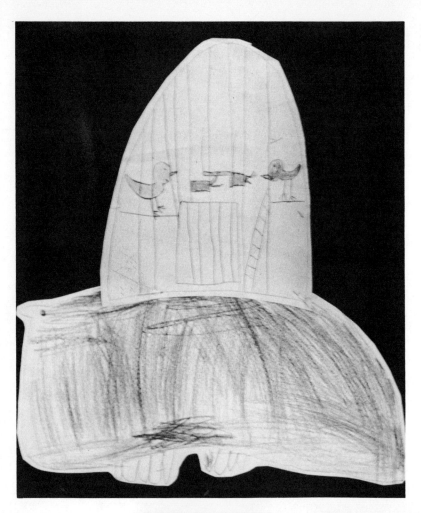

24-4. BIRD CAGE
East Orange, New Jersey, Public Schools.

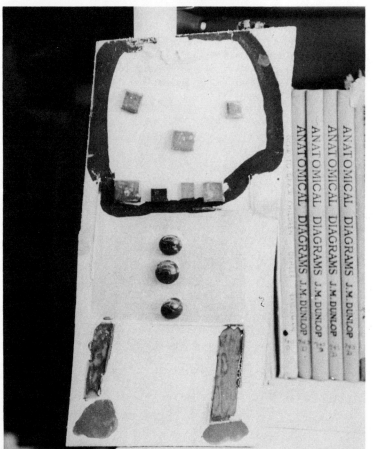

24-5. FIGURE
Wood and buttons. *East Orange, New Jersey, Public Schools.*

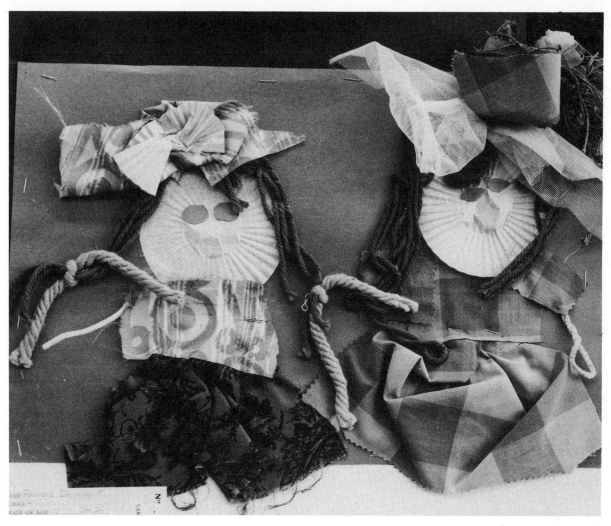

24-6. TWO FIGURES
Collage. *East Orange, New Jersey, Public Schools.*

24-7. PUPPET
East Orange, New Jersey, Public Schools.

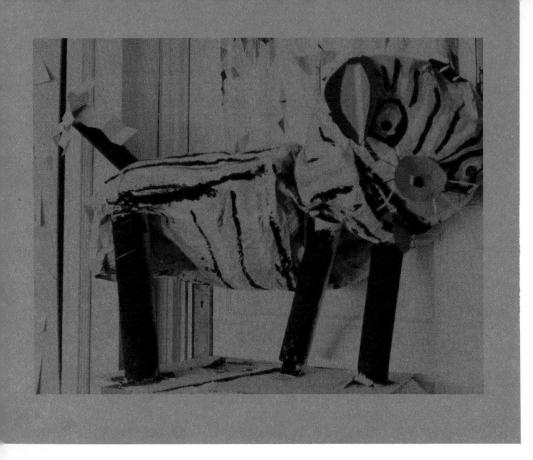

24-8. PAPER-BAG ANIMAL
Author's collection.

The children's decision to utilize two- or three-dimensional forms is largely dependent on the purpose for which their art objects are intended. Figures 24-7 and 24-8 are three-dimensional constructions. This makes them suitable props for a play, where they have to be carried and made to move like puppets. The expressional purpose, too, will often determine the kind of form to be used. An example of this is the bus trip painting experience shown in Figures 8-1 and 17-1 to 17-4.

PLANNING AND MOTIVATION: BEGINNING THE ART ACTIVITY

The bus trip paintings were made after the class had talked about a bus ride they had taken as part of a field trip. The bus experience was not the most important part of the trip; its objective had been a visit designed to implement a classroom study. But the bus ride was full of excitement for these children because they had had few previous opportunities to ride on buses. As a result of the discussion, led by the classroom teacher, the class agreed that a painting made by each member of the class would be a suitable means for describing the bus trip experience. The teacher asked the children, first, to think about the things they had seen and the various other experiences they had had; next, to describe these things; and, finally, to think of ways the sensations and happenings could be made clear and understandable to other people who had not been on the field trip.

The children's decision to make paintings was based on their expressed belief that the panorama of the landscape and the bus could be best expressed with color on large paper. This decision was made after a number of other art media had been discussed and the relative merits of different media had been studied in terms of an expressional purpose. The children agreed that a painting on paper makes it possible to create illusions of vast spaces—an advantage painting has over clay and most other three-dimensional forming materials. The conclusions regarding art processes, the media, and their suitability for the expressional purpose were made by the children. The teacher had no reason to believe that any particular medium would be selected by the class, but she felt that it was her responsibility to let the children develop their art activity on the basis of the decision they made. It did not matter whether the decision was a right one; what did matter was that the children have sufficient evaluation sessions—both individual and group—during the course of the activity, to arrive at some understanding of the value of their judgments.

The decision was not entirely the responsibility of the children: the teacher felt it necessary to tell them how much time could be devoted to the project. And time proved a factor in the decision finally made; paintings, the children had been told, would not take as much time as a diorama of a group mural made with three-dimensional forms. However, the decision was ultimately made by the children.

INTERACTION OF VICARIOUS AND FIRSTHAND EXPERIENCES

Not all of life can be directly experienced. There is an interaction of vicarious and firsthand experience that is important to the child at every level of the elementary-school experience. The amount of vicarious experience usable in the learning process probably increases as we move into the upper grades of the elementary school, and on up into the higher levels of the educational institutions.

Vicarious experience plays a comparatively insignificant role in the art activities of the kindergarten. At this early stage, the child seems to need direct contact with experience. Drawings by young kindergarten children appear to demonstrate this to be true. For example, the turtle in Figure 23-2 represents a pet kept by the children in the kindergarten room. The policeman in Figure 23-1 was drawn because of the intimate appreciation of the children for the policeman who protected them while they crossed a roadway on their way to school.

By the time children reach the first grade, they are becoming increasingly involved with vicarious experiences. At this point, art activity assumes additional importance in the learning processes: it becomes a means for making vicarious experience as vivid as possible. Murals, models, paintings, and clay forms can be made to represent and clarify the facts of the vicarious. Illustrations of historical events, charts and graphs representing the content of a geography lesson, of arithmetic, spelling, or literature help to make the experience more easily understood.

Mere duplication of an image does not neces-sarily provide for clarity and understanding; emotion and feeling must be present for thinking, logic, or the rational to function efficiently. The projection of the self into experience, which takes place before and during the art activity, provides this kind of blending of the emotional and the factual, the balance of thinking and feeling necessary for understanding.

The experience of participating in art activities should be designed to relate vicarious with first-hand experience so that art can give increased depth of understanding to the vicarious. The mural of a jungle (Figure 9-7) was painted by primary-grade children after they had both visited a zoo and dramatized the jungle through role playing. The visit supplemented the purely vicarious experience gained from reading, pictures, recordings, and the teacher's descriptions. The motivation period after the visit served to prompt the children to begin the art activity. The decision to make a mural was based on several factors, all discussed and understood by the children.

1. The view of the jungle had to be panoramic and colorful. This could be accomplished most suitably by a mural.
2. The children had painted pictures of animals on other occasions.
3. The children were ready to work in groups on common projects. A mural could be made by several children working together.
4. Enough time was available for this kind of job.
5. The children felt that a mural as colorful as that of a jungle would provide a pleasant decoration for the classroom.
6. There were twenty-five children in the class. If five children worked together on a mural, five murals could be made, and each group could elect to treat a special aspect of jungle life.

IMAGINATIVE PROJECTION AND PRECOGNITIVE THINKING

The imaginative faculty serves a useful function in the art education program at all grade levels. One evidence of this is what we shall call imaginative projection.

The natural need of all people to understand the things they experience results in their seeking useful closures. Closure is the perception of an incomplete experience as if it were complete. The missing parts are compensated for by imaginative

24-9. X-RAY DRAWING
Author's collection.

projection based on past experience. Obviously the store of past experience (what we have called the precognitive) can be drawn from (by the process of precognition called precognitive thinking) only insofar as it exists. One can project only from the experience one has had. Precognitive thinking seems to require a fairly rich background of experience as well as ability to select from this background in order to provide a richer texture for immediate experience. It is because of this that imaginative projection begins to assume importance only during the primary-grade period. Our task is to design a program that will help the precognitive store grow and that will, at the same time, provide children with the means for making useful selections from it. The natural tendency of primary-grade children to seek closures provides us in art education with an important technique for implementing the learning processes.

Figure 24-9 was drawn by a primary-grade child. It shows a bus with children looking out of the windows. But the children are drawn in full figure. We see not only their faces, but also their bodies that would otherwise be hidden from view. This is sometimes called x-ray drawing. The child is showing what he knew to be in the bus as well

as what he saw. Merely drawing the heads of children looking out of the windows would not have been a complete description of what the child knew. He knew that people are not just heads—they have heads that are attached to bodies. By projecting his thinking beyond the visual, this child knew that the children in the bus, while looking out of the window, were also sitting on the bus seats. This kind of description is extended to the bus itself. The steering wheel is shown connected to a steering linkage that is in turn connected to the front wheels. The child displays as much knowledge of the unseen elements in this bus as he has, or as much as interests him. He is aware that the driver steers the bus; his experience is not yet sufficiently profound for him to be concerned with the motor. His drawing shows the limits of his awareness as well as the things that are important to him.

The planning of the art program must take into account the limits of children's experience at each stage of their growing processes. The imaginative projections made by children in their drawings provide some understandings regarding their knowledges and interests. Through imaginative projection, children draw on their precognitive store of experience and give greater completeness to expression. The bus drawing could have been nothing more than a representation of a particular visual experience if it had not been made richer and more meaningful through the use of understandings from previous experiences.

IMAGINATIVE PROJECTION AND EMPATHY

The ability of the artist to know how other people feel in particular situations, the ability to place himself in "someone else's shoes," is evidence of the ability to use imaginative projection. Children often try to do this when they make drawings of other people. We all try to do it when we act a part in a play. Through art activities, it is possible to use this faculty in order to get a better understanding of experience. In an important sense empathy is a technique for developing our sensitivity to the world around us.

PLANNING FOR FANTASIES AND DAYDREAMS

Many kinds of experience form the basis of art activities in the elementary school. During the kindergarten year, children seem most concerned with their immediate consciousness of the surrounding world—perfectly naturally, because their awareness of reality is just beginning to develop. From the earliest grades, however, interest in the purely imaginative exists to some degree. As children grow older, they seem to become more concerned with fantasies and daydreams, and their imaginary experiences can be used as subject matter for art works.

As early as the primary-grade period, children apparently do some fanciful daydreaming. Each child considers himself the center of the universe, although the younger child's method for expressing this universe is perhaps less sophisticated than that of older children. Figures 24-10 and

24-10. PREHISTORIC ANIMAL
Author's collection.

24-11 are typical in this respect. Both of these drawings, made by first graders, show the freshness and unassuming innocence of the primary-grade child. Figure 24-10 was made by a little girl who was asked to draw a prehistoric animal. In a most refreshing way she places herself astride the monster. Figure 24-11, a chalk drawing, is a self-portrait. The little girl transforms herself into a ballet queen, alone on a stage, the curtains drawn back—there she is in all her finery. To emphasize the importance of the ballet queen, the figure is isolated in a form darker than the background. This adds contrast and calls attention to the dancer. Emphasis is further supplied by the massive frame formed by the stage curtains.

It is of special interest that emphasis on the highly imaginative, on fantasy, is often based on images of self. For some people, this childish mode of conception is never lost. This is not necessarily a sign of immaturity; it may be only one of the important ways in which the vicarious can be sufficiently imbued with feeling to become emotionally expressive. All children need to project themselves into imaginative situations, to establish themselves in the developing scheme of things, to form for themselves a glorious and important role in the eyes of their fellow creatures. There is no reason why they should not do this if it does not completely dominate their expressive work.

But the teacher must carefully discriminate among types of fantasy. Some fantasies can give color, emotional impact, strength, and force to an expressional purpose. Others are not so useful. Fantasies should be selected as subject matter for art activity because they can contribute to the achievement of some educational purpose. A rule of thumb is that fantasies are most educationally useful when they can be related to some real-life experience of a child. Proficient artists throughout history have had to resort to the products of firsthand experience in order to make artful fantastic forms. Metaphor is a parallel in literature: the unusual event, shape, or creature is compared with an aspect of known experience.

Many fantasies originate in daydreams. Al-

though most daydreaming has a source in reality, its relation to that source is often vague. When this is so, the art activity can serve another function: it can establish a purpose for the fantasy. When the teacher can help the child relate his fantasy to a source in reality, the fantasy can often motivate the child to art activity.

In Figure 24-10 the little girl is motivated to know more about prehistoric animals because she is a witness by virtue of the natural childish inclination to place herself in the experience. The result is a sharpening of the need for reality. This is an opportunity for the teacher to help the child increase the meaning of the experience by telling her about some of the characteristics of a particular prehistoric animal that would be particularly suitable. In much the same way, in Figure 24-11, the expressed egocentricity of the child is a means for sharpening her knowledge of the ballet costume and the stage.

Fantasy can be given a useful direction when such tales as those of Hans Christian Andersen are used as subject material for illustrations in paint or chalk. When children illustrate such stories, they can be asked to draw upon their own experience to supply images for their illustrations. The combination of the highly imaginative with the facts of daily living may serve to sharpen some of the useful moralizing of some fantasies, or it may give a meaning to the otherwise random mental wandering of much childish daydreaming. For example, self-portraits could be made as pictures of oneself doing exciting things in the future. One little girl will be a nurse, a boy may picture himself as a truck driver. In each case the daydream will be given a form that is real in terms of the world in which we live. The nurse will be pictured doing an important job. The truck driver will be operating a truck. The drawings must represent understandings that are the product of a growing knowledge of the realities of modern trucks and their operation, or the facts of the nursing profession.

Fantasies without substance are dead ends, insubstantial mental roamings.[1] Without direction,

24-11. BALLET QUEEN
Author's collection.

[1] Note that many fairy tales have purposes other than that of exciting the imagination. Some teach a moral lesson or develop concepts of right and wrong; others teach lessons related to social behavior or dramatically describe phenomena for which no immediate scientific explanation is available.

the fantasy can be a handicap, a hindrance to work. With direction, however, the free associations, the far-ranging imaginative flights that are the essence of fantasy can result in new insights and new forms. The art education program must use fantasy because free association is a tool of the processes of creative action: it stimulates precognitive thinking.

CHILDREN'S PLANNING AND DEVELOPMENT OF ART ACTIVITIES

The participation of children in the initiation of the art activity has been noted earlier—e.g., in the bus trip experience described in this chapter. In each case the art activity was planned as a continuation of experience. The children participated in the planning of art processes, the techniques for making art forms, and the organization of the class working schedule. Once the children are involved in the art activity, some mode must be developed for evolving the forms of the art expression.

Many paintings and constructions made by primary-grade children are noteworthy for their freshness and spontaneity. It is often assumed that this spontaneity is achieved by permitting the children to make their pictures or three-dimensional constructions entirely on the basis of the concepts formed in the motivation sessions that precede the activity. In many instances this is true, but not always. Many of the things young children do are carefully planned; each phase of the form-making process is deliberate. This is especially true in group art processes. Note the detailed planning of Figure 5-2, "The Circus," and Figure 9-7, "The Jungle," both by groups of first-grade children. On the other hand, a great many works are quickly and spontaneously formed. Note Figure 11-6, an abstraction, and Figures 11-2 and 11-3, pigs, drawn by primary-grade children.

One duty of the teacher is to help the children determine whether an art activity should be deliberative or spontaneous. The time factor was one reason that paintings were made of the bus trip. If time had been more plentiful, more elaborate work might have been done. On the other hand, it is not always desirable to spend much time on a single art activity. The im-

portance of the experience may determine how much time and planning should be devoted to a particular phase of art activity.

Not all art activities require detailed planning. But the spontaneous needs to be balanced by the very deliberative. The spontaneous offers children opportunity to record their early reactions, to draw freely and rapidly from their experience, to respond naturally, and to draw quickly upon their subconscious without the interference of the more selective and discriminating judgments of the deliberative, cognitive processes. Spontaneous painting is direct and rapid. Spontaneous forming is most usefully accomplished with clay or with quickly assembled constructions made from a collection of scrap materials available in the classroom. The youngest children enjoy making forms from soft wire bent into shapes and from arrangements of odd shapes and textures of papers and fabrics. Children also work quickly and easily with such materials as wax crayons, colored chalks, inks, and poster paints.

But children also need opportunity to exercise deliberativeness in their working processes. They need to make thoughtful, contemplative choices. For this reason they need opportunity to do detailed planning, to spend ample time critically discussing and evaluating their work as it progresses.

The deliberative processes have been subjected to much more critical study by art educators than have the spontaneous processes. We have long known that spontaneity is a characteristic of childhood and that children retain much of their wonderful sparkle and joyousness because of their natural liking for the quickly done painting or clay figure. On the other hand, many art teachers have looked with suspicion on the slowly and deliberately elaborated art project. These are the methods of the professional artist; it was felt that they are not often useful for young children.

A balance of thinking and feeling is necessary for effectiveness in art work (see Chapter Ten). Too much conscious rationalization, too much cognitive thinking *can* dull the excitement of the expressive painting or sculpture. Overintellectualization can lead to a dearth of inspirational thinking. It does not follow that careful planning and continuous evaluation of the progress of an art activity will destroy the effectiveness of the art work. The inspired concept, the spontaneously conceived metaphor, need not be lost because a process is planned and weighed.

First it is important that the children know how to use experience as a basis for art activity. Children need to formulate their own standards for their art work. It is usually true that, when they do, they can establish a working basis that lies within the scope of their level of achievement, their abilities, and their understandings. All too often the tightly drawn, overworked, and tired paintings are the result of a point of view that emphasizes adult rather than child standards.

Carefully planned and deliberately developed art form is not the sole province of upper-grade elementary-school art. The deliberative working processes are usefully explored as soon as children are able to relate art forming processes to their experiences. This occurs in the later phases of the kindergarten year. From that time on, art activities may be planned in detail and deliberatively executed.

Figure 24-12 is a drawing by a kindergarten child of a large building across the street from the school. It was drawn from sketches made when the entire class made sketches from the school steps. After the trip, the children tacked their sketches to the wall and talked about them. Most of the children were concerned about whether they had correctly represented the buildings. They talked about the things that needed to be done to make their drawings more satisfactory. This discussion indicated that the children saw and knew more than they had been able to show or record in their sketches. They said that the discussion made their omissions obvious to them

24-12. APARTMENT HOUSE
Drawing. *Author's collection.*

24-13. SKETCH AND DRAWING
East Orange, New Jersey, Public Schools.

and that it would be an easy matter to correct shortcomings.

In each of the completed drawings it is evident that freshness and spontaneity is retained in spite of the planning and detailed study.

Figure 24-12, drawn from a sketch after much critical discussion by the group and after the young artist had been asked to observe carefully the recommendations for improvements, bears the strong marks of a rhythmical kinaesthesia, of elements not consciously directed, despite the amount of cognitive thinking that went into it. In other respects the drawing has shortcomings, none of which were discussed during the period of evaluation before the final work. The evaluation was more concerned with details than with proportions; and the proportions in this drawing are rather arbitrary. The normally vertical rectangles of the windows are of different sizes; some are horizontal, others not. The square windows are smaller than the rectangular ones. Not all are equally divided into two parts; some appear to be casement windows. The child may well have drawn types of windows he knew about but did not see on the building. But detail, especially in view of the fact that this is a kindergarten child's work, is profuse. Note the elaborate chimneys, the head of a girl looking out a window, and the pair of entry doors at the bottom of the building.

Figure 24-13 is a sketch and a crayon drawing made from it, both by a first-grade child. The sketch is a pencil line drawing made on a small sheet (about 8½" × 11") of newsprint paper during a brief sketching trip by the entire class outside the school building. This child made several drawings of the houses across the street from the school. When the class returned from the trip, all the children selected one of their outdoor sketches from which to make crayon drawings. Their selection was made during a class discussion of the sketches in which the children talked about each other's work and made what they hoped would be useful comments to guide the development of the crayon drawings.

In no case did a child in the class exactly duplicate his sketch in the finished crayon drawing. Nearly all made drawings much more elaborate than their sketches.

There are many modes of thinking that are characteristic of the primary-grade child in the finished drawing shown in Figure 24-13. For example, an effort is made to give the building three-dimensional depth. This is accomplished on the right side of the building, and then the same thing is done to the left side, violating the rule of optical perspective that when the left side is visible, the right side is not. It is also curious to note that the window shade pulls are left outside the windows, as if the child felt himself to be inside and outside the building at the same time. In actuality, the child is representing what is true; he has to place himself, imaginatively, both inside and outside the building in order to draw it. In the sketch, the television antenna is large and important. In the crayon drawing, so much effort was given to the productive thinking required for forming the building that no provision was made for the antenna. The child evidently felt that he should include the antenna, and so it is crowded into the little space at the top of the paper. In the sketch, the chimney shows both the child's feeling that it should be at right angles to the pitched roof and his observation that it is really vertical. The feeling for correctness rather than the logic of a necessary verticality wins out in the final drawing.

The evidence we have of planning done by children leads to these conclusions:

1. Planning does not interfere with the freshness and spontaneity of children's art work.
2. Planning helps children gain a more detailed understanding of the subject material of the art activity.
3. Planning gives the children opportunity to formulate and work with goals that they devise in terms of their own levels of understanding, their motor skills, and their experiences.

GROUP AND INDIVIDUAL ACTIVITIES

All the activities discussed in this chapter are described as group activities. But all art activities need not, of course, be designed for group work. Individual children often need to work alone on jobs that suit their unique needs at a particular time. As a result, classrooms need to have some provision for children to continue art activities when the rest of the class is doing something else.

Children do not always work at the same speed.

If no provision is made for the children who finish their work before the rest of the group, they will simply do nothing and may well become restless. Such restlessness can become self-directed into useful channels; but it would be foolish for the teacher to assume that such a fortunate development will automatically take place. If the teacher determines that a child has finished before other members of the group, that there is no need for any continuing effort on the work the child has been doing, then provision must be made for individual art jobs. Space, materials, and equipment are needed, as well as help from the teacher or another student.

When a number of children finish a previous job at about the same time, several children can be grouped to work together, and members of the group can help each other. As other children finish art work, they may elect to join these groups. The latecomers can be helped by the children who have already started a new project. Encouraging children to help each other in this way is obviously desirable. When several groups are working at different art jobs, the separate groups can work on different projects and can gain the additional benefit of exchanging experiences.

Children are sometimes able to work alone to advantage. They learn to draw upon their own resources and, like the small working groups, they refer to the teacher those problems they believe require help for solution.

Group activities become increasingly important as children grow older. By the middle of the primary-grade period children usually need to participate in art activities that permit them to make contributions to some large group objective. They enjoy and profit from such group activity because it offers them a chance to be a contributing member of a social group and to gain recognition from it.

Almost any art activity in which a common goal is established can furnish the basis for group participation. Murals, puppets for puppet plays, scenery and costumes for dramatic production are only a few possibilities. Group activities give children opportunity to discuss the progress of their work, its effectiveness in achieving the expressional purpose, and the clarifications of the whole experience that each child is able, through his work, to make.

PERMISSIVE AND NONPERMISSIVE ART ACTIVITIES

Many art activities are directed by the teacher. It has been established in this text that teacher direction in art is just as important as teacher direction, or guidance, in reading, or spelling, civics, arithmetic or science.

One of the advantages of art education is that it often provides for self-motivation. Children, like all human beings, like to express themselves; they need to form metaphors uniquely their own. For this reason children are often asked to select their own art activities, to make their own choices of subject and materials and processes. This kind of permissive activity is often useful when it follows a series of nonpermissive activities. The ability of children to participate effectively in permissive art activities is evidence of a developing maturity.

Twenty-five

LEARNING THROUGH GESTURE,

DISCOVERY, AND IMAGINATION

The gestures of primary-grade children have to be developed into suitable expressional means as the children grow older. This development can be accomplished by relating the more complex experiences of older children to expressional gestures, such as kinaesthetic sensations.

Discovery and imagination are the beginning and the substance of art activity. Discovery is a learning device. Imagination is a means for developing an educationally effective process of creative action through art activities.

The structure of art processes and art experiences is comparatively simple for primary-grade children. The art processes for older children, however, are much more complex. Structuring art forms for the youngest children is mainly a matter of giving order and purpose to a gesture. Critical study at this stage is minimal. The physical forms begin to become effective communications when geometricity first appears.

Children in the intermediate and upper grades require a structure of art expression that will embrace their more complex experiences. The concepts the older children form from their experiences grow more detailed as the children mature. We expect these more complex concepts to grow in quality because the increasing critical awareness of the more mature children affects their understanding of their experiences. The application of increasing rational skill to the feelings children have in response to their experiences is expected to qualitatively influence their living patterns, their patterns of behaving and thinking. From this point of view, as children mature the art program should be planned to take advantage of possible useful interactions between experience, critical awareness, and emotional responses to experiences. The planning of the art program should provide for a means for the processes of forming from experience to contribute to the general living patterns of the children.

The purposes of the younger children are easily made clear to them. They find pleasure in manipulation; they are usually pleased with the color and structural characteristics of art materials, and they are seldom concerned with the detailed techniques of visual representation. For them, as was indicated in our discussion about early childhood art, generalizations are enough. Their limited concern with a detailed and critical evaluation of their efforts accounts, in part, for their satisfaction with what they produce. Their interest in what they produce may not last much longer than the span of attention required for the duration of their art activity. For them, the processes of art activity are most exciting. Their pleasure with the processes of doing is related to the emotional value of the descriptive gesture. During the later phases of their growth, they begin to create more deliberative and thoughtfully formed metaphors as they develop greater concern for productive techniques. When critical awareness becomes an important part of art activity, children gain an increased need to understand and know more about the techniques and structure of the art forming processes.

This whole process of growth in art activity, from the simple gesture to the thoughtful combination of feeling and thinking, is the process of learning through gesture, discovery, and imagination.

GESTURES IN ART ACTIVITIES OF OLDER CHILDREN

The simpler outlook of younger children made the gesture rich enough in its potential to satisfy their needs. For older children, however, the gesture is insufficient as a basis for forming the plastic metaphor. The gesture is important to older children, and it may form an elementary basis for their expressions. But the significance of the expressive gesture combined with increasingly differentiated experience requires the ability to probe both experiences and materials. This is a process that requires both a good precognitive store and technical knowledge, as well as acquaintance with the productive thinking processes.

For children in the early phases of the intermediate-grade period, the largest problem may be to maintain a significant relationship between expressive gestures, increasingly far-reaching experiences, and technical means for achieving the objectives that will later result from their maturing critical attitudes. This is the heart of the problem in program planning for the older child. If the child is not able to know the relationships between these various factors, and if he is not able to achieve them according to the skills he has accumulated, the whole of the forming process will lose its coherence. Lost relationships result in discontinuities. Discontinuity, in this sense, refers to the lack of harmonious relationships between the parts of an experience.

Figure 25-1 is a pen and ink line drawing by an eighth-grade child. In essence, this drawing is related to the simple line drawings of the primary-grade children's gesture phases. The simple kinaesthesia of the drawing of an apartment house, Figure 24-12, or the rhythmical movement associated with a concept as in Figure 18-2 has been developed to a higher level of accomplishment in Figure 25-1. In this picture, the expressive gesture has been the guiding rhythm for the drawing of a particular kind of man. The children who made the apartment house drawing (Figure 24-12) and the painting in Figure 18-2 were guided by a generalization. The rhythm of these paintings is the rhythm of generalized action related to an apartment building and to a cleaning action. In the more sophisticated gesture of the eighth-grade student (in Figure 25-1), there is evidence of a developed skill. The freedom with which the rhythmical and descriptive lines have

25-1. PEN AND INK PORTRAIT
New York City Public Schools.

been made is evidence of a willingness to experiment with line qualities to find out what lines can express. This is seen in the way lines follow the textured pattern of the hair, in the way they become hard and rigid in forming the man's eyeglasses, and in the way they become loose and flowing to describe the quality of the man's shirt.

The precision with which this ink drawing of a man is made indicates that the rhythmical movement of the underlying gesture is guided by a knowledge of form, a technical understanding of relationships, and a critical awareness of the structured pattern that is most satisfactorily expressive of the object being portrayed.

Figure 25-2 is a painting of a bouquet of flowers by an eighth-grade student. The white line embraces the over-all pattern of the gesture that defines the form of the bouquet. From this rhythmical generalization, masses that echo the first large gesture are loosely formed. Within the masses, the detail of a flower's textured surface completes the detailed structure of the whole concept.

25-2. FLOWERS
East Orange, New Jersey, Public Schools.

In addition to the older child's concern with achieving expressiveness from descriptive gestures, this painting of flowers is the product of experimental manipulations with paint. The child's critical awareness makes it possible for him to explore and discover unusual and unique patterns of color and shape that are associated with the qualities of a bouquet of flowers.

The completeness of this expression could have been the product of a spontaneous activity. But spontaneity is, in part, the product of previous experience. The habits of planning that are formed in early primary-grade experiences achieve more developed form in such a work as Figures 25-1 and 25-2.

THE GROWING NEED FOR AESTHETIC EXPERIENCE

The problems involved in planning for older children begin in the later phases of the primary-grade period. During the early phases of the intermediate period, these problems become increasingly insistent. If they are not properly handled at this time, they could become disruptive and might result in the gradual weakening and eventual complete loss of the educational value of art activity. This loss usually results from the frustrations children experience when they are unable to achieve expressive metaphoric forms with which to communicate the concepts they have formed during the early stages of the productive thinking phases of art activity.

If the natural modes of art activity, which are evidenced during the beginning of the primary period, can be developed throughout elementary school, useless frustrations may be avoided. For this reason, the expressive gesture should be cultivated until, at its more advanced stages, it is the product of the following:

1. Increasingly differentiated concepts.
2. Technical achievement.
3. Growing skill in carrying out experimental procedures in art.
4. Increasing critical awareness.

The correlation of natural modes of art activity with developing art skills and conceptual and forming skills is prerequisite for the achievement of aesthetic experience.

Frustration in art activity grows out of the lack of satisfaction that results from the inability to give form to one's aspirations. Frustration, in this sense, is a product of disharmony, of the incompleteness of experiences and associated forming processes. It is caused by a lack of aesthetic experience. The absence of the aesthetic is the sign of the incompleteness of experience.

THE ROLE OF DISCOVERY

The purpose we set for ourselves in planning for the art activity of older children must be to help the children find harmonies in their experiences and in their expressive metaphors. The bridge from forming to expression is the art activity.

Planning makes provision for discovery. Discovery is a result of experimentation with materials and ideas. The product of the interaction of experimentation with ideas and art materials is invention.

A function of the program for older children must be to make use of the values of the act of discovery and, in this way, to maintain and continue the pleasures younger children find in the forming processes. For older children, discovery must remain an exciting experience because it serves as the basic motivation to the forming of unique expressive metaphors.

We have indicated in our discussions about the structure of art education (see Chapter Eight) that discovery is the basis of the art education processes, just as it may be the source of a fruitful learning process. Joyce Cary describes discovery as an act of youth.[1] For Cary, pleasure in discovery is largely a gift of youthfulness. The pleasure of becoming aware is a precondition for becoming involved in expression through art activity, through the forming of artful metaphors. A function of art education processes must be to maintain this pleasure in discovery and to help young people develop their ability to respond to such pleasure.

We have some reason to believe that discovery is an ever growing capability. The natural increase in experience that can be an accumulative aspect of the growing processes, can increase a

[1] Joyce Cary, *Art and Reality* (New York: Anchor Books, Doubleday & Company, Inc., 1961), chapter 1.

child's ability to find pleasure in making discoveries. The teacher's problem is to conserve the growing children's tendency to find pleasure in their experiences and to stimulate them to seek means for giving form to their pleasurable responses. Encouraging children to be sensitive to the uniqueness of experience and to form habits of responding to the world around them is a responsibility of the teacher. The blasé child represents the teacher's failure to maintain curiosity, sensitivity, and pleasure in the ever changing panorama of daily living.

Planning for maintaining and developing the older child's sensitivity to his experiences and environment, for maintaining his pleasure in discovery, becomes interactive with the kinds of growth expected from children in the intermediate and upper grades. The usefulness of discovery increases as children mature. The increasing intellectual potency of growing children is aided by curiosity, which is an integral part of the processes of discovery. The processes of seeking relationships between concepts, of exploring materials, tools, and expressional techniques is related to both intellectual and emotional growth. Such processes provide an intense awareness that grows out of participation in expressive art activity and makes the values of the learning acquired increasingly effective.

The advantages of discovery for older children can be increased by the teacher's effective motivating devices and planning for art activity. This planning for art activity should be done in terms of the children's level of accomplishment.

The first problem in planning for the art activity of older children involves the planning of suitable motivation processes. The purpose of a motivation process must be to stimulate curiosity, to make the children want to probe the depth of experience, to seek out relationships between materials, tools, processes or techniques, and their conceptualizations.

The difference between the motivation processes used for the primary-grade and upper-grade groups consists of a difference in detail, depth, and breadth. The motivations provided for older children should provide technical means commensurate with the skills, conceptualizations, and critical understanding of the older children. The exact degree of depth, detail, and differentiated skill required for an older group will depend upon the accomplishments of the group, their previous experience, and their specific needs.

IMAGINATIVE PROJECTION AS A LEARNING DEVICE

The important advantage of the older child over the primary-grade child is the older child's store of precognitive sources, his greater knowledge, and his tendency to establish goals commensurate with his growth.

One of the useful means for achieving the goals of growth and invention suitable to meet the needs of the older child is through the development of techniques for encouraging discovery. Discovery may sometimes take place spontaneously, but we can not depend on the children's purely spontaneous drives to motivate it. Through planning, the teacher needs to take advantage of the children's natural inclinations to seek and find means for projecting their imaginings. Imaginative projection makes it possible to provide for habits of experimentation and invention, to foster creative imagination, and to establish habits and techniques of harnessing emotion to rationality.

A basic tendency among post-primary-grade children is the ordinary daydream. All children in elementary school are notable for their love of the imaginative fantastic daydream, a mode of behaving and thinking that grows as the children grow. The kind of fantasy acceptable to older children may be different from that acceptable to primary-grade children, but the difference is one of content. For example, as older children claim to lose interest in "Mother Goose" and fairy tales, they gain increased skill in finding means for projecting their imaginative flights of fancy. Even more than younger children, older children are inclined to daydream, to devise purely subjective explanations for things that escape their understanding, and to find pleasure in adventure stories or in various types of science fiction.

Older children need to be encouraged to permit their imagination to roam, to engage in flights of fancy. Such use of imagination results in the process of making free associations, which is the foundation of much creative thinking.

The mere imaginative whimsy or detached daydream is not the type of fantasy that will be a useful part of the art education program. Fantasy that has a source in the processes of free association can be most useful if it is applied to reality,

25-3. TUGBOAT
Brush and ink drawing.
Collection of Theodore Lynch.

if it is considered an extension of reality and a means for making reality more colorful, more vivid, or more suggestive of related concepts. When reality is freely explored, it is possible, through techniques of free association to achieve applications of factual situations to other related understandings. In this sense, reality becomes subjected to added meanings or it provides the means for suggesting new and fresh concepts.

Imaginative projection from reality can become a useful learning device because the exploration of reality in an inventive manner can lead to discoveries that cause more effective communication through previously unthought of forms.

In our discussion of the x-ray drawing, Figure 24-9, the x-ray mode was described as a form of imaginative projection. From this point of view, the mode has educationally desirable characteristics. Primary-grade children will use the x-ray method to give form to more than they can see during the course of simple visual experience. If this mode is perpetuated during the intermediate-grade period, it may become possible for the children to obtain more profound results because of their more refined and extensive precognitive store. The only question that remains concerns the advisability of using a technique that appears to belong to early childhood. The older children need not be encouraged to use the simple and naïve techniques of the primary period; they should be encouraged to explore the technique only if they find it a natural mode.

Figure 25-3 is an example of such a natural mode in the work of an older child. This brush and ink drawing of a tugboat was made by a boy in the fourth grade. The drawing is obviously more the product of a boy's than a girl's imagination. The x-ray views are restricted to those areas in which the boy was interested. Like most fourth-grade boys, this boy was interested in the captain who is pictured sitting at the controls guiding the boat. Behind the captain is the radio equipment and the other mechanisms. The rigging that extends from top to bottom of the rear of the tugboat and the radio and transmitting antenna are more imaginative than technically correct. Note that the captain is pulling the cord that causes the boat's horn to sound. In order to picture the loud and far-reaching sound of the horn, the boy painted the sound as lines coming from

25-4. UNDERWATER SCENE
Watercolor. *Collection of Theodore Lynch.*

the horn. The special character of the lines is based on the special character of the sound; loudness is represented as heavy lines, piercing sound as lines that travel from the horn in a slightly curving movement ascending diagonally into the sky. The movement of the sound is like the swift movement of a baseball; the sound travels high in a graceful curve that will land on the shore to be heard by those who are distant from the tugboat.

The difference between this fanciful drawing of a tugboat and the x-ray version of a bus in Figure 24-9 is a difference of imagination, skill, and a more differentiated concept in the work of the older child. The bus in Figure 24-9 is devoid of the same kind of fanciful detail; it is rather bare in conception. The tugboat (Figure 25-3) is full of detail: the horn at the front of the captain's position, the smokestack, the antenna, the details of wood texture, windows, life preservers, and some mechanical details such as the apparatus at the rear of the boat and at the front on the prow.

The painting by a sixth-grade child, shown in Figure 25-4, is an example of imaginative projec-

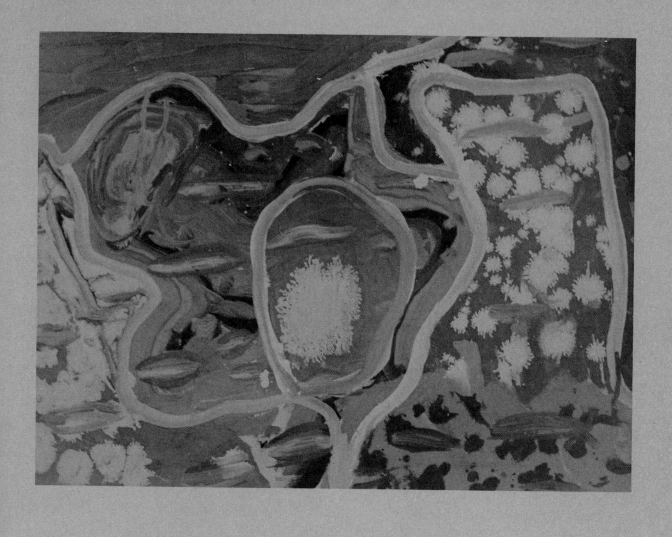

25-5. LANDSCAPE PAINTING
East Orange, New Jersey, Public Schools.

tion. In this painting, the point of view and the entire scene are imagined. In this respect, this painting is related to the x-ray picture (Figure 24-9). But unlike the x-ray picture this is not a cutaway picture; the scene is one that might be viewed by a diver. For the child, the images are the product of imaginative projection because they had to be pieced together from various bits of information. Like the drawing of a tugboat, this picture is useful because it represents an effort to describe reality through the techniques of imaginative projection. The details are those we would expect an older child to have learned.

Imaginative projection is a means for relating materials and forms to expressional purposes. This process requires the use of free associations. The manipulations of materials and the forming of concepts is a result of the individual child's ability to discover forms.

The painting in Figure 25-5, a landscape by an eighth-grade child, is the result of imagination projected from the free associations inspired by a process of freely manipulating paint. The child who made this painting did not know what would happen when the painting was started. In a general way, his purpose was to paint a landscape, but he permitted the exact forms to evolve out of the accidental formations made by the freely manipulated paint. Accidents were observed and imagination invented forms from the unexpected arrangements and configurations of the freely and sometimes unconventionally applied paint. For this kind of process, experimentation should involve sponges, sticks, and splatterings of paint.

SUMMARY

Planning the art program for older children requires that some emphasis be given to the need for strengthening and directing the natural modes of younger children. From the beginning of the intermediate-grade period, provision must be made for correlating gestures with art expression on a level commensurate with the developing experience of older children. The more highly developed forming processes of older children's gestures provide a basis for the achievement of aesthetic experience.

Planning art activities for older children also requires that provision be made for a program that places a large premium on learning through discovery. Discovery is considered to be the basis of learning; for this reason, planning must provide for the act of discovery as the first part of the processes of art activity.

Imaginative projection is a product of both discovery and expressive gestures, which are a source of expression. Imaginative projection provides the means for children to invent and to improvise; it is the essential aspect of the processes of creative action.

Twenty-six

SOME GUIDES

FOR PLANNING IN THE UPPER GRADES

Planning art activities for older children will be most effective if individual and group differences determine the nature of the plans made for art education activities and processes. The plan for the art program for the intermediate and upper grades of elementary school should be considered a continuation of the art program of the primary grades. The development of the program should be considered an accompaniment to the children's growing processes. The art program for older children will be most useful if it can foster all the varied aspects of this growth.

The art program for the older children, like the program for the primary groups, is planned as a means for providing children with opportunities to make their living as full, as exciting, and as complete as possible. The art program is not planned as a preparation for living in the future. The concept of planning is one that helps children find forms that extend their experiences, clarify their understandings, and provide them with aesthetic experiences in terms of their own level of development.

The fact that living is a progressive process and that a purpose of all education is to make children's growth progressive makes art planning an aid to progressive growth. Art education programs planned in terms of children's growth achieve a purpose that could be the purpose of all education: to make living rich, meaningful, and full of satisfactions. In art activity, satisfactions result from the individual's opportunities to find means to give form to his uniqueness. When the individual can express his uniqueness through physical forms, it may be possible for him to make a tangible contribution to the progressive achievement of the social group.

PLANNING SEQUENCES OF ART ACTIVITIES

The planning of art activities for older children, like the planning of art activities for primary-grade children, is not done in terms of problems that advance from the simple to the increasingly complex. Complexity evolves as a factor in the physical, emotional, and intellectual make-up of the children. The complexity of the problems in art forming results from the increasing complexity of the children as thinking and social beings. For this reason, we do not assume that watercolor is used at a certain age level or that construction paper, clay, or tempera paints are graded according to the difficulty of their manipulation. Whenever children are able to manipulate a material, they should use that material. Restrictions placed on the use of materials and tools should be determined by the individual child's physical ability to handle a hammer, a hand saw, a power saw, a chisel, a knife, a brush, clay or sand, plaster or wire, fabric, wood, or metals.

NEED FOR FLEXIBILITY IN ART PROGRAMS

The planning of the art program for the intermediate and upper grades must make provision for the differences that exist between groups of children in different environments. Children living in urban communities will have problems and modes of response to problems that are different from those of children in suburban communities. Similarly, children living in a group with a Spanish background will have different cultural influences acting upon them than children living in a group that is predominantly Irish. In some urban communities, the cultural atmosphere may even assume a new characteristic as a result of an eclectic environment arising from the blending of several cultural forces.

Formulas for planning for a particular group of children are not desirable. The best guide is for the teacher to recognize cultural characteristics in the children's backgrounds that will enrich or foster a good basis for art understandings and activity.

Program planning for children in the primary grades is a comparatively simple matter. We have found that it is possible to draw some general conclusions about the characteristics of patterns of growth in the art of early childhood. These definable patterns make it possible to offer some workable guidelines. For example, we know that spontaneous gestures can be related to experiences and art materials during the early processes of forming in the kindergarten. The children's efforts to relate plastic form to an expressional form may result in an ordering of shapes and colors known as geometricity, which is evidence of early success in art expression. These kinds of patterns of development make it possible to make a workable plan from existing guidelines. However, in the art of the upper grades, it is not possible to know exactly what all the children are ready and able to do at any one time. As the children mature, their critical awareness causes them to become increasingly self-conscious. This self-consciousness may cause them to increase their conscious thinking about their art work at the expense of their spontaneity, their expressive emotionalism. The result may be a growing awareness that their critical facility is too refined for their art skills in representation or their manipulative ability with tools and materials. For too many older children, this awareness may lead to frustration and a declining interest in art activity. Interest may decline because the children begin to believe that they aren't able to draw.

PLANNING FOR EXPRESSION

We have some reason to believe that children can become involved in art activity through similar motivations and in much the same manner as the professional artist. A child may be motivated by a desire to say something about experiences that interest him. The verbal forms, such as speech and poetry or body movements, such as clapping the hands or just "jumping with joy" may satisfy this need. The purpose of art activity should be to permit the child to become sufficiently sensitive to his experiences to want to give his concepts of them tangible forms. Such forms will be most meaningful to the child if they are able to communicate his increased notion of the importance of an experience and of the pleasure that results from its completeness and meaningfulness.

Planning for art activity must be designed to provide an aesthetic experience. Children should be given opportunity to make their experiences and concepts richer because the processes of art activity give them aesthetic meaning. Related to the aesthetic experience is the children's growing ability to communciate in plastic materials with ordered arrangements of the feelings and thinking necessary for growth in intelligence, in understanding, and in qualitative emotional responses.

If art planning does not provide for the aesthetic and the ability to communicate, as well as for the children's achievement of improved understanding, the art program will have failed in its educational purpose. Planning must, therefore, take note of the need to make critical thinking an important and contributing part of art activity. The natural inclination of children's growing critical facility to outstrip their forming and expressional skills should become a major concern of the program planner.

The difference between the child artist and the professional artist is the child's wide separation between forming skills and expressional purposes. The professional artist is able to achieve some success, some of the time, in finding a means that will give aesthetic form and meaning to the things he knows and wants to communicate.

The child, however, usually knows much more than he is able to communicate. This is especially noticeable in the work of primary-grade children. The youngest primary-grade children find it necessary to tell stories about the forms they make. They seem to be aware that their forms do not say as much as they want them to. Older children have much to say, but they become frustrated because their developed critical awareness makes them realize that they are not able to say as much as they feel they need to say.

Planning for the older children needs to help them narrow the gap between expressive skill and expressive need. Such planning must place a large emphasis on the kinds of skills the older children need to achieve their purposes.

ESTABLISHING PURPOSES

One of the first things the teacher needs to do is help the children know what their purposes are. After the children are aware of their purposes, they must know some of the most effective means for realizing them.

Skill in expression, skill in manipulation, and skill in relating ideas to materials must become the subjects of group and individual discussions and demonstrations. The most useful demonstrations of the skills children need for the accomplishment of their expressional purposes are those that grow out of a real situation. For this reason, art activity should begin with a motivation session that places some emphasis on techniques of research, investigation, and experimentation with materials. Planning must provide opportunities for the kind of activity described in Chapter Twenty-two. From time to time throughout the development of an art activity, it is most useful to have group discussions about the progress of the activity and to point out how some children are achieving their purposes. If some children are not achieving their purposes, it is necessary to demonstrate why they are not.

ROLE OF CREATIVE ACTION

The processes of discovery may also be related to the development of processes of creative action. We have techniques available that, like those used in the processes of experimentation and discovery, make much use of the critical faculties of older children. In Chapter Thirteen, examples were offered of the ways professional artists use materials and processes to discover forms and to invent forms that serve an expressional purpose. Such examples should be used to demonstrate methods for combining thinking, feeling, materials, and manipulative processes.

PLANNING FOR ART APPRECIATION AS PART OF ART ACTIVITY

Appreciation of the art of the great artists is not an isolated study in elementary school. The most rewarding appreciation is achieved by children when their appreciation results from the sympathetic understanding they gain when they realize that the artists solved problems similar to those that concern the children in their own art work.

THE ART GUIDE

There are a number of ways in which planning for the upper and intermediate grades can be effectively achieved. One of the most common and accepted methods has been to provide teachers within one school, or a group of schools of a large community, with a general guide rather than a rigid listing of specific kinds of art activities. The purpose of such a guide is to provide the teacher with a variety of methods and art activities. From this guide, the teacher can select those activities and methods that are valid at a particular time for a specific group of children. Another important function of the art guide is to allow the teacher to make changes in proposed plans in order to adapt the plans to a unique situation.

The art guide approach to planning need not be restricted to only the intermediate and upper grades. The same general method of planning is needed in the primary grades. However, prediction of the kind of art activity to be carried on in the kindergarten, first, and second grades, is easier than it is for the more complex situations that evolve in the more advanced grades.

The art guide is a convenience. An experienced teacher becomes adept in making diagnoses of the condition of her children; thus, she knows the needs of her group and can make the necessary provisions for planning and developing an educationally effective art program.

The planning of art work for the intermediate and upper grades can be accomplished in an effective manner if the teacher becomes acquainted with the kinds of things children do in specific situations under known conditions. The teacher must also be acquainted with expectancies in particular situations regarding skills, levels of readiness, emotional characteristics, needs, and interests. These understandings are gained through study of the work of various kinds of children. The application of these understandings by a teacher becomes a creative process based upon real knowledge.

Art guides are constructed in terms of the particular kinds of art activities that can be used for various kinds of learning purposes. The following are some of the considerations that must be provided for in the construction of an art guide:

1. The children's level of readiness must be related to the kind of art activity that will be proposed. Readiness in this respect refers to readiness for the following:
   a) Manipulative skills.
   b) Conceptualizations—understanding and interpretation of experience.
   c) Use of various types of media and tools.
   d) Understanding of subject materials.
   e) Understanding of the purposes of the art activity.

2. The kinds of art activities selected are largely determined by the kinds of activities provided by other subject areas of the school program. Many of the children's understandings are related to things they are learning in areas such as arithmetic, social studies, spelling, geography, civics, reading, literature, grammar, music, and science. The relation of art to general understanding and experience is often most useful for activities correlated with other learning areas. Similarly, the children's general experience level is often usefully related to the experiences that influence their readiness for various types of expression and forms of metaphoric communication. For example, the knowledge a group of children have acquired regarding the art of other people may influence the depth and breadth of their image-symbol concepts. Certainly, many of the learnings gained from other areas of the school curriculum will affect their store of precognitive knowledge. Children's modes of productive thinking may be strongly influenced by the concepts, knowledges, and experiences they gain in arithmetic, the sciences, literature, and languages. It must be understood that children will be able to relate these experiences to art activities most effectively if strong and meaningful correlations can be guided by a good teacher.

3. The art guide must provide for a variety of media, tools, and manipulative processes.

4. The art guide must provide for the strengthening of useful cultural traditions.

5. The art guide must provide for types of activities that will contribute to the emotional, intellectual, and expressional growth of children.

6. The art guide should include art activities that will aid in training the sensory receptors. Such art activities should provide opportunity for the children to exercise their senses of seeing, hearing, touching, smelling, and the sensations of movement. Specific kinds of art activities should emphasize the role of each of the sensory receptors, and provision should be made for the children to gain experience in relating sensory experience in effectively expressive art forms. Examples of this kind of experience are pictures made from materials that provide exercises in texture, color, and shape relations.

A GENERAL SUMMARY

The art program for older children must be developed within a framework of the following factors:

1. *Socio-cultural characteristics.* The unique socio-cultural characteristics of the children should be used in art activities. A means should be devised for making use of the natural heritage of a particular group of children. If the group is composed of children from several different kinds of cultural backgrounds, the class is especially fortunate. In such a case, the children will be able to benefit from a many faceted cultural experience. Art processes and activities can be used as a strong means for giving increased vitality to the children's understanding of the cultural differences existing in their own group. This goal can be accomplished by emphasizing the role of the different cultures in forming expressive art forms, by giving imaginative form to different aspects of the children's cultures, and by providing each representative of a cultural tradition with opportunities to dramatize the values his background can contribute to the group. Such opportunities can be provided by having the children work together on pictures, models, constructions, and other visual plastic forms related to a given cultural concept under the leadership of an individual or a group of individuals who represent a particular cultural background. In

this way, the children will be provided with an effective means for exchanging cultural experiences. This kind of activity is one that could be effectively related to other areas of the school program.

2. *Art skills.* Art skills involve the materials, processes, tools, and techniques with which the children are ready to work, as well as the typical characteristics of intermediate- and upper-grade art work. In most cases, these skills will be more complex than those employed by children in the primary grades, although the older children will perform similar kinds of manipulations, and will work with similar processes, techniques, subject matter, and purposes. Art activities should not be graded from easy to difficult. Children must be allowed to work with skills and to perfect skills according to their experiences, their level of achievement, their natural manipulative abilities, and the purposes that have been established for their group.

Each group of children at each grade level in the intermediate and upper grades will evolve skills in the following general areas:

a) Drawing. Skills in drawing will involve two-dimensional processes that make use of ink, pencil, and brush.

b) Painting. Painting will involve knowledge about the various kinds of coloring materials. Such materials might include synthetic colors that the children can make from stains and dyes, earth materials such as colored clays, or the many available types of paint. Children in elementary school most often use poster paints, watercolors, or water temperas.

c) Construction. The manipulation of three-dimensional materials involves problems in relating materials. Structuring requires processes such as fastening, gluing, pasting, nailing, and tying together of the separate parts of a structure. In some instances, an element that we shall call engineering will be involved. In many cases, construction will include the building of puppet stages, marionette stages, props and sets for dramatic productions, and models intended to illustrate concepts formed as part of the general learning program.

d) Skill in perception. Children need to become increasingly observant in order to be able to recognize the usefulness of details and to see relations between details and general ideas. For example, the color of a body of water, the characteristics of the waves or ripples, and the reflections on the water may be important details that can contribute to the metaphoric effectiveness of a finished picture if they are properly related to the purpose of an expression.

The art program must be planned to develop skills in making use of the activities of the sensory receptors. The way to develop such skills has been demonstrated in art activities that make use of the various kinds of sensory experience that serve to give completeness and fullness, to an experience. Such sensitivities include the senses of touching, hearing, smelling, tasting, and movement sensations. It is evident that some of these sensitivities are more important than others in art activities. For example, the most important sensory responses are those of seeing, touching, and moving. However, we have evidence that some art forms require or are enriched by other sensory experiences. The sense of hearing is often usefully expressed through color and rhythm or other unexpected means.

It often happens that a program of correlating art with other areas of subject matter provides for and strengthens the interaction of sensory experience. We have already noted, in our discussion regarding the characteristics of primary-grade art, that there is some useful sensory activity in the art of even the youngest children. During intermediate- and upper-grade art activities, it becomes possible to place a larger emphasis on techniques for increasing the effectiveness of the interaction and sensitivities of the sensory receptors. The art program for the intermediate and upper grades must, therefore, make specific provisions for accomplishing this kind of increase in sensitivity to the stimuli provided by experience.

e) Skill in invention. Plans for the art program must make provision for the development of skills in invention. Skill in invention requires skill in the techniques of experimentation and improvisation, as well as the ability to recognize results that will be useful in the forming of expressive metaphors. This ability to make discoveries leads to processes of learning, which are the essence of the processes of art education.

APPENDICES

Appendix One

THE PROCESSES OF EVALUATION

Evaluation is a part of all art activities. Evaluation criteria are not rigid. New criteria must be formulated for each group of children because children are constantly growing and changing in their thinking, their abilities, and their knowledges. The processes of evaluation help to build guides and to define and clarify the purposes and accomplishments of the educational processes. In art education, the evaluation processes are natural parts of art activity.

Children need effective evaluation processes in order to help them find meaning and purpose in their art activities.

CONTINUITY OF THE EVALUATION PROCESSES

Evaluation in art education is a continuous process; it should begin the moment art activity is thought about. For this reason, the teacher needs to plan for processes of evaluation from the beginning of the first motivation session. The last evaluation of an accomplishment in art should be the first evaluation of the next art activity. The processes of evaluation continue from one art activity to another. This continuity aids in the establishment of relationships between separate art activities.

Evaluation and motivation in art activity are inseparable. Effective motivation makes the purpose of an art activity clear to the children. Knowledge regarding purposes is related to the children's desire to participate in art activities. This desire consists of enthusiasm for the art activity; it is an emotional conviction that the forming of concepts into

271

physically structured metaphors is a useful and satisfying way to communicate. If children do not have this kind of emotional impetus to participate in art activity, it is evident that the motivation techniques used are not good.

EVALUATION AND GRADING

Evaluation is not the same as grading. To grade a child's art work is to determine how good or bad a child's work is according to some predetermined standard. Grading is a technique that is often used for purposes of making a report of a child's progress for parents, for administrative record keeping, or for other teachers or for the child's information. Such reporting usually takes the form of a letter grade for a report card, transcript of credits, or for permanent records of academic accomplishment. Evaluation can furnish such information, but this is not its primary function.

PURPOSES OF EVALUATION

Evaluation is a means for helping children know what they have accomplished and what they need to accomplish in order to improve their work. Evaluation helps children formulate directions for their future work, and it helps them participate with the teacher in planning the work they need to do in order to achieve mutually understood objectives. The most effective evaluation processes are those in which the children always participate.

The teacher should help the children evaluate their work by acting as the leader or guide for the development of effective evaluation procedures and techniques. In order to effectively help the children evaluate their work, the teacher must be able to:

1. Evaluate herself as a leader and guide in the development of effective evaluation techniques.

2. Evaluate the effectiveness of the children's evaluation techniques.

Evaluation is a tool that can be used to implement the processes of art activity. The processes of evaluation find their basic purpose in their uses as aids to children's intellectual, emotional, physical, and social growth.

STRUCTURE OF THE EVALUATION PROCESSES

The kind of evaluation used for art activity must depend upon the philosophy of art and education governing the art education program. If the emphasis in the art program is on the growth of the children, the purpose of the evaluation procedure will be to insure the most useful kinds of growth through the processes of art activity.

The approach to art education developed in this text has been one that places emphasis on the education of children. Consequently our concept of evaluation must be concerned with determining the effectiveness of art as a process of education for all children. Art education is conceived of as a means for developing the unique characteristics of each individual child. Evaluation must, therefore, be a process that serves this purpose.

The purpose of evaluation must be to help children grow in a variety of general areas, which can be described as follows:

1. *Each individual grows in his ability to express his own uniqueness.* As a child matures, his individuality will mature also and will become an increasingly effective means for making the child a useful member of his social group.

2. *Each individual grows in his ability to form concepts into physical forms that become expressive metaphors.* The child's skill in making each formed metaphor a contribution to experience and learning requires an evolving sensitivity and a developing understanding of environment and ideas.

3. *As each child grows through art activities his patterns of behavior change.* Behavior changes and growth are indicators of the effectiveness of the art education program. Emphasis is placed on the modes of action, the patterns of behavior, formed by a child as a result of his participation in art activities. Behavior patterns grow as skill in expression grows. Skill in expression is made possible by the child's improving ability to relate thinking to feeling, or to make his rational and emotional responses to experience reinforce each other. In this way, the child continuously increases his ability to give quality to his thinking about all kinds of activities. Such transfer of ability from the art activity should be encouraged through processes of evaluation.

A program of evaluation must be based upon a recognition of the purposes and goals for the elementary-school art education program. These goals are defined in terms of children, their relation to their environment, their individuality, their social relationships, and their growth. After a determination has been made regarding the areas of concern for evaluation, the next step must be to formulate means for implementing the processes of evaluation. This procedure requires the development of techniques for evaluation.

Techniques for evaluation involve the formulation of methods for gathering information that will serve as a basis for the evaluation processes and as a means for interpreting the material gathered. Related to the techniques for interpreting information is the process of formulating directions for future work.

The areas of concern for the evaluation processes are related to questions regarding the ways in which art can meet the general purposes of elementary-school education, as well as the special purposes of the more limited areas of art education.

The evaluation program should be based upon a set of goals that draw their substance from the following three general areas:

1. *A point of view about the purposes of education in the elementary school.* The purposes of art education for children in elementary school must be structured within the context of the general educational purposes.

2. *The relation of children to the society in which they live.* We have seen that the cultural forces surrounding our children do much to shape and direct their behavior, modes of thinking, and performance. Goals that form the framework of the evaluation processes must be formulated in terms of the social environment in which the children live. The art activity, and the nature of the results secured in art activities, should be evaluated in terms of the children's cultural, as well as their economic environment. The children's socioeconomic environment must be understood in terms of the broad goals of our democratic tradition, which include our hopes for a strong democratic society in the future. For this reason, the goals we formulate must draw their strength from the belief that all children are entitled to the fullest possible intellectual, social, and economic life.

3. *Each child is a growing human being.* A purpose of the art program must be to encourage each child's growth in all of its phases. In terms of evaluation, criteria should be formulated to take into account the patterns of maturation our sciences tell us can be expected. Our knowledge of children's biological and social maturation provides us with goals for art education. A purpose of the evaluation program should be to know what is expected of children in certain places, at certain times, and under certain conditions. We must also realize that it is not reasonable to assume that children will conform to a rigid developmental pattern. It is possible to establish general guiding principles; however, each teacher must formulate new criteria for each group of children. No two children, or no two groups of children, can be expected to exactly duplicate any other child or group of children.

4. *Above all else, the purpose of the art education program in elementary school finds its roots in the education of children.* Evaluation programs are devised to help children live and grow happily. The evaluation program is not designed to make the children better artists; it is designed to discover how art and children interact with each other and how children benefit from their association with the processes of art activity.

GENERAL CRITERIA

The formulation of general criteria for evaluation is necessary and desirable. Our discussion about the structure of evaluation criteria suggests means for establishing criteria suitable for each separate classroom situation. According to this idea, criteria should be formulated according to the following principles:

1. Evaluation must be continuous.

2. Evaluation must be a part of all phases of the art activity.

3. Evaluation and grading are two separate things. Grading may be an outcome of evaluation, but it is not its purpose. The purpose of evaluation is to implement and aid the whole of the processes of education through art education activities.

4. Criteria for evaluation are based on the philosophy of education that guides the whole education program in a particular elementary school. It is assumed that this will be a philosophy intended to strengthen the education of elementary-school children.

5. Evaluation criteria are based on the needs of children.

6. Children at all grade levels in elementary school should participate in the formulation of criteria. Children need to discuss the criteria they establish. Through discussion, the teacher can help children formulate meaningful criteria.

7. Criteria must change as children change.

The criteria for art education may be conceived as being concerned with three large areas: attitudes, knowledges, and habits and skills. If evaluative criteria are divided into these three areas, it is possible to construct a chart that can serve as a checklist, with each criterion graded according to some scale. The following suggestions are proposed as a basis from which teachers can make a chart that can be used as part of their permanent or working record.

1. Attitudes

Participates in art experiences.

Demonstrates confidence and self-reliance in art work.

Reveals growth from one project to another in manipulative skill and sensitivity to organization.

Can formulate purposes for each art activity.

Is sympathetic and tolerant of the work of others.

Accepts and evaluates criticism in an intelligent manner.

Experiments with materials and ideas.

Evaluates the great art of history with understanding and withholds judgments if understandings are not sufficiently mature.

Displays a growing critical skill.

Knows that art problems may have many solutions.

Understands how art may have many applications to many phases of living.

Understands how art forms may provide many different kinds of satisfaction.

Is sensitive to the relations between processes, materials, tools, and ideas.

Demonstrates aesthetic sensitivity.

2. Knowledges

Knows the meaning of art terms.

Knows how to approach problems of expression with imagination and inventiveness.

Knows how to evaluate results in order to make useful discoveries.

Knows some necessary facts about art in the home, community, industry, and religion.

Knows facts about materials, tools, and processes.

3. Habits and skills

Evaluates with a growing critical awareness.

Is consistently original in his work, avoids the stereotype.

Selects appropriate materials and processes for his expressions.

Is habitually cooperative in social and working relations.

Uses tools and materials with consideration and contributes to maintaining good organization in the classroom.

Reveals the effects of art experiences in reconstructed behavior in both general and particular forms.

Continues art activity after class time on a voluntary basis.

Constantly reveals, in conversation and in work, the habit of seeking and finding art applications in activities outside the classroom, both in and out of school.

Demonstrates increasing skill in drawing, painting, and in the use of standard art materials.

Criteria for evaluation purposes should be flexible; criteria should be changed whenever the need is evident. Children do not always need to be evaluated, nor do they need to evaluate themselves according to a rigid listing of standards. For example, the following two lists are variations of the criteria previously listed.

I.

Personal growth

Interest in art expression.
Originality of ideas.
Use and choice of color.
Skill in use of tools and media.
Neatness and general appearance of art work.
Responsibility for completion of art work.
Appreciation of work of other children.
Evaluation of own efforts.

Social growth

Ability to follow general directions.
Contributions to group projects.
Willingness to cooperate.
Responsibility for care of materials.
Cooperation in "cleaning up" at end of period.

II.

Personal growth

Interest in art.
Originality.
Skill in use of tools and media.
Neatness and general appearance of work.
Responsibility for tools, materials, and cleanup.

Social growth

Contributions to the group.
Cooperation with others.
Respect for work of others.

Growth in art skills

Design skill—ability to organize ideas.
Skill with paint, crayon, chalk, ink, etc.
Skill with three-dimensional materials.
Inventiveness.
Techniques of experimentation.

Evaluation processes are most effective for the individual child if the child can be evaluated in terms of his own growth. Although we expect children to achieve levels of accomplishment that accord with a general standard for their group, we

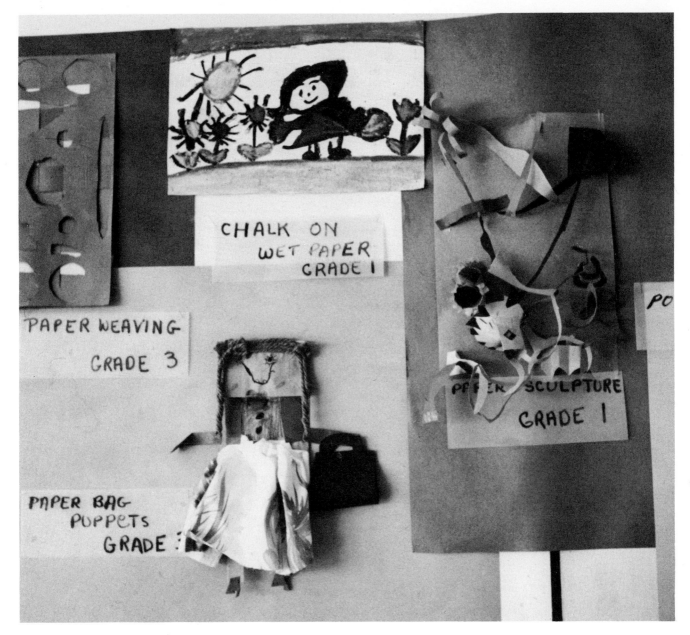

Text visible within the display image:

CHALK ON WET PAPER GRADE 1

PAPER WEAVING GRADE 3

PAPER BAG PUPPETS GRADE

PAPER SCULPTURE GRADE 1

PO

must realize that each child is a unique entity. In order to know how much growth a particular child makes, it is most useful to compare his present work with his past work. A simple means for recording growth is to keep a file of the work a student has done over a period of time. Each separate art job should be dated so that it will be possible to study the amount and sequence of change and growth. It is desirable to maintain such a file for at least a semester or for half a school year.

A record sheet of a child's growth serves as a useful source of information. The record should contain information regarding the number of jobs done, the date on which each was begun and completed, and a general estimate of what was accomplished. It is helpful to include on such a record estimates by the teacher, the individual child, and (when feasible) by the group. The group estimate may be one developed during a group evaluation session.

TYPES OF EVALUATION

Evaluation may be a group or individual project. Group evaluation may consist of a general class discussion about the work being done. Individual evaluation will consist of a private discussion between the teacher and the student.

Group evaluations are related to and are motivated by displays of class work on classroom walls and bulletin boards and in school corridors or other exhibition places. Group understanding of techniques and expressional means may be improved or increased if displays are designed to facilitate evaluation.

Figure A-1 is an example of a display intended to provide children with opportunity and resource for discussing expressional techniques. Such displays act as evaluation criteria. By observing the displays, children can discuss the success with which each art form achieves an expressional purpose, the ways in which the expressional purpose could be improved, and the techniques the displays suggest that would be most suitable for use in the children's future work.

Individual evaluations are usually limited to discussions by the teacher and student of the work accomplished and of formulations of directions for future work. Individual students might evaluate themselves on a self-evaluation form, using criteria similar to those suggested for general evaluation purposes. A student's self-evaluations

can be compared with those made by the teacher and can be used as a basis for discussion between the student and the teacher.

Form 1 is an example that might be used for the individual student's self-evaluations.

FORM 1.

The individual work record of_____ Class_____

No.	Description	Date begun	Date finished	Evaluation

EVIDENCES OF ART EDUCATION

IN THE ELEMENTARY SCHOOL

What do we look for when we try to determine if an effective art education program exists in an elementary school? Many of the things we consider necessary for learning through art activities are not always visible to the casual observer. The subjective nature of the art processes makes it difficult to use objective criteria for determining the success or lack of success of an art program.

It is possible, however, to walk through an elementary-school building and take note of the presence or the absence of art activity. Such evidence will be found in displays of the children's art work and in art activities in progress in the classrooms.

PHYSICAL FACILITIES FOR GENERAL CLASSROOMS

Art activity can take place anywhere, but the best kinds of activities require certain minimum physical facilities. If these facilities are available, we can assume that there is a basis for the existence of an art education program.

Every classroom in which art is taught should have sinks, bulletin boards, tables, and storage space. Because not all of the kinds of art activities in which children participate can be carried on in the general classroom, a special art room is provided in some of the best situations. Children need lots of space, heavy workbenches, and freedom from concern about easily marred floors, tables, and walls. The special art room should be designed to make this kind of freedom possible. When

277

some art activities are carried on in the general classroom, they may cause interference with other kinds of learning activities. For example, some kinds of work with paste, paints, sand, or plaster require cleaning facilities that are not available in the average classroom. Although it might be argued that such facilities can be provided, in terms of economy it is cheaper to provide a specially equipped art room than to equip every classroom as an art room.

Some facilities, however, should be installed in every classroom to make it possible for children to engage in art work as a part of their other educational activities. For this purpose, each classroom should have a sink equipped with an oversize drain and trap, which decrease the danger of the sink's becoming clogged from clay, plaster, or other kinds of waste. Bulletin boards should always be available in the general classroom. For evaluation purposes, alone, it is necessary to have wall space on which the children can tack their work. Wall surfaces are also useful as working surfaces, especially for large drawings and paintings or for murals. Storage space which should be designed to accommodate large papers, supplies, and tools, is also necessary in every classroom. Every classroom should also be provided with tables or other kinds of large working surfaces.

EVIDENCE OF SPECIALIZED ART ACTIVITY

The evidence of art activity in a school building, other than that of the children's art work and the observable art facilities in each classroom, should be as follows:

1. A *special art workshop.* Such a room should be at least twice the size of the average classroom. Children working on art jobs need room to move their arms and bodies. A minimum of fifty square feet per student would not be too much.

Sinks in the special art classroom should be stainproof and large. It is best if the sinks have a number of faucets and basins in order to accommodate several children at one time.

The floors in the art room should be made from a material that can be cleaned easily. The floors should be resistant to the destructive effects of varnishes, oils, solvents, and various kinds of paints.

The special art room should provide facilities for storing clay. Clay storage requires the installation of clay bins as well as shelves enclosed in a tight cabinet lined with a rust resistant metal, such as zinc. The interiors of such cabinets should be kept damp in order to retard the drying of the children's clay work. Slow drying of clay is necessary to keep the clay from cracking. For the finishing of the clay work, a ceramic kiln will be required.

The special art room must be equipped with tool cabinets and storage cabinets for supplies and student work. Furniture should include workbenches with vises, large tables, easels, and stools. Wall surfaces in the art room should be constructed so that pins and tacks can be used freely. In this way, all wall surfaces may be used as working surfaces or as display areas.

2. *Evidence of specialized art activities should be seen in the behavior of the children.* The child who has good experience in art education displays an appreciation of the work he accomplishes and shows respect and understanding of the work of others. Appreciation of the work of other children is one of the important social understandings that can be achieved through an educationally useful art program. Appreciation, understanding, and respect for the art work of others should lead to the child's ability to participate intelligently in group evaluations of art activities.

A child's familiarity with the techniques and processes of art activity should help him respond with useful ideas when faced with problems that demand inventiveness, imagination, creativity, and the ability to utilize all useful senses for the solution of art problems. A child should display confidence, interest, and ability in attacking problems that demand creative-imagination.

The art activity should help a child accept responsibility for making improvements in his work when the evaluations of the group and teacher suggest possibilities for new directions and additional solutions to problems. There is evidence of an increasing maturity when a child is able to accept the recommendations of others, evaluate the recommendations, and then use them to solve problems according to his unique capabilities.

A SUGGESTED CHECKLIST

The following is a suggested checklist that indicates the ways in which we can determine whether or not an effective program of art education exists in an elementary school.

1. Are essential facilities for daily art education available to the child?

Evidence

a) There is a general art workshop in the building.
b) The workshop includes essential features agreed upon by the staff, such as running water, teachers' storage, pupils' storage, worktables, and exhibit space.
c) A wide variety of materials for art work is provided.
d) Per pupil expenditures for art materials compare favorably with expenditures for books.
e) The child's homeroom provides art materials and opportunities, both as special art activities and in other subject areas.
f) The child's home provides some opportunity and materials for art experience.

2. Is every child given constant opportunity for the essential activities of growth?

Evidence

a) Has constant opportunity to use his muscles and his senses in the manipulation of various materials.
b) Has opportunities to explore his environment—materials, forces, people.
c) Carries out his own purpose.
d) Makes his own plans and choice of tools and materials.
e) Achieves his own creative adjustments and results.
f) Works both alone and in groups.
g) Develops mastery of materials and of himself.
h) Solves problems in construction and art.
i) Enjoys art activities.
j) Appreciates art products—his own and others'.
k) Criticizes art work—his own and others'.

3. Is the child building a healthy sense of belonging and emotional security?

Evidence

a) Talks comfortably to adults and speaks fearlessly to strangers.
b) Participates easily with other children in his group.
c) Consults readily with the teacher for help or for mere sociability.
d) Responds with ideas when faced with an art problem.
e) Tackles materials with confidence and interest.
f) Shows his work to others when he is ready to.
g) Talks easily about his work.
h) Takes his membership in the group for granted.
i) Turns to art activity to relieve tension.

4. Is the child achieving recognition and ego satisfaction through his art work?

Evidence

a) Insists on finishing his own work.
b) Takes pride in exhibiting his results.
c) Accepts suggestions but carries them out in his own way.
d) Accepts opportunities for leadership.
e) Takes pride in personal responsibility.
f) Protects his own work from accidental or purposeful injury.
g) Demands individual storage space for his things.

5. Is the child growing in freedom of expression?

Evidence

a) Talks freely with other children.
b) Moves about the workshop at will without interfering with others.
c) Keeps himself busy.
d) Readily chooses a project and makes plans for carrying it out.
e) Makes evaluative judgments without fear.
f) Defends his own ideas and his work to other children and to the teacher.
g) Argues with good temper over workshop matters.
h) Keeps his originality as his art work becomes more complex.

6. Is the child growing in his art skills and techniques?

Evidence

a) Improves his mastery of tools, including simple power tools.
b) Adds to his repertory of mediums.
c) Increases his manipulative skill.
d) Grows in his mastery of resistances in materials, such as the grain in wood, the plasticity of clay, the kinkiness of wire, the flimsiness of paper.
e) Grows in his control of lines with brush, crayon, and pencil.
f) Increases in his ability to work from crude to precise results.
g) Gradually sees more things that suggest art expression.
h) Gains more accurate perceptions of color, size, and shape.
i) Sharpens his sense of qualities such as heaviness, clumsiness, frailness, smoothness, softness, and brittleness.
j) Gains speed and accuracy in expressing what he sees.
k) Improves in muscular coordination; for example, he improves the balance of his own body, the sureness of his muscular movements, and his deftness in handling tools, instruments, and materials.

7. Is the child increasing his knowledge and information by means of art experiences?

Evidence

a) Grows in his awareness of the nature of different materials—the texture of textiles, the warmth of wood or leather, the brittleness of glass, the "runniness" of watercolors.

b) Recognizes with interest more and more adaptations of materials in machinery, furniture, clothing, and the like.

c) Increases his understanding of industrial processes that make and shape materials.

d) Becomes acquainted with the specific work of a growing number of craftsmen.

e) Increases his ability to feel in his own muscles the economy of movement of skilled workers.

f) Learns more and more of the social uses of the various arts and techniques.

g) Improves his sense of order and design in various forms.

h) Grows in his ability to analyze design.

i) Builds an acquaintanceship with the work of current artists and craftsmen.

j) Begins to be able to recognize different styles peculiar to individual artists.

k) Gradually learns some of the history of art, including knowledge of both the artists and of the tools and materials with which they worked.

l) Gains confidence in defending his judgments of ugliness and beauty in his surroundings.

8. Is the child building the personal, emotional, and aesthetic attitudes that lead to a mature personality and an individual style of life?

Evidence

a) Likes to experiment; he is adventurous and approaches any new experience with courage.

b) Constantly makes efforts to achieve good order, good design, and functional beauty.

c) Grows in his respect for excellent accomplishment and for the authority of good workmen.

d) Builds a discipline of his impulses in order to finish jobs, to create imagined effects, and to express himself with artistic simplicity and restraint.

e) Builds respect for himself, the integrity of the honest workman, and the self-reliance of the experienced worker.

f) Grows in his disposition to share with his fellow workers; he shows consideration, cooperation and group-consciousness in his dealings with them.

g) Grows in his affection and respect for others as fellow workers.

h) Expresses frank enjoyment in his art activities.

i) Tends to develop hobbies that have artistic significance.

j) Finds increasing interest in art activity as recreation.

k) Increasingly criticizes ugliness in his environment and shows a disposition to improve it.

l) Increasingly recognizes the arts as tools for living and tends to use them in this way.

m) Gradually builds a recognizable personal style in his tastes in both practical and cultural matters.

9. Is the child experiencing a reasonable variety of personally chosen art forms?

Evidence

a) Frequently experiments with dramatics.

b) Takes varied parts in organizing dramatic enterprises—building scenery, making costumes, playing roles, or stage managing.

c) Takes a regular part in some musical activity.

d) Makes simple musical instruments.

e) Sings alone or in choral groups.

f) Shows growing bodily controls (such as balance, rhythm, precision, and ease of movement) that are related to dance or to athletics.

g) Paints, draws, models, or builds things on his own initiative in and out of school.

BOOKS FOR REFERENCE

AND ADDITIONAL READING

ART HISTORY AND THEORY OF ART

ARNHEIM, RUDOLF, *Art and Visual Perception.* Berkeley and Los Angeles: University of California Press, 1957.

JANSON, H. W., *History of Art.* Englewood Cliffs, N. J.: Prentice-Hall, Inc. and New York: Harry N. Abrams, Inc., 1962.

KEPES, GYORGY, *Language of Vision.* Chicago: Paul Theobald and Co., 1945.

LOWRY, BATES, *The Visual Experience, an Introduction to Art.* Englewood Cliffs, N. J.: Prentice-Hall, Inc. and New York: Harry N. Abrams, Inc., 1961.

MOHOLY-NAGY, LASZLO, *Vision in Motion.* Chicago: Paul Theobald and Co., 1947.

SEIBERLING, FRANK, *Looking into Art.* New York: Holt, Rinehart & Winston, Inc., 1959.

ART EDUCATION

BARKAN, MANUEL, *Through Art to Creativity.* Boston: Allyn and Bacon, Inc., 1960.

BLAND, JANE COOPER, *Art of the Young Child.* New York: The Museum of Modern Art, 1958.

CANE, FLORENCE, *The Artist in Each of Us.* New York. Pantheon Books, Inc., 1951.

COLE, NATALIE, *The Arts in the Classroom.* New York: The John Day Company, Inc., 1940.

ERDT, MARGARET HAMILTON, *Teaching Art in the Elementary School* (rev. ed.) New York: Holt, Rinehart & Winston, Inc., 1962.

GAITSKELL, CHARLES D., and MARGARET R. GAITSKELL, *Art Education in the Kindergarten.* Peoria: Chas. A. Bennett Co., Inc., 1952.

HENRY, EDITH M., *Evaluation of Children's Growth Through Art Experience.* Washington, D. C.: National Art Education Association, 1959.

KEILER, MANFRED L., *The Art in Teaching Art.* Lincoln: University of Nebraska Press, 1961.

LINDSTROM, MIRIAM, *Children's Art.* Berkeley and Los Angeles: University of California Press, 1960.

LOGAN, FREDERICK M., *Growth of Art in American Schools.* New York: Harper & Row, Publishers, 1955.

LOWENFELD, VIKTOR, *Creative and Mental Growth*

(rev. ed.). New York: The Macmillan Company, 1963.

MCFEE, JUNE KING, *Preparation for Art*. Belmont, California: Wadsworth Publishing Company, Inc., 1961.

MENDELOWITZ, DANIEL M., *Children Are Artists*. Stanford: Stanford University Press, 1953.

NATIONAL ART EDUCATION ASSOCIATION, *Planning Facilities for Art Education*. Washington, D. C.: N.E.A., n.d.

READ, HERBERT, *Education Through Art*. New York: Pantheon Books, Inc., 1945.

ZIEGFELD, EDWIN, ed., *Education and Art*. Paris: UNESCO, 1953.

ART TECHNIQUES

ARGIRO, LARRY, *Mosaic Art Today*. Scranton: International Textbook Company, 1961.

BARANSKI, MATTHEW, *Graphic Design: A Creative Approach*. Scranton: International Textbook Company, 1960.

————, *Mask Making*. Worcester: Davis Publications, Inc., 1954.

BETTS, VICTORIA, *Exploring Papier-Mâché*. Worcester: Davis Publications, Inc., 1955.

BRYCE, MAYO, and HARRY B. GREEN, *Teacher's Craft Manual: A Handbook for Teachers*. San Francisco: Fearon Publishers, Inc., 1955.

COLLIER, GRAHAM, *Form, Space, and Vision: Discovering Design Through Drawing*. Englewood Cliffs, N. J.: Prentice-Hall, Inc., 1963.

COX, DORIS, and BARBARA WARREN, *Creative Hands*. New York: John Wiley & Sons, Inc., 1951.

DUNCAN, JULIA HAMLIN, and VICTOR D'AMICO, *How to Make Pottery and Ceramic Sculpture*. New York: Simon and Schuster, Inc., 1947.

HUGHES, TONI, *How to Make Shapes in Space*. New York: E. P. Dutton & Co., Inc., 1955.

JOHNSON, PAULINE, *Creating with Paper*. Seattle: University of Washington Press, 1958.

LANCHESTER, WALDO, *Hand Puppets and String Puppets*. Peoria: Chas. E. Bennett Co., Inc., 1953.

LORD, LOIS, *Collage and Construction in Elementary and Junior High Schools*. Worcester: Davis Publications, Inc., 1958.

MATTIL, EDWARD L., *Meaning in Crafts*. Englewood Cliffs, N. J.: Prentice-Hall, Inc., 1959.

MOSELEY, SPENCER, PAULINE JOHNSON, and HAZEL KOENING, *Crafts Design*. Belmont, California: Wadsworth Publishing Co., Inc., 1962.

RANDALL, ARNE W., *Murals for Schools*. Worcester: Davis Publications, Inc., 1956.

REED, CARL, and JOSEPH ORZE, *Art from Scrap*. Worcester: Davis Publications, Inc., 1960.

ROTTGER, ERNST, *Creative Paper Design*. New York: Reinhold Publishing Corporation, 1962.

WANKELMAN, WILLARD, PHILIP WIGG, and MARIETTA WIGG, *A Handbook of Arts and Crafts for Elementary and Junior High School Teachers*. Dubuque: William C. Brown Company, Publishers, 1961.

INDEX

INDEX